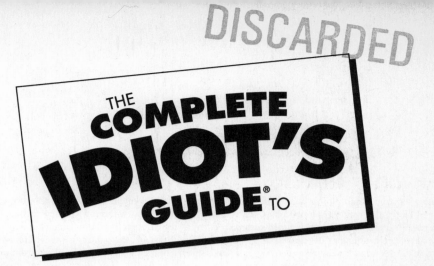

# THE COMPLETE IDIOT'S GUIDE® TO

# Spanish Verbs

*by Gail Stein*

## ALPHA

A member of Penguin Group (USA) I

*This book is dedicated to:*
*My tremendously patient and supportive husband, Douglas*
*My incredibly loving and understanding sons, Eric and Michael*
*My proud parents, Jack and Sara Bernstein*
*My extremely artistically gifted sister, Susan J. Opperman*
*My superior consultant and advisor, Roger Herz*

International Standard Book Number: 1-59257-000-3
Library of Congress Catalog Card Number: 2003104299

07   06   05       8   7   6   5   4   3

Interpretation of the printing code: The rightmost number of the first series of numbers is the year of the book's printing; the rightmost number of the second series of numbers is the number of the book's printing. For example, a printing code of 03-1 shows that the first printing occurred in 2003.

*Printed in the United States of America*

**Note:** This publication contains the opinions and ideas of its author. It is intended to provide helpful and informative material on the subject matter covered. It is sold with the understanding that the author and publisher are not engaged in rendering professional services in the book. If the reader requires personal assistance or advice, a competent professional should be consulted.

The author and publisher specifically disclaim any responsibility for any liability, loss, or risk, personal or otherwise, which is incurred as a consequence, directly or indirectly, of the use and application of any of the contents of this book.

Most Alpha books are available at special quantity discounts for bulk purchases for sales promotions, premiums, fund-raising, or educational use. Special books, or book excerpts, can also be created to fit specific needs.

For details, write: Special Markets, Alpha Books, 375 Hudson Street, New York, NY 10014.

**Publisher:** *Marie Butler-Knight*
**Product Manager:** *Phil Kitchel*
**Senior Managing Editor:** *Jennifer Chisholm*
**Senior Acquisitions Editor:** *Renee Wilmeth*
**Development Editor:** *Michael Koch*
**Senior Production Editor:** *Katherin Bidwell*
**Copy Editor:** *Cari Luna*
**Illustrator:** *Jody Schaeffer*
**Cover/Book Designer:** *Trina Wurst*
**Indexer:** *Angie Bess*
**Layout/Proofreading:** *John Etchison, Ayanna Lacey*

# Contents at a Glance

# Contents

# Introduction

If you want to really learn, understand, and conquer Spanish verbs, this is the book for you. Some people speak a foreign language only in infinitives. Others quickly slur over their verbs with the hope that no one will notice that they can't differentiate the past from the present or the future, let alone cope with the intricacies of the dreaded subjunctive. Still others take the easy way out by purchasing verb books that simply spoon-feed forms in a rapid succession of pages without any clear-cut explanations that would encourage and enhance mastery. Let's face it, when it comes to speaking a foreign language properly, you need to fine-tune your conjugation skills. There's a lot in this book that will give you the practice you need to use Spanish verbs the way native speakers do.

In addition to providing you with verb charts showing everything from simple regular verbs, to spelling-change verbs, to stem-changing verbs, to every imaginable irregular verb, this book also explains how to apply what you've learned to any verb you may encounter. Every verb tense and mood is explored and explained in great detail to enable you to express events, actions, and situations in the proper time frame. Numerous examples are provided to show you how to manipulate the language with ease. Finally, you are afforded the opportunity to practice what you've learned through a series of exercises intended to hone your foreign language skills. The more you use the knowledge you've acquired, the faster you'll be able to communicate on a more advanced level.

I have written this book so that it will be an instructive tool and an instrument that will guide you to a more complete understanding of Spanish verbs and not merely enable you to copy them off a page. This book is extremely user-friendly and will make the task of verb conjugation a pleasant, satisfying, and rewarding experience. You'll find that the straightforward, clear-cut, simple approach will instill you with the knowledge you need to use Spanish verbs with ease and confidence.

## How This Book Is Organized

This book is organized into three parts and appendixes. The three parts provide you with the basic tools necessary for everyday conversation, reading, and writing tasks involving high-frequency verbs in simple tenses and with the higher degree of expertise and competence necessary to use more sophisticated structures in compound tenses in more complex sentences. This book is one-of-a-kind in that it provides you with the rules, explanations, and practice you need so that you can be in control and demonstrate proficiency and competency in any situation with any Spanish verb. It is appropriate, and will prove extremely useful, for people from all walks of life:

students, travelers, business people—in short, anyone who wants a richer, more meaningful command of the language. Here's what this book has to offer:

- ◆ **Part 1, "Tenses and Moods,"** helps you understand the sometimes subtle nuances between verb tenses and moods. It also explains the differences between simple, compound, and progressive tenses so that you can develop a clear understanding of which tense is appropriate to use in the context of your conversation and writing. This section introduces you to the ins and outs of Spanish regular verbs, verbs with stem and spelling changes, and completely irregular verbs.

- ◆ **Part 2, "Comparing Tenses,"** goes into very specific detail about each verb tense or mood, providing concrete explanations and examples. You'll learn to unlock the mysteries of verb conjugations and how to add endings that enable you to express exactly what you're trying to say. This part also explains the intricacies of the enigmatic subjunctive, as well as the complexities surrounding the formation of commands. You'll also be given plenty of opportunities to ponder and to practice what you've learned through a wide variety of challenging exercises that will put you in charge.

- ◆ **Part 3, "Verbal Distinctions and Expressions,"** presents you with verbal idioms and expressions that not only give you practice with the verbs you've mastered, but also give you the idiomatic, conversational vocabulary you need to speak Spanish more proficiently. If your intention is to speak Spanish like a native, this section certainly brings you closer to realizing your goal by providing you with the necessary explanations and tools.

Take special note of the appendixes that accompany this book. Appendix A provides the answer key to all exercises in this book. Appendix B provides a complete list of verb charts with examples of every type of verb with every conceivable change or irregularity. Appendixes C, D, and E list the regular -*ar*, -*er*, and -*ir* verbs along with any verbs requiring spelling and/or stem changes. Refer to Appendix B to correctly conjugate any verb on the list. Appendix F lists compound irregular verbs, those where a prefix is added to an already irregular verb. Reflexive verbs are listed in Appendix G and an example of how these verbs are conjugated in each tense is provided. Lastly, Appendix H lists the irregular past participles you'll need to form any of the seven compound tenses.

# Extras

To spice up a seemingly dry topic and to make this book more fun and informative to read, a few important sidebars have been added:

**¡Mira!** _____

This box points out those pesky little rules we sometimes lose sight of. The *¡Mira!* sidebar tells you how to work with verbs more easily and more efficiently to get the most correct results.

**¡Cuidado!** _____

Read these warnings to avoid making unnecessary, un-intentional, or embarrassing mistakes.

**¿Qué quiere decir...?**

This box provides you with definitions of terms that you may not know or may have forgotten. Use these boxes as a quick refresher course.

## Acknowledgments

The author would like to acknowledge the contributions, input, support, and interest of the following people: Raymond C. Elias, Martin S. Hyman, Michael Koch, Christina Levy, Renee Wilmeth, Katherin Bidwell, and Cari Luna.

## Special Thanks to the Technical Reviewer

*The Complete Idiot's Guide to Spanish Verbs* was reviewed by an expert who double-checked the accuracy of what you'll learn here, to help us ensure that this book gives you everything you need to know about Spanish verbs. Special thanks are extended to Daniel Gonzalez.

## Trademarks

All terms mentioned in this book that are known to be or are suspected of being trademarks or service marks have been appropriately capitalized. Alpha Books and Penguin Group (USA) Inc. cannot attest to the accuracy of this information. Use of a term in this book should not be regarded as affecting the validity of any trademark or service mark.

# Part 1

# Tenses and Moods

We rarely, if ever, think about tenses, let alone moods, when we speak our native language—they just seem to flow naturally. When we speak a foreign language, however, we have to make a conscious effort to properly express what we're trying to say. Our work is cut out for us until we internalize the rules of the language.

In this part I'll introduce you to the world of Spanish tenses and moods. I'll explain the difference between simple and compound tenses and what you'll have to do to form each of them. I'll introduce you to the formation of Spanish progressive tenses, and I'll help you form present and past participles so that you'll be able to confidently use any verb listed in the appendixes in the back of this book. Finally, I'll give you all the practice you'll need before tackling Part 2.

# All About Verbs

## In This Chapter

- ◆ Spanish subject pronouns
- ◆ Spanish moods and tenses
- ◆ Forming and using the past participle
- ◆ Forming compound tenses
- ◆ Forming and using progressive tenses

Want to know where the action is? Just look at a verb! Verbs are words that show movement: *eat, dance, run, play*. They also show a state of being or thinking: *be, believe, think, hope*. Without a verb, you can't form a sentence, yet the shortest sentence imaginable can be formed with just one small verb: *Go!* In any language, if you know the verb that expresses your thought, you will be able to communicate with a native speaker and make yourself understood.

A native language is learned by first listening, then speaking, then reading, and finally, by writing. We learn our first language automatically as children without giving any thought whatsoever to how we are constructing our sentences. We use moods and put verbs in tenses routinely by following the models we've listened to and internalized. When learning a second or foreign language, however, if we are not immersed in the language there are certain guidelines and rules we have to learn and memorize that will enable us to communicate in a proper, educated fashion. In this chapter you'll learn what you need to know to unlock the mystery behind Spanish verbs.

# What Kind of Verb Is It?

In Spanish there are three families of regular verbs, those whose infinitives end in -*ar* (the largest group), -*er*, and -*ir*. All verbs within each of the families follow the same rules for conjugation, the change that must be made to the verb so that it agrees with the subject. So once you've learned the endings for each respective family of verbs, you can conjugate any regular verb in that family.

Within each of these families there are verbs that have changes within their stem (the part of the verb to which the infinitive ending is added), and the changes, once learned, may be applied to any verb with the stem change. There are other verbs with certain endings that require special spelling changes in some, but not necessarily all, tenses. Once you recognize the ending, you will be able to apply the rules you've learned to successfully conjugate that verb.

Spanish also contains many irregular verbs that follow no pattern whatsoever. They may be memorized or you can look them up in your *Complete Idiot's Guide*.

# And the Subject Is ...

Although subject pronouns are not used as much in Spanish as they are in English, you still have to know what the subject is to properly conjugate the verb. In most instances, the Spanish verb ending clearly identifies the subject. In Spanish, therefore, the subject pronouns are mainly used for clarity, for emphasis, and to be polite. Table 1.1 lists the Spanish subject pronouns.

## Table 1.1    Spanish Subject Pronouns

|  | **Singular** |  | **Plural** |  |
|---|---|---|---|---|
| 1st person | yo | I | nosotros (nosotras) | we |
| 2nd person | tú | you | vosotros (vosotras) | you |
| 3rd person | él | he | ellos | they |
|  | ella | she | ellas | they |
|  | usted (Ud.) | you | ustedes (Uds.) | you |

Note the following about Spanish subject pronouns:

◆ *Yo* is only capitalized at the beginning of a sentence.

◆ *Tú* is used when speaking to one friend, relative, pet, or person with whom one is very familiar. *Ud.* is the more polite form used to show respect.

◆ *Ud.* and *Uds.* are not generally omitted in Spanish.

◆ *Nosotras* and *vosotras* are used to speak about female subjects only. *Nosotros*, *vosotros*, and *ellos* refer to male subjects or to a group of male and females, regardless of the number of either gender within the group.

◆ *Vosotros* and *vosotras* are used in Spain but are uncommon in Latin America, where *Uds.* is preferred.

# Are You in the Right Mood?

If your first language is English and you've studied in the United States, undoubtedly none of your language arts teachers has ever referred to a verb mood. Even those of us who went through the tedious drill of diagramming sentences under the tutelage of a strict grammarian were never introduced to the concept of *mood* (also referred to as *mode*). Let's take a closer look at this overlooked and elusive term.

The mood of a verb indicates the manner in which the action or state of being is conceived or the way in which the person looks at the action or state of being that is expressed. In English there are three moods: the indicative, the imperative, and the subjunctive. In Spanish there are two additional moods: the conditional and the infinitive.

◆ The indicative mood is, by far, the most commonly used mood in both English and Spanish. The indicative mood states a fact or asks a question: *Is he tall? No, he's short.*

◆ The imperative mood expresses a command: *Please help me understand this rule.*

◆ The subjunctive mood indicates wishing, emotion, doubt, fear, and supposition, among other things, in sentences generally consisting of more than one clause: *I am afraid that she will be late for her appointment.* The subjunctive is used more frequently in Spanish than in English and will require a fair amount of study.

> **¿Qué quiere decir...?**
>
> A mood shows the way a person looks at the action or state of being that he or she wants to express.

◆ The conditional mood shows what the subject *would do* or *would have done* under certain circumstances or situations: *If I had the money, I would travel around the world.*

◆ The infinitive mood is the verb in its "to" form: to eat, to dance, to run, to play, to be. Think of the phrase "To be or not to be, that is the question" as an example of a verb being used in its infinitive mood.

# What Time Is It?

The tense of a verb refers to the time period in which the action or state of being occurs. Tenses can be either simple (consisting of one verb form) or compound (consisting of two parts). English has three simple tenses: past, present, and future, and three compound tenses: past perfect, present perfect, and future perfect. In Spanish, however, there are seven simple tenses that have corresponding compound tenses. At first glance, this may seem overwhelming. A careful look at Table 1.2, however, which shows how the simple and compound tenses are related and formed, will help dispel any worries you might have that this task is too burdensome:

## Table 1.2   Corresponding Simple and Compound Tenses

| Simple Tense | Compound Tense |
| --- | --- |
| present<br>*presente de indicativo*<br>do/does; am/are/is | present perfect<br>*perfecto de indicativo*<br>have |
| preterit<br>*pretérito*<br>did | preterit perfect<br>*pretérito anterior*<br>had |
| imperfect<br>*imperfecto*<br>was; used to | pluperfect<br>*pluscuamperfecto*<br>had |
| future<br>*futuro*<br>will | future perfect<br>*futuro perfecto*<br>will have |
| conditional<br>*potencial simple*<br>would | conditional perfect<br>*potencial compuesto*<br>would have |
| present Subjunctive<br>*presente de subjuntivo*<br>may | perfect subjunctive<br>*perfecto de subjuntivo*<br>may have |

| Simple Tense | Compound Tense |
| --- | --- |
| imperfect subjunctive | pluperfect subjunctive |
| *imperfecto de subjuntivo* | *pluscuamperfecto de subjuntivo* |
| might | might have |

Each simple tense has specific endings that help identify it. These endings remain the same whether the verb is regular or irregular, or whether it has spelling or stem changes. Once you become adept at recognizing and using the various endings, you will be able to communicate in any mood or any tense. Each simple tense will be presented separately with its corresponding compound form in the forthcoming chapters, affording ample opportunity for you to become familiar with it and to practice it.

Despite the fact that compound tenses are made up of two parts, once you understand the concept of how they are formed, they should present no problem whatsoever. If you look carefully at the previous table, you will notice that the word "perfect" appears in one form or another in the title of each compound tense. Any perfect tense is formed by taking the corresponding simple tense of the helping verb *haber* (to have) and adding the past participle of the action performed (see the following diagram). One verb, the verb *haber*, will have to be memorized in all of its forms in order to construct a verb in a compound tense or to recognize a compound

**¡Mira!**

Conjugate the verb *haber* (to have) in any simple tense, add a past participle and you have the corresponding compound tense. If the simple conditional tells you what the subject *would* do, then the conditional perfect tells you what the subject *would have* done. One note of caution: The helping verb *haber* (to have) cannot be used interchangeably with the verb *tener* (to have).

structure when reading. Because the past participle of any verb remains the same no matter which compound tense is formed, and since the number of irregular past participles is limited, to a certain degree forming compound tenses is easier than forming simple tenses! Follow this easy formula to form a compound tense:

| | | |
| --- | --- | --- |
| Present | | Present Perfect |
| Preterit | | Preterit Perfect |
| Imperfect | | Pluperfect |
| Future | of *haber* + Past Participle = | Future Perfect |
| Conditional | | Conditional Perfect |
| Present Subjunctive | | Perfect Subjunctive |
| Imperfect Subjunctive | | Pluperfect Subjunctive |

# Forming Past Participles

To form the past participle of an *-ar* verb, drop the *-ar* infinitive ending and add *-ado*. To form the past participle of *-ir* and *-er* verbs, drop the *-ir* or *-er* infinitive ending and add *-ido* as shown in Table 1.3.

### Table 1.3    Forming the Past Participle of Regular Verbs

| Ending | Verb | Meaning | Past Participle | Meaning |
|---|---|---|---|---|
| -ar | hablar | to speak | hablado | spoken |
| -er | comer | to eat | comido | eaten |
| -ir | recibir | to receive | recibido | received |

If an *-ir* or *-er* verb stem ends in a vowel, add an accent to the vowel as shown in Table 1.4.

### Table 1.4    Past Participles with Accents

| Verb | Meaning | Past Participle | Meaning |
|---|---|---|---|
| caer | to fall | caído | fallen |
| creer | to believe | creído | believed |
| leer | to read | leído | read |
| traer | to bring | traído | brought |
| oír | to hear | oído | heard |
| reír | to laugh | reído | laughed |

The verbs in Table 1.5 and their compounds (a prefix is added to the main verb) are irregular and must be memorized.

¡Mira! _____

Verb compounds are made by adding a prefix to a verb that already exists, for example: *cubrir* (to cover) and *descubrir* (to discover or to uncover). These compounds can be found in Appendix C.

## Table 1.5    Irregular Past Participles

| Verb | Meaning | Past Participle | Meaning |
| --- | --- | --- | --- |
| abrir | to open | abierto | opened |
| cubrir | to cover | cubierto | covered |
| decir | to tell, say | dicho | said |
| escribir | to write | escrito | written |
| freír | to fry | frito | fried |
| hacer | to make | hecho | made |
| imprimir | to print | impreso | printed |
| morir | to die | muerto | died |
| poner | to put | puesto | put |
| proveer | to provide | provisto | provided |
| resolver | to resolve | resuelto | resolved |
| romper | to break | roto | broken |
| satisfacer | to satisfy | satisfecho | satisfied |
| ver | to see | visto | seen |
| volver | to return | vuelto | returned |

### Práctica 1

Try your hand at forming the past participles of the following Spanish verbs. Pay attention to any irregular verbs or their compounds.

1. ayudar (to help): _____

2. mirar (to look at): _____

3. beber (to drink): _____

4. prometer (to promise): _____

5. decidir (to decide): _____

6. vivir (to live): _____

7. atraer (to attract): _____

8. suponer (to imagine): _____

9. contradecir (to contradict): _____

10. revolver (to turn over): _____

# Using *Haber* to Form a Compound Tense

Let's take a closer look at the simple forms of the verb *haber* to see how we can use it in our formula for compound tense formation:

|  | Present | Preterit | Imperfect | Future | Conditional | Subjunctive | Imperfect Subjunctive |
|---|---|---|---|---|---|---|---|
| yo | he | hube | había | habré | habría | haya | hubiera |
| tú | has | hubiste | habías | habrás | habrías | hayas | hubieras |
| él | ha | hubo | había | habrá | habría | haya | hubiera |
| nosotros | hemos | hubimos | habíamos | habremos | habríamos | hayamos | hubiéramos |
| vosotros | habéis | hubisteis | habíais | habréis | habríais | hayáis | hubierais |
| ellos | han | hubieron | habían | habrán | habrían | hayan | hubieran |

Note that the imperfect subjunctive can also be: *hubiese, hubieses, hubiese, hubiésemos, hubieseis, hubiesen.*

Now you can form the compound tenses as follows:

| | | |
|---|---|---|
| Present Perfect: | Yo he cantado. | I have sung. |
| Preterit Perfect: | Yo hube cantado. | I had sung. |
| Pluperfect: | Yo había cantado. | I had sung. |
| Future Perfect: | Yo habré cantado. | I will have sung. |
| Conditional Perfect: | Yo habría cantado. | I would have sung. |
| Past Subjunctive: | … que yo haya cantado | … that I may have sung |
| Imperfect Subjunctive: | … que yo hubiera cantado | … that I might have sung |

## Práctica 2

Try your hand at forming the compound tenses. You'll see that you'll get the hang of it in no time flat.

Express in Spanish what everyone did and then give the English meaning.

1. bailar (to dance); present perfect

   Yo _____. _____.

2. escribir (to write); preterit perfect

   Tú _____. _____.

3. comer (to eat); pluperfect

   Él _____. _____.

4. leer (to read); future perfect

   Nosotros _____. _____.

5. reír (to laugh); conditional perfect

   Vosotros _____. _____.

6. escribir (to write); past subjunctive

   Es imposible que ellos _____. _____.

7. volver (to return); pluperfect subjunctive

   Era urgente que Uds. _____. _____.

# Using Past Participles in Other Ways

Past participles may also be used in the following ways:

◆ As adjectives that agree in number and gender with the nouns they modify:

   Él es muy conocido.          Ellas fueron muy conocidas.
   He is very well-known.       They were very well-known.

◆ With *estar* (see later in this chapter) to express a condition that is the result of an action:

   La puerta está cerrada.      Los coches serán vendidos.
   The door is closed.          The cars will be sold.

◆ With *ser* (see Chapter 2) to express the passive voice:

   La carta fue escrita por él. El vuelo será suspendido.
   The letter was written by him. The flight will be canceled.

◆ To form a noun from a verb:

   Los invitados llegan.        Los desconocidos no pueden entrar.
   The guests arrive.           The unknown can't enter.

# Progressing Along

In Spanish there are also progressive tenses that show that an action or event is, was, will be, or would be in progress or continuing at the moment indicated. The progressive tenses are usually formed by taking either the present, preterit, imperfect, future, or conditional of the irregular verb *estar* (to be) and adding a present participle, referred to in Spanish as the *gerundio* (gerund). Progressive tenses can also be formed by using the proper tense of the verbs *seguir* (to keep on, continue), *continuar* (to continue), *ir* (to go), *venir* (to come) and *andar* (to walk) and adding a gerund.

**¡Mira!**

In English both present participles and gerunds end in -*ing*. In English, unlike in Spanish, there is a difference between the present participle (While *eating*, I watched TV) and a gerund (*Eating* fish is healthy). In the second example, *eating*, the subject of *is*, is a gerund. In Spanish, however, the present participle may not be used as a noun subject and an infinitive is used: *Comer pescado es saludable*.

# Forming Gerunds

To form the gerund of an -*ar* verb, drop the -*ar* infinitive ending and add -*ando*. To form the past participle of -*ir* and -*er* verbs, drop the -*ir* or -*er* infinitive ending and add -*iendo* as shown in Table 1.6.

### Table 1.6    Forming the Gerund of Regular Verbs

| Ending | Verb | Meaning | Past Participle | Meaning |
|--------|------|---------|-----------------|---------|
| -ar | hablar | to speak | hablando | speaking |
| -er | comer | to eat | comiendo | eating |
| -ir | recibir | to receive | recibiendo | receiving |

If an -*ir* or -*er* verb stem ends in a vowel, drop the infinitive ending and add -*yendo* as shown in Table 1.7.

## Table 1.7    Gerunds with Accents

| Verb | Meaning | Gerund | Meaning |
|------|---------|--------|---------|
| caer | to fall | cayendo | falling |
| construir | to construct | construyendo | constructing |
| creer | to believe | creyendo | believing |
| destruir | to destroy | destruyendo | destroying |
| huir | to flee | huyendo | fleeing |
| leer | to read | leyendo | reading |
| traer | to bring | trayendo | bringing |
| oír | to hear | oyendo | hearing |

Certain *-ir* verbs with stem changes require a vowel change in the gerund. Table 1.8 shows that the *e* before the *-ir* infinitive ending becomes an *i* and the *o* before the *-ir* infinitive ending becomes a *u*.

## Table 1.8    Gerunds of *-ir* Stem-Changing Verbs

| Change | Verb | Meaning | Gerund | Meaning |
|--------|------|---------|--------|---------|
| e to i | corregir | to correct | corrigiendo | correcting |
|        | decir | to say, tell | diciendo | saying, telling |
|        | divertir | to divert | divirtiendo | diverting |
|        | freír | to fry | friendo | frying |
|        | mentir | to lie | mintiendo | lying |
|        | pedir | to ask | pidiendo | asking |
|        | repetir | to repeat | repitiendo | repeating |
|        | sentir | to feel | sintiendo | feeling |
|        | servir | to serve | sirviendo | serving |
|        | venir | to come | viniendo | coming |
|        | vestir | to dress | vistiendo | dressing |
| o to u | dormir | to sleep | durmiendo | sleeping |
|        | morir | to die | muriendo | dying |

Verbs with irregular gerunds include:

| | | | |
|---|---|---|---|
| ir | to go | yendo | going |
| poder | to be able to | pudiendo | being able to |

**¡Mira!**

All compounds of stem-changing and irregular verbs form their gerunds in the same manner: *traer* (to bring), *trayendo*; *atraer* (to attract), *atrayendo*.

---

**Práctica 3**

Try forming the gerunds of the following Spanish verbs. Pay attention to any irregular verbs or their compounds.

1. buscar (to look for): _____

2. aprender (to learn): _____

3. asistir (to attend): _____

4. reconstruir (to reconstruct): _____

5. sonreír (to smile): _____

6. despedir (to say good-bye): _____

7. desvestir (to undress): _____

8. prevenir (to prevent): _____

# Using *Estar* to Form the Progressive Tenses

Follow this easy formula to form a progressive tense:

Present

Preterit

Imperfect

Future        } of *estar* + Gerund = Progressive

Conditional

Present Subjunctive

Imperfect Subjunctive

Let's take a closer look at the simple forms of the verb *estar* to see how we can use it in our formula for progressive tense formation:

|  | **Present** | **Preterit** | **Imperfect** | **Future** | **Conditional** |
|---|---|---|---|---|---|
| yo | estoy | estuve | estaba | estaré | estaría |
| tú | estás | estuviste | estabas | estarás | estarías |
| él | está | estuvo | estaba | estará | estaría |
| nosotros | estamos | estuvimos | estábamos | estaremos | estaríamos |
| vosotros | estáis | estuvisteis | estabais | estaréis | estaríais |
| ellos | están | estuvieron | estaban | estarán | estarían |

Now you can form the *progressive* tenses as follows:

| | | |
|---|---|---|
| Present Progressive: | Yo estoy comiendo. | I am eating |
| Preterit Progressive: | Yo estuve comiendo. | I was eating. |
| Imperfect Progressive: | Yo estaba comiendo. | I was eating. |
| Future Progressive: | Yo estaré comiendo. | I will be eating. |
| Conditional Progressive: | Yo estaría comiendo. | I would be eating. |

**¡Mira!**

The gerund is often the equivalent of *by* + an English present participle: *Leyendo, aprenderá mucho.* (By reading, you'll learn a lot.) *Trabajando mucho, gano mucho dinero.* (By working a lot, I earn a lot of money.)

## Práctica 4

Express what everyone does by using the progressive tenses. Give the English meaning.

1. estudiar (to study); present progressive:

   Yo _____

2. aplaudir (to applaud); preterit progressive:

   Tú _____

*continues*

*continued*

3. correr (to run); imperfect progressive:

Él _____

4. leer (to read); future progressive:

Nosotros _____

5. reír (to laugh); conditional progressive:

Vosotros _____

6. dormir (to sleep); present progressive:

Ellos _____

Although used somewhat less frequently, *andar* (to walk), *continuar* (to continue), *entrar* (to enter), *ir* (to go), *salir* (to go out), *seguir* (to keep on, continue), and *venir* (to come) can serve as helping verbs to form the progressive tenses. The complete conjugations of these verbs appear in the verb charts in Appendix B.

| | |
|---|---|
| Él anda cantando. | He is walking along singing. |
| Continué comiendo. | I continued eating. |
| Ella entró gritando. | She entered screaming. |
| Iban corriendo. | They were running. |
| Saldrá llorando. | She will go out crying. |
| ¡Siga leyendo! | Keep on reading. |
| Vendrían riendo. | They would come laughing. |

### ¿Qué quiere decir...?

The perfect participle expresses *having done something*. It is formed by combining the present participle of *haber* with the past participle of the verb showing the action: *Habiendo terminado, él fue a casa.* (Having finished, he went home.) *Habiendo pagado, ella salió de la tienda.* (Having paid, she left the store.)

# Repaso

◆ Spanish regular verbs end in *-ar*, *-er*, and *-ir*. All verbs within the *-ar*, *-er*, and *-ir* families follow the same rules of conjugation.

◆ Spanish also contains verbs with stem changes, spelling changes, and totally irregular verbs.

◆ Spanish subject pronouns are used only for clarity, emphasis, or to be polite.

◆ The mood of a verb indicates the way in which the person looks at the action or state of being that is expressed.

◆ The tense of a verb indicates the time period in which the action occurred.

◆ Simple tenses consist of one verb form, whereas compound tenses require the helping verb *haber* (conjugated in the appropriate simple tense) plus a past participle.

◆ Progressive tenses show that an action or event in progress or continuing at the moment indicated.

◆ Progressive tenses are usually formed by taking either the present, preterit, imperfect, future, or conditional of the irregular verb, *estar* (to be) and adding a present participle, referred to in Spanish as the *gerundio* (gerund).

◆ *Andar* (to walk), *continuar* (to continue), *ir* (to go), *salir* (to go out), *seguir* (to keep on, continue), and *venir* (to come) can serve as helping verbs to form the progressive tenses.

## The Least You Need to Know

◆ All Spanish verbs end in *-ar*, *-er*, or *-ir*.

◆ A mood indicates how a person views an action while a tense indicates the time of the action.

◆ Tenses may be simple (one verb form), compound (two verb forms: the helping verb *haber* + a past participle) or progressive (*estar* + a gerund).

# Regularities and Irregularities

## In This Chapter

- ◆ All about regular verbs
- ◆ All about spelling-change verbs
- ◆ All about stem-changing verbs
- ◆ Verbs with both changes
- ◆ All about irregular verbs

Every language has its share of regular and irregular verbs. As children we learn to express ourselves in our native language without any knowledge or understanding of the rules and regulations governing verb conjugation. We listen to those around us and pick up speech patterns based upon what we hear from our role models. As we get older, our command of the language increases as we read and develop a more extensive vocabulary. We communicate automatically with ease and with little forethought.

Gone are the days of diagramming sentences and labeling the parts of speech of various sentences. Indeed, most native speakers are unaware of which verbs in their language are regular or irregular or why certain verbs are spelled in a certain way or have certain changes. If it sounds right, then it must be right and the rules are inconsequential as long as one's ideas can be communicated and understood. Most people speak well, but not perfectly, and it's rarely much of a problem. For the non-native, however, an understanding of how verbs work is essential for good communication. In this chapter you'll learn how to recognize regular verbs, verbs with spelling changes, verbs with stem changes, and verbs that follow no rules at all: irregular verbs.

# Regular Verbs

All Spanish verbs end in -*ar*, -*er*, or -*ir*. The good news is that the overwhelming majority of Spanish verbs within each of these groups are regular: that means they follow simple rules for conjugation in all simple and compound tenses. These verbs are predictable, and if you follow the rules and know your endings, you will not make any mistakes. Many of these verbs are cognates. That means that they are easily recognizable because they resemble English verbs in spelling and/or pronunciation.

The bad news is that although there are relatively few completely irregular verbs, they tend to be the ones that are most frequently used and that are the basis for idiomatic expressions in Spanish. These verbs have to be memorized because there are no rules to explain why they undergo the changes they do.

---

### Práctica 1

Give the English meaning of these regular Spanish verbs:

| | | | |
|---|---|---|---|
| 1. aceptar | _____ | 7. omitir | _____ |
| 2. decidir | _____ | 8. responder | _____ |
| 3. comprender | _____ | 9. funcionar | _____ |
| 4. persuadir | _____ | 10. admitir | _____ |
| 5. considerar | _____ | 11. vender | _____ |
| 6. ofender | _____ | 12. participar | _____ |

---

# Verbs with Spelling Changes

In Spanish, the spelling of some verbs changes in order for that verb to retain its proper sound. In other words, verbs with spelling changes sound regular to the ear, but when written, they look different from the original infinitive.

There are two groups of verbs in this category:

- ◆ Verbs with a consonant change.
- ◆ Verbs with a vowel change.

The first group consists of verbs where there is a change in the spelling of a consonant while the second group consists of verbs where there is a change in a vowel. The following diagram illustrates this more clearly.

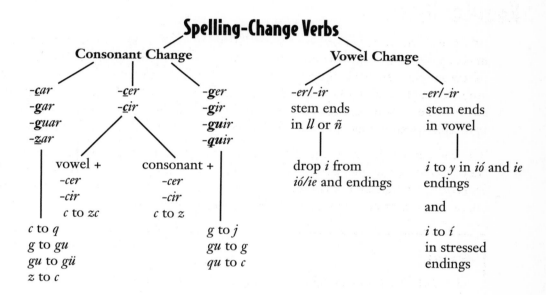

# Spelling-Change Verbs

**Consonant Change**

- -*car*
- -*gar*
- -*guar*
- -*zar*

- -*cer*
- -*cir*

- -*ger*
- -*gir*
- -*guir*
- -*quir*

vowel +
-*cer*
-*cir*
*c* to *zc*

consonant +
-*cer*
-*cir*
*c* to *z*

*c* to *q*
*g* to *gu*
*gu* to *gü*
*z* to *c*

*g* to *j*
*gu* to *g*
*qu* to *c*

**Vowel Change**

-*er*/-*ir*
stem ends
in *ll* or *ñ*

-*er*/-*ir*
stem ends
in vowel

drop *i* from
*ió/ie* and endings

*i* to *y* in *ió* and *ie*
endings

and

*i* to *í*
in stressed
endings

Spelling changes only occur in certain tenses and only before certain letters to maintain correct sound and stress. Table 2.1 shows which tenses require changes and gives examples.

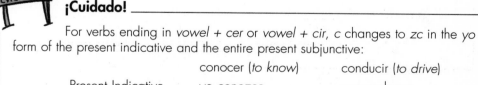

## ¡Cuidado!

For verbs ending in *vowel + cer* or *vowel + cir*, *c* changes to *zc* in the *yo* form of the present indicative and the entire present subjunctive:

|  | conocer (*to know*) | conducir (*to drive*) |
|---|---|---|
| Present Indicative | yo conozco | yo conduzco |
| Present Subjunctive | que yo conozca | que yo conduzca |

## Table 2.1   Spelling-Change Verbs

| Verbs | Change | Tenses and Examples |
|---|---|---|
| **Group 1: Verbs with a change in consonant** | | |
| **-ar** | | |
| *-car* | *c* to *qu* before *e* | bus**c**ar (*to look for*) <br> Preterit: yo bus**qu**é <br> Present subjunctive: que tú bus**qu**es |
| *-gar* | *g* to *gu* before *e* | lle**g**ar (*to arrive*) <br> Preterit: yo lle**gu**é <br> Present subjunctive: que él lle**gu**e |
| *-guar* | *gu* to *gü* before *e* | averi**gu**ar (*to find out*) <br> Preterit: yo averi**gü**é <br> Present subjunctive: que Ud. averi**gü**e |
| *-zar* | *z* to *c* before *e* | cru**z**ar (*to cross*) <br> Preterit: yo cru**c**é <br> Present subjunctive: que ellos cru**c**en |
| **-er/-ir** | | |
| *-cer/-cir* | *c* to *z* before *o* and *a* | ven**c**er (*to conquer*) <br> Present: yo ven**z**o <br> Present subjunctive: que yo ven**z**a <br> espar**c**ir (*to spread out*) <br> Present: yo espar**z**o <br> Present subjunctive: que yo espar**z**a |
| *-ger/-gir* | *g* to *j* before *o* and *a* | esco**g**er (*to choose*) <br> Present: yo esco**j**o <br> Present subjunctive: que tú esco**j**as <br> diri**g**ir (*to direct*) <br> Present: yo diri**j**o <br> Present subjunctive: que tú diri**j**as |
| *-guir* | *gu* to *g* before *o* and *a* | distin**gu**ir (*to distinguish*) <br> Present: yo distin**g**o <br> Present subjunctive: que él distin**g**a |
| *-quir* | *qu* to *c* before *o* and *a* | delin**qu**ir (*to offend*) <br> Present: yo delin**c**o <br> Present subjunctive: que ellos delin**c**an |

| Verbs | Change | Tenses and Examples |
|---|---|---|
| **Group 2: Verbs with a vowel change** | | |
| Verbs whose stem ends in *ll, ñ* | drop *i* from *ió* and *ie* ending | empeller (*to push, shove*)<br>Gerund: empellendo<br>Preterit: él empelló, ellos empelleron<br>Imperfect subjunctive: que él empellera<br><br>bruñir (*to polish, coll. to put on make-up*)<br>Gerund: bruñendo<br>Preterit: él bruñó, ellos bruñeron<br>Imperfect subjunctive: que ella bruñera |
| Verbs ending in *eer* | *i* to *y* in *ió* and *ie* endings | creer (*to believe*)<br>Gerund: creyendo<br>Preterit: él creyó, ellos creyeron<br>Imperfect subjunctive: que Ud. creyera |
| | *i* to *í* in stressed endings | Preterit: tú creíste<br>     nosotros creímos<br>     vosotros creísteis<br>Past participle: creído |
| The verb *oír* | *i* to *y* in *ió* and *ie* endings | oír (*to hear*)<br>Gerund: oyendo<br>Preterit: él oyó, ellos oyeron<br>Imperfect subjunctive: que Uds. oyeran<br>Imperative: tú oye |
| | *i* to *í* in stressed endings | Present: nosotros oímos<br>Preterit: tú oíste<br>     nosotros oímos<br>     vosotros oísteis<br>Past participle: oído<br>Imperative: vosotros oíd |

## Práctica 2

All of the following sentences are in the present subjunctive. Complete the verb with the letter that's missing to explain what it is necessary that you do:

1. (tocar) Es necesario que yo to____e el piano.

2. (llegar) Es necesario que yo no lle____e tarde.

*continues*

*continued*

3. (pagar) Es necesario que yo pa___e mis facturas.

4. (organizar) Es necesario que yo organi___e mis cosas.

5. (apaciguar) Es necesario que yo apaci___e a los niños.

6. (obedecer) Es necesario que yo obede___a a las reglas.

7. (zurcir) Es necesario que yo zur___a estos pantalones.

8. (dirigir) Es necesario que yo diri___a mis pasos hacia el centro.

9. (escoger) Es necesario que yo esco___a bien.

10. (distinguir) Es necesario que yo distin___a entre lo bueno y lo malo.

# Verbs with Stem Changes

The irregularity of verbs with stem changes occurs in the stem vowel in certain forms. These verbs are often referred to as shoe verbs because changes in the vowel take place in all singular forms (*yo, tú, él*) and the third person plural form (*ellos*) of the present tense, thus forming the outline of a shoe:

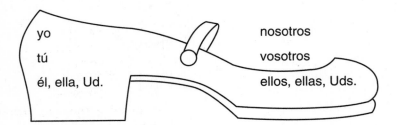

These verbs have changes in other tenses and moods as well. They may be divided into four different classes as shown in the following diagram.

## Stem-Changing Verbs

| Class 1 | Class 2 | Class 3 | Class 4 |
|---------|---------|---------|---------|
| *-ar* verbs | *-ir* verbs | *-ir* verbs | *-ar* verbs |
| *-er* verbs | | | *-er* verbs |
| | | | *-ir* verbs |
| *e* to *ie* | stressed | stressed | *ai* to *aí* |
| *o* to *ue* | *e* to *ie* | *e* to *i* | *au* to *aú* |
| | stressed | unstressed | *eu* to *eú* |
| | *o* to *ue* | *e* to *i* | |
| | unstressed | | |
| | *e* to *i* | | |
| | unstressed | | |
| | *o* to *u* | | |

Once again, these changes only occur in certain moods and tenses and depend upon particular endings. Table 2.2 illustrates this more clearly:

## Table 2.2  Stem-Changing Verbs

| Verbs | Change | Tenses and Examples |
|-------|--------|---------------------|
| **Class 1** | | |
| *-ar* | *e* to *ie* | cerrar (*to close*) |
| | | Present: yo c**ie**rro |
| | | tú c**ie**rras |
| | | él c**ie**rra |
| | | ellos c**ie**rran |
| | | Subjunctive: (que yo) c**ie**rre |
| | | Imperative: c**ie**rra (tú) |
| *-ar* | *o* to *ue* | mostrar (*to show*) |
| | | Present: yo m**ue**stro |
| | | tú m**ue**stras |
| | | él m**ue**stra |
| | | ellos m**ue**stran |
| | | Subjunctive: (que yo) m**ue**stre |
| | | Imperative: m**ue**stra (tú) |

*continues*

## Table 2.2    Stem-Changing Verbs (continued)

| Verbs | Change | Tenses and Examples |
|---|---|---|
| **Class 1** | | |
| -er | e to ie | perder (*to lose*)<br>Present: yo p**ie**rdo<br>tú p**ie**rdes<br>él p**ie**rde<br>ellos p**ie**rden<br>Subjunctive: (que yo) p**ie**rda<br>Imperative: p**ie**rde (tú) |
| -er | o to ue | morder (*to bite*)<br>Present: yo m**ue**rdo<br>tú m**ue**rdes<br>él m**ue**rde<br>ellos m**ue**rden<br>Subjunctive: (que yo) m**ue**rda<br>Imperative: m**ue**rde (tú) |
| **Class 2** | | |
| -ir | stressed<br>e to ie | mentir (*to lie*)<br>Present: yo m**ie**nto<br>tú m**ie**ntes<br>él m**ie**nte<br>ellos m**ie**nten<br>Subjunctive: (que yo) m**ie**nta<br>Imperative: m**ie**nte (tú) |
| | unstressed<br>e to ie<br>followed by<br>a, ió, ie<br>endings | Gerund: m**i**ntiendo<br>Preterit: él m**i**ntió<br>ellos m**i**ntieron<br>Subjunctive: (que nosotros) m**i**ntamos<br>(que vosotros) m**i**ntáis<br>Imperfect subjunctive: (que yo) m**i**ntiera |
| | stressed<br>o to ue | dormir (*to sleep*)<br>Present: yo d**ue**rmo<br>tú d**ue**rmes<br>él d**ue**rme<br>ellos d**ue**rmen<br>Subjunctive: (que tú) d**ue**rmas<br>Imperative: d**ue**rme (tú) |

| Verbs | Change | Tenses and Examples |
|---|---|---|
| | unstressed *o* to *ue* followed by *a, ió, ie* endings | Gerund: durmiendo<br>Preterit: él durmió<br>  ellos durmieron<br>Subjunctive: (que nosotros) durmamos<br>  (que vosotros) durmáis<br>Imperfect subjunctive: (que tú) durmieras |
| **Class 3** | | |
| *-ir* | stressed *e* to *i* | pedir (*to ask*)<br>Present: yo pido<br>  tú pides<br>  él pide<br>  ellos piden<br>Subjunctive: (que él) pida<br>Imperative: pide (tú) |
| | unstressed *e* to *ie* | Gerund: pidiendo<br>Preterit: él pidió<br>  ellos pidieron<br>Subjunctive: (que nosotros) pidamos<br>  (que vosotros) pidáis<br>Imperfect subjunctive: (que yo) pidiera |
| **Class 3 (There are very few verbs in this class)** | | |
| *-ar*<br>*-er*<br>*-ir* | stressed *ai* to *aí*<br>*au* to *aú*<br>*eu* to *eú* | reunir (*to join*)<br>Present: yo reúno<br>  tú reúnes<br>  él reúne<br>  ellos reúnen<br>Subjunctive: (que Ud.) reúna<br>Imperative: reúne (tú) |

# Verbs Ending in *-iar* and *-uar*

For some verbs ending in *-iar* and for all verbs ending in *-uar* (except those ending in *-cuar* and *-guar* listed in Appendix D), *i* changes to *í* and *u* changes to *ú* in the *yo*, *tú*, *él*, and *ellos* forms of the present and the present subjunctive, and the *tú* form of the imperative as shown in Table 2.3.

### Table 2.3 Verbs Ending in *-iar* and *-uar* with Changes

|  | variar (*to vary*) | continuar (*to continue*) |
|---|---|---|
| Present | yo varío | yo continúo |
|  | tú varías | tú continúas |
|  | él varía | él continúa |
|  | nosotros variamos | nosotros continuamos |
|  | vosotros variáis | vosotros continuáis |
|  | ellos varían | ellos continúan |
| Present Subjunctive | que yo varíe | que yo continúe |
|  | que tú varíes | que tú continúes |
|  | que él varíe | que él continúe |
|  | que nosotros variemos | que nosotros continuemos |
|  | que vosotros variéis | que vosotros continuéis |
|  | que ellos varíen | que ellos continúen |
| Imperative | varía | continúa |

## Verbs Ending in *-uir*

For verbs ending in *-uir* (except for those ending in *-guir*, listed in Appendix F), a *y* is inserted after the *u* in the *yo*, *tú*, *él*, and *ellos* forms of the present, in the *él* and *ellos* forms of the preterit, and in all forms of the present and imperfect subjunctive, and the *tú* form of the imperative as shown in Table 2.4.

### Table 2.4 Verbs Ending in *-uir* (but not *-guir*)

|  | concluir (*to conclude*) |
|---|---|
| Present | yo concluyo |
|  | tú concluyes |
|  | él concluye |
|  | nosotros concluimos |
|  | vosotros concluís |
|  | ellos concluyen |
| Present Subjunctive | que yo concluya |
|  | que tú concluyas |
|  | que él concluya |
|  | que nosotros concluyamos |
|  | que vosotros concluyáis |
|  | que ellos concluyan |

| | concluir (*to conclude*) |
|---|---|
| Imperfect Subjunctive | que yo concluyera |
| | que tú concluyeras |
| | que él concluyera |
| | que nosotros concluyéramos |
| | que vosotros concluyerais |
| | que ellos concluyeran |
| Imperative | concluye |

## Práctica 3

All of the verbs are in the present tense. Express what each person does:

1. (despertar) Julio desp____rta a los niños.

2. (remendar) María rem____nda la camisa.

3. (acostar) Juan ac____ta a sus hijas.

4. (contar) Paco c____nta historias increíbles.

5. (perder) Susana p____rde la paciencia.

6. (volver) Carlos v____lve temprano.

7. (preferir) Juanita pref____re ir al cine.

8. (dormir) Eduardo d____rme hasta tarde.

9. (expedir) Sofía exp____de un paquete a su amiga.

10. (distribuir) Ricardo distribu____e folletos.

11. (enviar) Luz env____a cartas a su familia.

12. (continuar) Elena contin____a estudiando.

# Spelling-Change Verbs with Stem Changes

Be aware that some verbs with spelling changes also undergo changes within their stems, which means that when they are conjugated in the various tenses, they are subject to two different irregularities. If, therefore, a verb ends in *-car*, *-gar*, *-zar*, *-cer*, *-ger*, or *-guir*, you must take a careful look at the stem vowel. If that vowel is an *e* or an *o*, it is quite possible that the verb also undergoes a stem change according to Table 2.2. The following high-frequency verbs fall into this category:

♦ The following -*car* verbs with the *o* to *ue* spelling change will be irregular in the *yo*, *tú*, *el*, *ellos* forms of the present, in the present subjunctive, in the *yo* form of the preterit, and the *tú* imperative:

> volcar (to overturn, empty)
> revolcar (to knock down)

♦ The following -*gar* verbs with the *e* to *ie* spelling change will be irregular in the *yo*, *tú*, *el*, *ellos* forms of the present, in the present subjunctive, in the *yo* form of the preterit, and in the *tú* imperative:

> abnegar (to forego)
> cegar (to blind)
> denegar (to reject)
> desplegar (to unfold)
> fregar (to rub)
> negar (to deny)
> plegar (to fold)
> regar (to water)
> renegar (to renege)
> sosegar (to calm)

♦ The following -*gar* verbs with the *o* to *ue* spelling change will be irregular in *yo*, *tú*, *el*, *ellos* forms of the present, in the present subjunctive, in the *yo* form of the preterit, and in the *tú* imperative:

**¡Mira!**
The verb *jugar* (to play) changes the internal *u* to *ue*.

> colgar (to hang up)
> descolgar (to unhook)
> j**u**gar (to play)
> rogar (to beg)

♦ The following -*zar* verbs with the *e* to *ie* spelling change is irregular in *yo*, *tú*, *el*, *ellos* forms of the present, in the present subjunctive, in the *yo* form of the preterit, and in the *tú* imperative:

> comenzar (to begin)
> empezar (to begin)
> tropezar (to hit, stumble)

**¡Mira!**
The verb *avergonzar* (to shame) changes the internal *o* to *üe*.

♦ The following -*zar* verbs with the *o* to *ue* spelling change will be irregular in *yo*, *tú*, *el*, *ellos* forms of the present, in the present subjunctive, in the *yo* form of the preterit, and in the *tú* imperative:

almorzar (to eat lunch)
avergonzar (to shame)
esforzar (to strain)
forzar (to force)
reforzar (to reinforce)

◆ The following -*cer* verbs with the *o* to *ue* spelling change will be irregular in *yo*, *tú*, *el*, *ellos* forms of the present, in the present subjunctive, and in the *tú* imperative:

cocer (to cook, boil)
torcer (to twist)

◆ The following -*gir* verbs with the *e* to *i* spelling change will be irregular in *yo*, *tú*, *el*, *ellos* forms of the present, in the present subjunctive, in the *él*, *ellos* forms of the preterit, in the imperfect subjunctive, and in the *tú* imperative:

corregir (to correct)
elegir (to elect)
regir (to rule)

◆ The following -*guir* verbs with the *e* to *i* spelling change will be irregular in *yo*, *tú*, *el*, *ellos* forms of the present, in the present subjunctive, in the *él*, *ellos* forms of the preterit, in the imperfect subjunctive, and in the *tú* imperative:

conseguir (to get)
perseguir (to pursue)
proseguir (to continue)
seguir (to follow)

**¡Cuidado!**

Not all verbs that look alike have the same irregularities. The verbs *negar* (to deny), *abnegar* (to forego) and *renegar* (to renege) have an *e* to *ie* spelling change, while the verb *anegar* (to overwhelm, to flood) does not.

## Práctica 4

All of the verbs are in the present subjunctive. Fill in the two spelling changes for each verb that tell what it is important that these people do.

1. (denegar) Es importante que ellos den___ ___en esto.

2. (jugar) Es importante que ellos j___ ___en bien.

*continues*

*continued*

3. (empezar) Es importante que ellos emp___ ___en el trabajo.

4. (almorzar) Es importante que ellos alm___r___en rápidamente.

5. (descolgar) Es importante que ellos desc___l___en el teléfono.

6. (cocer) Es importante que ellos c___ ___an el pollo.

7. (corregir) Es importante que ellos corr___ ___an sus tareas.

8. (seguir) Es importante que ellos s___ ___an practicando.

# Irregular Verbs

It is important to familiarize yourself with the high-frequency irregular verbs commonly used in everyday conversation and writing. Recognizing that a verb is irregular will help you to avoid making unnecessary mistakes in conjugation and usage and will enable you to speak Spanish correctly. Since these verbs do not fit into any pattern, they must be memorized.

The most common irregular verbs, illustrated in Appendix B, are:

caber (to fit)

caer (to fall)

conocer (to know)

dar (to give)

decir (to say, tell)

dormir (to sleep)

estar (to be)

haber (to have; helping verb used to form compound tenses)

hacer (to make, do)

ir (to go)

oír (to hear)

oler (to smell)

poder (to be able to)

poner (to put)

querer (to wish, want)

reír (to laugh)

saber (to know)

salir (to go out)

satisfacer (to satisfy)

ser (to be)

tener (to have)

traer (to bring)

valer (to be worth)

venir (to come)

ver (to see)

Lesser-used verbs that are irregular and are included in Appendix B include:

| | |
|---|---|
| adquirir<br>(to acquire) | argüir<br>(to argue) |
| bendecir<br>(to bless) | delinquir<br>(to transgress) |
| erguir<br>(to raise, lift up) | errar<br>(to wander; to err) |
| garantir<br>(to guarantee) | inquirir<br>(to inquire) |
| yacer<br>(to lie down) | |

**¡Mira!**

The verb *haber* (to have) is used as a helping verb (an auxiliary verb) to form all of the compound tenses of all verbs.

# Repaso

◆ All Spanish verbs end in *-ar*, *-er*, or *-ir*.

◆ All regular verbs with each infinitive ending are conjugated in the same manner in all tenses.

◆ There are two groups of verbs with spelling changes: those with an irregular stem spelling where a consonant changes, and those with an irregular ending spelling where a vowel changes.

◆ Consonant changes are as follows:

    *-car* verbs change *c* to *qu*

    *-gar* verbs change *g* to *gu*

    *-guar* verbs change *gu* to *gú*

    *-zar* verbs change *z* to *c*

    consonant + *-cer* and *-cir* verbs change *c* to *z*

    vowel + *-cer* and *-cir* verbs change *c* to *zc*

    *-ger* and *-gir* verbs change *g* to *j*

    *-guir* verbs change *gu* to *g*

    *-quir* verbs change *q* to *c*

- Vowel changes are as follows:

  -*er* and -*ir* verbs that end in *ñ* or *ll* drop *i* from *ió/ie*

  -*er* and -*ir* verbs ending in a vowel change *i* to *y* before *ió/ie*

  -*er* and -*ir* verbs ending in a vowel change *i* to *í* in stressed endings

- There are four classes of stem-changing verbs:

  Class 1 -*ar* and -*er* verbs change *e* to *ie* and *o* to *ue*.

  Class 2 -*ir* verbs change stressed *e* to *ie* and *o* to *ue* and unstressed *e* to *i* and *o* to *u*.

  Class 3 -*ir* verbs change stressed *e* to *i* and unstressed *e* to *i*.

  Class 4 -*ar*, -*er*, and -*ir* verbs change stressed *ai* to *aí*, *au* to *aú*, and *eu* to *eú*.

- Some verbs ending in -*iar* and all verbs ending in -*uar* change *i* to *í* and *u* to *ú*, respectively, in the *yo*, *tú*, *él*, and *ellos* forms of the present and the present subjunctive, and in the imperative *tú* form.

- Verbs ending in -*uir* (but not -*guir*) insert a *y* after the *u* in the *yo*, *tú*, *él*, and *ellos* forms of the present, in the *él* and *ellos* forms of the preterit, in all forms of the present and imperfect subjunctive, and in the imperative *tú* form.

- Some spelling-change verbs ending in -*car*, -*gar*, -*zar*, -*cer*, -*ger*, and -*guir* also have stem changes.

- Irregular verbs, which tend to be the most frequently used verbs, must be memorized.

## The Least You Need to Know

- Verbs with spelling changes require a change to the consonant before the infinitive ending or to the vowel of the infinitive ending to maintain the proper pronunciation of the verb.

- Verbs with stem changes require an internal change to a vowel within the verb.

- Verbs with spelling or stem changes do not change in every tense.

- Some Spanish verbs are completely irregular.

# Part 2

# Comparing Tenses

Let's face it, for effective communication you have to know your verbs: You won't get very far without understanding their meaning or conjugating them properly. Naturally, you don't want to be labeled a "gringo" because your vocabulary and structural skills are lacking. The more you study and practice, the more proficient you'll become.

In this part I'll lead you into the world of Spanish tenses and moods, where you'll slowly progress from tenses that are relatively easy to those that require more time, more patience, and more memorization. I'll explain what the different tenses and moods are, how to form them, and when to use them. Lastly, I'll give you enough exercises to leave you feeling like a pro.

# The Present and the Present Perfect

## In This Chapter

- ◆ Forming the present tense of regular verbs
- ◆ Forming the present tense of spelling-change and stem-changing verbs
- ◆ How to use reflexive verbs
- ◆ Forming the present tense of irregular verbs
- ◆ When to use the present tense
- ◆ Forming and using the present perfect and the present progressive

Action that is taking place now, in the present, can be expressed in three ways in Spanish: by using the present, the present progressive, or the present perfect. This may at first seem confusing, but careful consideration of how each tense is used by native speakers will clear up any difficulties.

The present tense is a simple tense that expresses an action or state of being that occurs now: *I leave, I am leaving, I do leave*. While the present tense expresses what the subject generally does at any given time, the present progressive expresses what the subject is doing now, at this very moment in time: I am typing a manuscript. Finally, the present perfect is a compound tense that describes an action or state of being that started in the past and continues in the present: He has lived here for three years. It may also refer to an action that took place in the past and is somehow connected to the present: I have organized the party for Mike. In this chapter you'll learn how to comfortably use all three tenses for Spanish verbs.

# The Present Tense of Regular Verbs

A verb expresses an action or state of being and is normally shown in its infinitive form, the "to" form: to speak. In English, regular verbs and many irregular verbs have only two different forms:

| | |
|---|---|
| I **speak** | We speak |
| You speak | You speak |
| He/She **speaks** | They speak |

In Spanish, however, regular verbs have several different forms, which must be memorized. Let's take a look at the Spanish verb *hablar* (to speak):

| | |
|---|---|
| Yo habl**o** | Nosotros habl**amos** |
| Tú habl**as** | Vosotros habl**áis** |
| Él, Ella habl**a** | Ellos, Ellas habl**an** |

All regular verbs within each infinitive group (*-ar*, *-er*, and *-ir*) follow the same rules of conjugation: Each subject has its own ending that does not change. Once the endings have been learned, they may be applied to any regular verb with the corresponding infinitive ending.

## The Present Tense of *-ar* Verbs

The largest infinitive group is that of *-ar* verbs. To form the present tense of these verbs, drop the *-ar* infinitive ending and add the endings shown in Table 3.1.

### Table 3.1   *-ar* Verb Conjugation

| Infinitive | Meaning | Subject | Ending | Conjugated Verb |
|---|---|---|---|---|
| bailar | to dance | yo | -o | bail**o** |
| cantar | to sing | tú | -as | cant**as** |

| Infinitive | Meaning | Subject | Ending | Conjugated Verb |
|---|---|---|---|---|
| preparar | to prepare | él | -a | prepara |
| estudiar | to study | ella | -a | estudia |
| ayudar | to help | Ud. | -a | ayuda |
| trabajar | to work | nosotros | -amos | trabaj**amos** |
| ganar | to win | vosotros | -áis | gan**áis** |
| telefonear | to phone | ellos | -an | telefone**an** |
| saludar | to greet | ellas | -an | salud**an** |
| comprar | to buy | Uds. | -an | compr**an** |

You should now feel comfortable working in the present tense with any of the *-ar* verbs listed in Appendix D.

## Práctica 1

Express what each person does by giving the correct form of the verb:

1. (caminar) ellos _____
2. (gritar) yo _____
3. (celebrar) nosotros _____
4. (viajar) Ud. _____
5. (nadar) tú _____
6. (esperar) vosotros _____
7. (descansar) ella _____
8. (mirar) Uds. _____
9. (dibujar) él _____
10. (enseñar) ellas _____

# The Present Tense of *-er* Verbs

The next group is that of *-er* verbs. To form the present tense of these verbs, drop the *-er* infinitive ending and add the endings shown in Table 3.2.

## Table 3.2  -er Verb Conjugation

| Infinitive | Meaning | Subject | Ending | Conjugated Verb |
|---|---|---|---|---|
| acceder | to agree | yo | -o | accedo |
| aprender | to learn | tú | -es | aprendes |
| correr | to run | él | -e | corre |
| depender | to depend | ella | -e | depende |
| esconder | to hide | Ud. | -e | esconde |
| pretender | to try to | nosotros | -emos | pretendemos |
| ofender | to insult | vosotros | -éis | ofendéis |
| creer | to believe | ellos | -en | creen |
| sorber | to sip | ellas | -en | sorben |
| vender | to sell | Uds. | -en | venden |

The regular -er verbs in Appendix E should now be easy to conjugate in the present tense.

**¡Mira!**

Verbs ending in -eer are regular in the present tense. These verbs include: *leer* (to read), *creer* (to believe) and *proveer* (to provide).

## Práctica 2

Express what each person does by giving the correct form of the verb:

1. (beber) nosotros  _____

2. (comer) ellos  _____

3. (leer) Ud.  _____

4. (prometer) tú  _____

5. (comprender) ella  _____

6. (deber) vosotros  _____

7. (responder) Uds.  _____

8. (corresponder) él  _____

9. (interceder) yo _____

10. (tejer) ellas _____

## The Present Tense of *-ir* Verbs

To form the present tense of *-ir* verbs, drop the *-ir* infinitive ending and add the endings shown in Table 3.3.

### Table 3.3    *-ir* Verb Conjugation

| Infinitive | Meaning | Subject | Ending | Conjugated Verb |
|---|---|---|---|---|
| aplaudir | to applaud | yo | -o | aplaudo |
| combatir | to fight | tú | -es | combates |
| discutir | to discuss | él | -e | discute |
| disuadir | to dissuade | ella | -e | disuade |
| omitir | to omit | Ud. | -e | omite |
| abrir | to open | nosotros | -imos | abrimos |
| cubrir | to cover | vosotros | -ís | cubrís |
| persistir | to persist | ellos | -en | persisten |
| asistir | to attend | ellas | -en | asisten |
| prohibir | to prohibit | Uds. | -en | prohiben |

Use the verbs in Appendix F in conjunction with Table 3.3. to practice the *-ir* verb present-tense conjugation.

### Práctica 3

Express what each person does by giving the correct form of the verb:

1. (sufrir) ellos _____

2. (escribir) Ud. _____

3. (vivir) nosotros _____

*continues*

*continued*

4. (recibir) él     _____

5. (partir) ellas     _____

6. (decidir) tú     _____

7. (describir) Uds.     _____

8. (insistir) vosotros     _____

9. (permitir) yo     _____

10. (subir) ella     _____

# The Present Tense of Spelling-Change Verbs

In the present tense, all verbs ending in *-car*, *-gar*, *-guar*, and *-zar* are regular if they do not also have a stem change. Simply drop the *-ar* infinitive ending and add the endings shown in the previous table. Table 3.4 shows how this is done.

## Table 3.4    The Present Tense of *-car*, *-gar*, *-guar*, and *-zar* Verbs

| Subject | *-car* verbs | *-gar* verbs | *-guar* verbs | *-zar* verbs |
| --- | --- | --- | --- | --- |
| yo | busco | llego | averiguo | cruzo |
| tú | buscas | llegas | averiguas | cruzas |
| él, ella, Ud. | busca | llega | averigua | cruza |
| nosotros | buscamos | llegamos | averiguamos | cruzamos |
| vosotros | buscáis | llegáis | averiguáis | cruzáis |
| ellos, ellas, Uds. | buscan | llegan | averiguan | cruzan |

In the present tense, verbs ending in a consonant + *cer* and *cir* change *c* to *z*, those ending in a vowel + *cer* or *cir* change *c* to *zc*, those ending in *-ger* and *-gir* change *g* to *j*, those ending in *-guir* change *gu* to *g*, and those ending in *-quir* change *qu* to *c* only in the *yo* form. All other forms of the present tense are regular, as shown in Table 3.5. (Caution: Verbs ending in a vowel + *cir* change *c* to *zc* in the *yo* form of the present tense.)

## Table 3.5 The Present Tense of *-cer/-cir*, *-ger/-gir*, *-guir*, and *quir* Verbs

| Subject | *-cer* | *-cir* | *-ger* | *-gir* | *-guir* | *-quir* |
|---|---|---|---|---|---|---|
| | vencer<br>conocer | esparcir<br>conducir | escoger | dirigir | distinguir | delinquir |
| yo | venzo<br>conozco | esparzo<br>conduzco | escojo | dirijo | distingo | delinco |
| tú | vences<br>conoces | esparces<br>conduces | escoges | diriges | distingues | delinques |
| él,<br>ella, Ud. | vence<br>conoce | esparce<br>conduce | escoge | dirige | distingue | delinque |
| nosotros | vencemos<br>conocemos | esparcimos<br>conducimos | escogemos | dirigimos | distinguimos | delinquemos |
| vosotros | vencéis<br>conocéis | esparcís<br>conducís | escogéis | dirigís | distinguís | delinquís |
| ellos,<br>ellas, Uds. | vencen<br>conocen | esparcen<br>conducen | escogen | dirigen | distinguen | delinquen |

*The English meanings of the Spanish verbs used in this table are as follows:* vencer *(to conquer),* esparcir *(to frown),* conocer *(to know),* conducir *(to drive),* escoger *(to choose),* dirigir *(to direct),* distinguir *(to distinguish),* delinquir *(to offend).*

---

### Práctica 4

Express what you do by giving the correct form of the verb:

1. (vencer) Yo _____ a mis enemigos.

2. (apaciguar) Yo _____ a mis amigos.

3. (fruncir) Yo _____ el ceño cuando tengo un problema.

4. (escoger) Yo _____ bien a mis amigos.

5. (explicar) Yo _____ bien mis ideas.

6. (padecer) Yo _____ del corazón.

7. (analizar) Yo _____ demasiado.

8. (traducir) Yo _____ todas las frases al español.

9. (exigir) Yo _____ mucho.

10. (investigar) Yo _____ todo.

# The Present Tense of Stem-Changing Verbs

In the present tense, all stem changes occur in the "shoe" formation, or in the *yo, tú, él, ella, Ud., ellos, ellas, Uds.* forms.

The following changes occur in the stem vowel of *-ar* and *-er* verbs:

$\left.\begin{array}{l} e \text{ to } ie \\ \\ o \text{ to } ue \end{array}\right\}$ in all present-tense forms except *nosotros* and *vosotros*

**¿Qué quiere decir...?**

A present-tense "shoe verb" is a verb that requires a change in the spelling of the vowel in the stem in the *yo, tú, él, ella, Ud., ellos, ellas,* and *Uds.* forms. The *nosotros* and *vosotros* forms retain the vowel from the infinitive.

The following changes occur in the stem vowel of *-ir* verbs:

$\left.\begin{array}{l} e \text{ to } ie \\ i \text{ to } ie \\ e \text{ to } i \\ o \text{ to } ue \end{array}\right\}$ in all present-tense forms except *nosotros* and *vosotros*

**¡Cuidado!**

Some verbs, because of their meanings, are only conjugated in the third person singular form: *llover* (to rain), *llueve* (it rains); *nevar* (to snow), *nieva* (it snows).

"Shoe" changes also occur in the *-iar* verbs listed in Appendix D where *i* becomes *í* within the shoe (***envío, envías, envío,*** *enviamos, enviáis,* ***envían***), in all *-uar* verbs (except *-cuar* and *-guar* verbs) where *u* becomes *ú* within the shoe (***continúo, continúas, continúa,*** *continuamos, continuáis,* ***continúan***) (see Appendix D), and in *-uir* verbs (except *-guir* verbs) where a *y* is inserted after the *u* (***concluyo, concluyes, concluye,*** *concluimos, concluís,* ***concluyen***) (see Appendix F) in all present-tense forms except *nosotros* and *vosotros*.

Examples of all "shoe" conjugations appear in Tables 2.2, 2.3, and 2.4 of Chapter 2.

## Práctica 5

Following the rules given above, fill in the chart for the verbs listed. Consult the appendixes if you are unsure of the verb.

| Verb | Meaning | Yo | Nosotros | Ellos |
|------|---------|-----|----------|-------|
| enc**o**mendar | to trust | _____ | _____ | _____ |
| m**o**strar | to show | _____ | _____ | _____ |
| esqu**i**ar | to ski | _____ | _____ | _____ |
| ade**cuar** | to fit, adapt | _____ | _____ | _____ |
| atesti**guar** | to attest | _____ | _____ | _____ |
| eval**uar** | to evaluate | _____ | _____ | _____ |
| ent**e**nder | to understand | _____ | _____ | _____ |
| res**o**lver | to resolve | _____ | _____ | _____ |
| excl**uir** | to exclude | _____ | _____ | _____ |
| extin**guir** | to extinguish | _____ | _____ | _____ |
| inqu**i**rir | to inquire | _____ | _____ | _____ |
| m**e**dir | to measure | _____ | _____ | _____ |

Refer to Chapter 2 for verbs that have both a spelling change and a "shoe" stem change in the present tense. These verbs are also listed in Appendixes D, E, and F in the back of the book.

# The Present Tense of Reflexive Verbs

A reflexive verb is easily identifiable by the *-se* that is tagged on to the end of a verb: *llamarse* (to call oneself). Reflexive verbs show that the subject is performing an action upon itself. The reflexive verb has a reflexive pronoun as its direct or indirect object. The subject (which may be omitted, but which should be kept in mind) and the reflexive pronoun refer to the same person(s) or thing(s): *(Yo) Me llamo Gail*. I call myself Gail or My name is Gail.

In many instances, you can use the same verb, without the reflexive pronoun, when performing the action *upon* or *for* someone else. The verb is then no longer reflexive.

| | |
|---|---|
| Me llamo Gail. | I call myself Gail. (My name is Gail.) |
| Llamo a Carlos. | I call Carlos. |

Some verbs that are usually not used as reflexives may be made reflexive by adding the reflexive pronoun:

|                     |                      |
|---------------------|----------------------|
| Preparo la comida.  | I prepare the meal.  |
| Me preparo.         | I prepare myself.    |

A list of common reflexive verbs can be found in Appendix G.

Take note of the following verbs that are always used reflexively in Spanish but are not necessarily used that way in English. Boldface type indicates a spelling/stem changing or irregular verb:

| | |
|---|---|
| ac**or**darse (de) | to remember |
| apoderarse (de) | to take possesion (of) |
| apresurarse (a) | to hurry |
| aprovecharse (de) | to avail oneself (of) |
| arrep**en**tirse (de) | to repent, regret |
| atreverse (a) | to dare (to) |
| burlarse (de) | to mock |
| empeñarse (en) | to insist (on) |
| enterarse (de) | to find out about |
| escaparse (de) | to escape from |
| fiarse (de) | to trust |
| figurarse | to imagine |
| fijarse (en) | to notice |
| **ir**se | to go away |
| **negar**se (de) | to refuse (to) |
| olvidarse (a) | to forget |
| pare**cer**se (a) | to resemble |
| quejarse (de) | to complain |
| **reír**se (de) | to laugh at |
| tratarse (de) | to concern |

## Using Reflexive Pronouns

Reflexive verbs must be conjugated in all tenses with their reflexive pronouns. The verb is then conjugated according to its ending and any spelling/stem changes or irregularities. Each subject has its own pronoun that is generally placed before the conjugated verb in the present tense, as shown in Table 3.6.

### Table 3.6    The Present Tense of Reflexive Verbs

| Subject | Reflexive Pronoun | Verb |
| --- | --- | --- |
| yo | me | parezco |
| tú | te | apresuras |
| él, ella, Ud. | se | divierte |
| nosotros | nos | olvidamos |
| vosotros | os | figuráis |
| ellos, ellas, Uds. | se | acuestan |

Me levanto temprano.        No me acuesto tarde.
I get up early.        I don't go to bed late.

When the subject is followed by a conjugated verb and an infinitive, the reflexive pronoun may be placed before the conjugated verb or after and attached to the infinitive to which its meaning is linked:

Me voy a sentar.        Deseo divertirme.
I'm going to sit down.        I want to have fun.

Reflexive verb constructions are often used to replace verbs in the passive voice (where the subject is acted upon) as follows:

Aquí se habla español.
Spanish is spoken here.

### Práctica 6

Express what each person does by using a reflexive pronoun and by conjugating the verb.

*continues*

*continued*

1. (acordarse) Él _____ de todo.

2. (casarse) Ellos _____.

3. (enfadarse) Yo _____ a menudo.

4. (equivocarse) Ud. _____ de vez en cuando.

5. (despedirse) Ellas _____ a las ocho.

6. (preocuparse) Nosotros _____.

7. (despertarse) Tú _____ temprano.

8. (negarse) Vosotros _____ a trabajar.

# The Present Tense of Irregular Verbs

In the present tense, some verbs are irregular only in the *yo* form. You will find that you use these high-frequency verbs in Table 3.7 quite often.

## Table 3.7    Present-Tense Verbs Irregular in the *Yo* Form

| Verb | Meaning | Yo Form |
| --- | --- | --- |
| caber | to fit | quepo |
| caer | to fall | caigo |
| dar | to give | doy |
| hacer | to make, do | hago |
| poner | to put | pongo |
| saber | to know a fact, to know how to | sé |
| salir | to go out | salgo |
| traer | to bring | traigo |
| valer | to be worth | valgo |
| ver | to see | veo |

The verbs listed in Table 3.8 are the most commonly used verbs in Spanish that are irregular in the present tense. Some have regular *nosotros* and *vosotros* forms. All irregular forms are indicated in bold type.

## Table 3.8    Irregular Spanish Verbs

| Verb | Meaning | yo | tú | él | nosotros | vosotros | ellos |
|------|---------|-----|-----|-----|----------|----------|-------|
| decir | to tell | **digo** | **dices** | **dice** | decimos | decís | **dicen** |
| estar | to be | **estoy** | **estás** | **está** | estamos | estáis | **están** |
| haber | to have | **he** | **has** | **ha** | **hemos** | habéis | **han** |
| ir | to go | **voy** | **vas** | **va** | **vamos** | **vais** | **van** |
| oír | to hear | **oigo** | **oyes** | **oye** | **oímos** | **oís** | **oyen** |
| oler | to smell | **huelo** | **hueles** | **huele** | olemos | oléis | **huelen** |
| reír | to laugh | **río** | **ríes** | **ríe** | **reímos** | reís | **rien** |
| ser | to be | **soy** | **eres** | **es** | **somos** | **sois** | **son** |
| tener | to have | **tengo** | **tienes** | **tiene** | tenemos | tenéis | **tienen** |
| venir | to come | **vengo** | **vienes** | **viene** | venimos | venís | **vienen** |

These verbs, and others, are irregular in other tenses and some have irregular present or past participles. They will be addressed in the sections that pertain to them in particular. Bear in mind that all compounds of these verbs, listed in Appendix C follow the same rules of conjugation.

---

### Práctica 7

Complete each sentence using the correct form of the verb in parentheses to speak about each person:

1. (decir) Julia siempre _____ la verdad.

2. (venir) Ellos _____ en coche.

3. (ser) Nosotros _____ inteligentes.

4. (reír) Tú _____ todo el tiempo.

5. (oír) Vosotros _____ bien.

6. (tener) Yo _____ un coche nuevo.

7. (ir) Él _____ al cine.

8. (estar) Ud. _____ contento hoy.

# Using the Present Tense

The present tense is used as follows:

◆ To describe or introduce people or events:

Te presento a Carlos. (Let me introduce you to Carlos.)

Tiene treinta años. (He's thirty years old.)

> **¡Mira!** _____
>
> Hay, the impersonal form of
> *haber*, means there is or there
> are: *Hay sol*. (There's sun; it's
> sunny.)

◆ To give information about events taking place:

Elena va a la fiesta. (Elena is going to the party.)

◆ To express habitual actions:

Generalmente, leo mucho. (Generally, I read a lot.)

◆ To ask for instructions or to discuss an action that will take place in the immediate future:

¿Empiezo a leer? (Shall I begin to read?)

Te llamo pronto. (I'll call you soon.)

◆ To express an event or action that began in the past and is continuing in the present by using *hace (que)* or *desde hace*:

| | |
|---|---|
| ¿Cuánto tiempo hace que estudias? | Hace una hora (que estudio). |
| ¿Desde cuándo estudias? | Estudio desde hace una hora. |
| How long have you been studying? | I've been studying for an hour. |

---

## Práctica 8

Express what each person does by giving the correct form of the present tense.

1. (tener) Uds. _____ buena suerte.

2. (acostarse) Tú _____ temprano.

3. (entender) Él no _____ nada.

4. (coger) Yo _____ cada oportunidad.

5. (seguir) Ellos _____ cantando.

6. (adquirir) Vosotros _____ mucho dinero.

7. (habituarse) Ella _____ a trabajar duro.

8. (distribuir) Ellas _____ los libros.

9. (saber) Yo _____ cocinar.

10. (ser) Nosotros _____ profesores.

11. (enviar) Tú _____ el paquete.

12. (adecuarse) Nosotros _____ a todo.

# Forming and Using the Present Perfect

The present perfect is a compound tense, which means that it is made up of more than one part. The two elements that are needed to form the present perfect are:

1. The present tense of the helping verb *haber*, which expresses that something has taken place.

2. The past participle of the verb: which expresses what the action was.

The following diagram shows how the present perfect is formed:

Present Perfect of verb =      when + what

/    \

Present Perfect of verb =    (what) has + happened

/      \

Present Perfect of verb =   helping verb + main verb

/        \

Present Perfect of verb = haber (to have) + past participle

The formula for the formation of the present perfect is:

| subject noun or pronoun + haber in present + past participle |

The formation of past participles was explained in Chapter 1. To review:

> for -*ar* verbs drop *ar* and add -*ado*

> for -*er* verbs drop *er* and add -*ido*

> for -*ir* verbs drop *ir* and add -*ido*

If an -*er* or -*ir* verb ends in a vowel, simply add an accent to *ído.*

Irregular past participles are listed in Table 1.3 and in Appendix H.

Note the following about the use of the present perfect:

♦ The present perfect tense is used to express an action that took place at no definite time in the past, thus it's other name, the past indefinite.

♦ The helping verb *haber* must be used in Spanish even though we often omit this auxiliary verb in English:

> He recibido un regalo. (I [have] received a gift.)

♦ The past participle remains invariable for the different subject pronouns:

> Yo he escrito una carta. (I wrote a letter.)

> Ellos han escrito una carta. (They wrote a letter.)

♦ The past participle cannot be separated from the helping verb:

> Ellos no han llegado. (They haven't arrived.)

> Siempre he dicho la verdad. (I always told the truth.)

> ¿Has visto a los niños? (Have you seen the children?)

> ¿Ella no ha comido? (Hasn't she eaten?)

**¡Mira!** _____

The past participle always ends in -o when it follows *haber:*

> *Ella ha escrito una carta.*
> She has written a letter.

---

## Práctica 9

Express what each person has done to break a record:

1. (consumir) Nosotros _____ 50 hamburguesas en un día.

2. (estudiar) Vosotros _____ 10 lenguas extranjeras en un año.

3. (beber) Ella _____ 25 vasos de agua en una hora.

4. (ver) Yo _____ 10 películas en un día.

5. (hacer) Tú _____ tus tareas en 5 minutos.

6. (escribir) Uds. _____ 500 postales en 5 horas.

# Forming and Using the Present Progressive

The present progressive expresses what the subject is doing right now: it speaks about an action that is in progress. As discussed in Chapter 1, the two elements that are needed to form the present perfect are:

1. The present tense of the verb *estar:* which expresses that something is taking place.

2. The gerund of the verb: which expresses what the action is.

The following diagram shows how the present progressive is formed:

Present Perfect of verb =        when + what

/    \

Present Perfect of verb =     (what) is + happening

/    \

Present Perfect of verb = estar (present) + main verb pres. part.

The formula for the formation of the present perfect is:

subject noun or pronoun + *estar* in present + gerund

Nosotros estamos hablando.
We are speaking.

The formation of gerunds was explained in Chapter 1. To review:

for *-ar* verbs drop *ar* and add *-ando*

for *-er* verbs drop *er* and add *-iendo*

for *-ir* verbs drop *ir* and add *-iendo*

If an *-er* or *-ir* verb ends in a vowel, simply add *-yendo*:

| | |
|---|---|
| caer (to fall) | cayendo |
| construir (to build) | construyendo |
| creer (to believe) | creyendo |
| huir (to flee) | huyendo |
| leer (to read) | leyendo |
| oír (to hear) | oyendo |
| traer (to bring) | trayendo |

Stem-changing *-ir* verbs and their compounds change the stem vowel from *e* to *i* and from *o* to *u*:

| | |
|---|---|
| corregir (to correct) | corrigiendo |
| decir (to say, tell) | diciendo |
| divertir (to amuse) | divirtiendo |
| dormir (to sleep) | durmiendo |
| freír (to fry) | friendo |
| morir (to die) | muriendo |
| mentir (to lie) | mintiendo |
| pedir (to ask) | pidiendo |
| repetir (to repeat) | repitiendo |
| sentir (to feel) | sintiendo |
| venir (to come) | viniendo |
| vestir (to dress) | vistiendo |

*Ir* (to go) and *poder* (to be able to) have the following irregular gerunds respectively: *yendo* and *pudiendo*.

## Práctica 10

Express what each person is doing in the street:

1. (huir) Dos hombres _____.

2. (cantar) Yo _____.

3. (servir) Ella _____ bebidas.

4. (conducir) Tú _____.

5. (recoger) Nosotros _____ papeles.

6. (dormir) Vosotros _____.

# Repaso

1. To conjugate regular -*ar* verbs, drop the -*ar* infinitive ending and add: *o, as, a, amos, áis, an.*

2. To conjugate regular -*er* verbs, drop the -*er* infinitive ending and add: *o, es, e, emos, éis, en.*

3. To conjugate regular -*ir* verbs, drop the -*ir* infinitive ending and add: *o, es, e, imos, ís, en.*

**¡Mira!**

With reflexive verbs the reflexive pronoun may precede the conjugated verb form or may be attached to the gerund. In the latter case, an accent mark is placed on the stressed vowel: *Se está peinando. Está peinándose.* (He's combing his hair.)

4. Spelling-change -*car*, -*gar*, -*guar*, and -*zar* verbs are regular in the present.

5. Verbs ending in consonant + -*cer*/-*cir* change *c* to *z*, vowel + *cer*/vowel + *cir* change *c* to *cz*, -*ger*/-*gir* change *g* to *j*, -*guir* change *gu* to *g*, and -*quir* change *q* to *c* only in the *yo* form of the present tense.

6. The following stem changes occur within the "shoe" (the *yo, tú, él,* and *ellos* forms): in -*ar* and -*er* verbs *e* changes to *ie* and *o* changes to *ue*, in -*ir* verbs *e* changes to *ie*, *e* changes to *i* or *o* changes to *ue*.

7. Reflexive verbs can be identified by *se* that is attached to the end of the infinitive. Reflexive verbs show that the subject is acting upon itself and require the use of reflexive pronouns that agree with the subject.

8.  Reflexive pronouns precede the conjugated verb. When there are two verbs, the reflexive pronoun may precede the conjugated verb or may follow the infinitive to which it is attached.

9.  The following verbs have irregular *yo* forms in the present tense: *caber, caer, dar, hacer, poner, saber, salir, traer, valer,* and *ver.*

10. The following verbs are irregular in most or all forms of the present: *decir, estar, haber, ir, oír, oler, reír, ser, tener, venir.*

11. The present perfect expresses what has occurred and is formed by conjugating *haber* in the present tense and adding a past participle (which remains the same for all subject pronouns).

12. The present progressive expresses what is occurring and is formed by conjugating the verb *estar* in the present tense and adding a gerund. Reflexive pronouns may precede *estar* or may be placed after and attached to the gerund. In this case, the stressed vowel is accented.

## The Least You Need to Know

- The endings for regular *-ar* verbs are: *o, as, a, amos, áis, an.*

- The endings for regular *-er* verbs are: *o, es, e, emos, éis, en.*

- The endings for regular *-ir* verbs are: *o, es, e, imos, ís, en.*

- Verbs with spelling and stem changes require special attention.

- Irregular verbs must be memorized.

- The present perfect is formed by taking the present of *haber* and adding a past participle.

- The present progressive is formed by taking the present of *estar* and adding a gerund.

# Chapter 4

# The Preterit and the Preterit Perfect

## In This Chapter

◆ Forming the preterit of regular verbs

◆ Forming the preterit of spelling-change and stem-changing verbs

◆ How to use reflexive verbs in the preterit

◆ Forming the preterit of irregular verbs

◆ When to use the preterit

◆ Forming and using the preterit perfect and the past progressive

In Spanish, actions or events that took place in the past may be expressed using the preterit (to express an action that was completed in the past) or the imperfect (to express a continuous action in the past). There are rules and guidelines to determine which past tense may be used appropriately in any given situation. Chapter 4 focuses on the preterit while Chapter 5 will focus on the imperfect.

The preterit tense is a simple tense that expresses an action, event, or state of mind that occurred in the past and was completed at a specific moment in time: I left. The preterit perfect is a compound tense that is mainly used in formal writing, such as literary and historical works. It is replaced by the *preterit* or *pluperfect* (see Chapter 5) in conversation and informal writing. The preterit perfect expresses an action that had happened in the past: After he had spoken, the audience applauded. Finally, the past progressive expresses what was going on and completed in the past. In this chapter you'll learn how to form and use the preterit and the past progressive and how to recognize the preterit perfect when it is used in writing.

# The Preterit Tense of Regular Verbs

The preterit tense of regular verbs is formed by dropping the *-ar*, *-er*, or *-ir* infinitive ending and by adding the endings shown in Table 4.1. (Note that *-er* verbs and *-ir* verbs have the exact same endings in the preterit tense.)

## Table 4.1 The Preterit of Regular Verbs

| Subject | *-ar* verbs | *-er* verbs | *-ir* verbs |
|---|---|---|---|
| | **hablar** (*to speak*) | **beber** (*to drink*) | **abrir** (*to open*) |
| yo | habl**é** | beb**í** | abr**í** |
| tú | habl**aste** | beb**iste** | abr**iste** |
| él, ella, Ud. | habl**ó** | beb**ió** | abr**ió** |
| nosotros | habl**amos** | beb**imos** | abr**imos** |
| vosotros | habl**asteis** | beb**isteis** | abr**isteis** |
| ellos, ellas, Uds. | habl**aron** | beb**ieron** | abr**ieron** |

You should now feel comfortable working in the present tense with any of the regular verbs listed in Appendix B.

---

## Práctica 1

Express what happened at Susana's party by giving the correct form of the preterit:

1. (invitar) Susana _____ a todos sus amigos.

2. (preparar) Sus amigos _____ muchas cosas para comer.

3. (bailar) Nosotros _____.

4. (cantar) Tú _____.

5. (pasar) Vosotros _____ un buen rato allí.

6. (regresar) Yo _____ tarde.

## Práctica 2

Express what happened over the weekend by giving the correct form of the preterit:

1. (salir) Los niños _____ con sus amigos.

2. (comer) Yo _____ en un restaurante.

3. (asistir) Vosotros _____ a una fiesta.

4. (correr) Julio _____ por la playa.

5. (recibir) Tú _____ un regalo de tus abuelos.

6. (aprender) Nosotros _____ un poema.

# The Preterit of Spelling-Change Verbs

In the preterit tense, verbs ending in *-cer/-cir*, *-ger/-gir*, *-guir*, and *-quir* have no spelling changes and follow the regular rules of preterit formation. Other verbs, however, do change.

## The Preterit of *-car*, *-gar*, *-guar*, and *-zar* Verbs

In the preterit tense, all verbs ending in *-car*, *-gar*, *-guar*, and *-zar* (see Appendix D) change only in the *yo* form. Table 4.2 shows how this is done.

## Table 4.2 Spelling Changes in -car, -gar, -guar, and -zar Verbs

| Ending | Infinitive | Meaning | Change | Yo/Preterit |
|--------|-----------|---------|--------|-------------|
| -car | sacar | to take out | c to qu | saqué |
| -gar | pagar | to pay | g to gu | pagué |
| -guar | averiguar | to find out | u to ü | averigüé |
| -zar | lanzar | to throw | z to c | lancé |

### Práctica 3

Express what you did yesterday:

1. almorzar a las dos _____

2. tocar el piano _____

3. castigar a los niños _____

4. amortiguar la luz en mi cuarto _____

5. abrazar a mi amigo _____

6. encargar libros _____

7. pescar _____

8. apaciguar a mi hermano _____

## The Preterit of Verbs Ending in Vowel + -er/-ir

Verbs ending in vowel -er/-ir (see Appendix B) change the third person singular form (el, ella, Ud.) from io to yó and the third person plural form (ellos, ellas, Uds.) from -ieron to -yeron. All other preterit forms have an accented i – í as shown in Table 4.3.

## Table 4.3 Spelling Changes in Vowel + -er/-ir Verbs

| Subject | caer (to fall) | leer (to read) | oír (to hear) |
|---------|----------------|----------------|----------------|
| yo | caí | leí | oí |
| tú | caíste | leíste | oíste |
| él, ella, Ud. | cayó | leyó | oyó |

| Subject | caer (*to fall*) | leer (*to read*) | oír (*to hear*) |
|---|---|---|---|
| nosotros | caímos | leímos | oímos |
| vosotros | caísteis | leísteis | oísteis |
| ellos, ellas, Uds. | cayeron | leyeron | oyeron |

## Verbs Ending in -*uir*

Verbs ending in -*uir* (but not -*guir*) change the third person singular form (*el, ella, Ud.*) from *io* to *yó* and the third person plural form (*ellos, ellas, Uds.*) from -*ieron* to -*yeron*. Unlike the verbs mentioned immediately above, all other preterit forms except *yo* remain without an accent on the *i*:

distribuir (to distribute)

| | |
|---|---|
| yo distribuí | nosotros distribuimos |
| tú distribuiste | vosotros distribuisteis |
| él distribuyó | ellos distribuyeron |

**¡Cuidado!**

The verbs *decir, traer,* and all verbs ending in -*ducir* are irregular in the preterit.

## Verb Stems Ending in *ñ* and *ll*

Verb stems ending in *ñ* and *ll* before the infinitive ending drop the *i* of the preterit endings for the third person singular (*él, ella, Ud.*) and plural (*ellos, ellas, Uds.*) forms, as shown in Table 4.4.

## Table 4.4    Verb Stems Ending in *ñ* or *ll*

| Subject | gruñir (*to grunt*) | tañer (*to ring*) | bullir (*to boil*) |
|---|---|---|---|
| yo | gruñí | tañí | bullí |
| tú | gruñiste | tañiste | bulliste |
| él | **gruñó** | **tañó** | **bulló** |
| nosotros | gruñimos | tañimos | bullimos |
| vosotros | gruñisteis | tañisteis | bullisteis |
| ellos | **gruñeron** | **tañeron** | **bulleron** |

---

**Práctica 4**

Express what each person did:

1. (leer) Él _____ muchos libros.

2. (oír) Ellos _____ decir que nosotros vamos a estudiar español.

3. (concluir) Las muchachas _____ sus estudios.

4. (bullir) La ciudad _____ de actividad.

5. (caer) El niño ____ de su bicicleta.

6. (poseer) Esas mujeres _____ una fortuna.

---

# The Preterit of Stem-Changing Verbs

The only verbs with stem changes in the preterit are those whose infinitive ends in -*ir*. Verbs ending in -*ir* that have a stem change in the present tense also have a stem change in the preterit.

## -*ir* Verbs with *e* to *ie* or *e* to *i* Stem Changes

Verbs whose stems change from *e* to *ie* or from *e* to *i* in the present (see Appendix F), change their stems from *e* to *i* in the preterit in the third person singular (*él, ella, Ud.*) and in the third person plural (*ellos, ellas, Uds.*) forms as shown in Table 4.5.

## Table 4.5   Verbs with *e* to *ie* or *e* to *i* Stem Changes

| Preterit (*e* to *ie* in present) | Preterit (*e* to *i* in present) |
|---|---|
| preferir (*to prefer*) | servir (*to serve*) |
| yo preferí | yo serví |
| tú preferiste | tú serviste |
| él prefirió | él sirvió |
| nosotros preferimos | nosotros servimos |
| vosotros preferisteis | vosotros servisteis |
| ellos prefirieron | ellos sirvieron |

The verbs *reír* (to laugh) and *sonreír* (to smile) both have the same changes but drop *i* in the stem of the third person singular (*él, ella, Ud.*) and third person plural (*ellos, ellas, Uds.*) forms. All other preterit forms have an accented *i - í:*

| | |
|---|---|
| yo (son)reí | nosotros (son)reímos |
| tú (son)reíste | vosotros (son)reísteis |
| **él (son)rió** | **ellos (son)rieron** |

## Verbs with *o* to *ue*

Verbs whose stem changes from *o* to *ue* in the present (see Appendix F), change their stems from *o* to *u* in the preterit in the third person singular (*él, ella, Ud.*) and in the third person plural:

dormir (to sleep)

| | |
|---|---|
| yo dormí | nosotros dormimos |
| tú dormiste | vosotros dormisteis |
| él d<u>u</u>rmió | ellos d<u>u</u>rmieron |

---

### Práctica 5

Express what each person did at a party:

1. (sonreír) Ana y Marta _____ dos veces.
2. (dormir) José _____ en la hamaca.
3. (preferir) Julio y Juan _____ cantar.
4. (pedir) Clara _____ algo de comer.
5. (consentir) Unos muchachos _____ a tocar la guitarra.
6. (servir) La madre y el padre _____ refrescos.

---

# The Preterit of Reflexive Verbs

In the preterit tense, the reflexive pronoun precedes the conjugated verb:

Ayer yo me quedé en casa y me aburrí.
Yesterday I stayed home and I became bored.

Ellos se divirtieron mucho.
They had a lot of fun.

---

### Práctica 6

Express what each person did yesterday before going to work:

Ejemplo:
Ana/levantarse tarde. Ana se levantó tarde.

1. Yo/cepillarse los dientes _____

2. Ellos/vestirse rápidamente _____

3. Nosotros/despertarse temprano_____

4. Tú/bañarse _____

5. Vosotros/desayunarse con vuestra familia _____

6. Él/afeitarse _____

---

# The Preterit of Irregular Verbs

Many high-frequency Spanish verbs are irregular in the preterit and most of them are also irregular in the present tense. These irregular verbs, however, may be grouped according to their changes, making them, perhaps, easier to learn and remember. A few verbs are completely irregular and must be memorized. Let's look first at the verbs that may be grouped.

Verbs that may be grouped have the same preterit endings (regardless of their infinitive ending), which differ from the endings for regular verbs. These endings are:

| yo | -e | nosotros | -imos |
|----|-----|----------|-------|
| tú | -iste | vosotros | -isteis |
| él | -o | ellos | -ieron (or -jeron if the stem ends in j or -ducir) |

Some verbs change the vowel before the infinitive ending (e or a) to i as shown in Table 4.6. Note that some verbs also use a different consonant in the stem.

## Table 4.6    Verbs with *i* in the Preterit Stem

|  | decir (*to say*) | venir (*to come*) | querer (*to want*) | hacer (*to make*) | satisfacer (*to satisfy*) |
|---|---|---|---|---|---|
| yo | dije | vine | quise | hice | satisfice |
| tú | dijiste | viniste | quisiste | hiciste | satisficiste |
| él | dijo | vino | quiso | hizo* | satisfizo* |
| nosotros | dijimos | vinimos | quisimos | hicimos | satisficimos |
| vosotros | dijisteis | vinisteis | quisisteis | hicisteis | satisficisteis |
| ellos | dijeron | vinieron | quisieron | hicieron | satisficieron |

Some verbs change the vowel before the infinitive ending (*a* or *o*) to *u* as shown in Table 4.7. Note that some verbs also use a different consonant in the stem.

## Table 4.7    Verbs with *u* in the Preterit Stem

|  | caber (*to fit*) | haber (*to have*) | saber (*to know*) | poner (*to put*) | poder (*to be able*) |
|---|---|---|---|---|---|
| yo | cupe | hube | supe | puse | pude |
| tú | cupiste | hubiste | supiste | pusiste | pudiste |
| él | cupo | hubo | supo | puso | pudo |
| nosotros | cupimos | hubimos | supimos | pusimos | pudimos |
| vosotros | cupisteis | hubisteis | supisteis | pusisteis | pudisteis |
| ellos | cupieron | hubieron | supieron | pusieron | pudieron |

Some verbs drop the infinitive ending (*-ar* or *-er*) and add *uv* before the preterit ending as shown in Table 4.8. Note that *tener* also drops *en*.

## Table 4.8    Verbs with *uv* in the Preterit Stem

|  | andar (*to walk*) | estar (*to be*) | tener (*to have*) |
|---|---|---|---|
| yo | anduve | estuve | tuve |
| tú | anduviste | estuviste | tuviste |
| él | anduvo | estuvo | tuvo |
| nosotros | anduvimos | estuvimos | tuvimos |
| vosotros | anduvisteis | estuvisteis | tuvisteis |
| ellos | anduvieron | estuvieron | tuvieron |

Some verbs have *-j* in their preterit stem. These verbs include all those that end in *-ducir* (see Appendix F), as shown in Table 4.9. Note that this occurs in the verb *decir*, shown in Table 4.6.

### Table 4.9 Verbs with *j* in the Preterit Stem

|  | traer (*to bring*) | conducir (*to drive*) |
|---|---|---|
| yo | traje | conduje |
| tú | trajiste | condujiste |
| él | trajo | condujo |
| nosotros | trajimos | condujimos |
| vosotros | trajisteis | condujisteis |
| ellos | trajeron | condujeron |

## Dar and Ver

The verbs *dar* (to give) and *ver* (to see) have the same irregular preterit endings, which are added to the *d-* and *v-* of these verbs respectively, as shown in Table 4.10.

### Table 4.10 The Preterit of *dar* and *ver*

|  | dar (*to give*) | ver (*to see*) |
|---|---|---|
| yo | di | vi |
| tú | diste | viste |
| él | dio | vio |
| nosotros | dimos | vimos |
| vosotros | disteis | visteis |
| ellos | dieron | vieron |

## Ser and Ir

*Ser* (to be) and *ir* (to go) have the exact same preterit forms. You must understand the context of the sentence in order to distinguish which verb is being used. The highly irregular forms of these two verbs are:

| yo fui | nosotros fuimos |
|--------|-----------------|
| tú fuiste | vosotros fuisteis |
| él fue | ellos fueron |

Note that there are no accents in the preterit forms of the verbs *dar* (to give), *ver* (to see), *ser* (to be), and *ir* (to go).

---

## Práctica 7

Express what the following people did while on a trip to a Spanish-speaking country:

1. (ir) Yo _____ al cine.
2. (hacer) Nosotros _____ una excursión.
3. (poner) Vosotros _____ tarjetas postales.
4. (tener) Uds. _____ ganas de ir al centro.
5. (poder) Tú _____ ver un museo de arte moderno.
6. (andar) Ella _____ por la ciudad.
7. (estar) Ellos _____ en el teatro.
8. (querer) Ud. _____ visitar los jardines.
9. (conducir) Ella _____ por el campo.
10. (ver) Él _____ un desfile.

---

# Using the Preterit

The preterit is used as follows:

♦ To express an action or event that began at a specific time in the past:

Empecé a trabajar a las ocho.
I began to work at 8 o'clock.

◆ To express an action or event that was completed at a specific time in the past:

> Fui al cine anoche.
> Last night I went to the movies.

◆ To express an action that was completed in the past:

> Visité a mi hermana.
> I visited my sister.

◆ To express a series of events that were complete within a definite time period in the past:

> Me desperté temprano, me vestí, y salí.
> I got up early, I got dressed, and I went out.

## Verbs Whose Meaning Changes in the Preterit

Some verbs that express a mental state or state of mind have a different meaning when used in the preterit, as shown in Table 4.11.

### Table 4.11    Verbs Whose Meaning Changes in the Preterit

| Verb | Present | Preterit |
|------|---------|----------|
| conocer | to be acquainted with (know) Yo la conozco. I know her. | to meet La conocí en España. I met her in Spain. |
| poder | to be able to, can Él puede hacerlo. He can do it. | to manage Él pudo hacerlo. He managed to do it. |
| querer | to wish, want No quieren salir. They don't want to go out. | to refuse No quisieron salir They refused to go out. |
| saber | to know Sé la verdad. I know the truth. | to find out Supe la verdad. I found out the truth. |
| tener | to have Tengo un regalo de él. I have a gift from him. | to receive Tuve un regalo de él. I received a gift from him. |

**Práctica 8**

Below is a list of what Alicia did yesterday. Express what she did:

1. dormir hasta las ocho _____

2. ir al supercado _____

3. hacer una cita con el doctor _____

4. sacar dinero del banco _____

5. pagar las cuentas _____

6. dar un regalo a Marta _____

7. almorzar en el centro con Juanita _____

8. traer a sus niños a la escuela _____

9. poner un anuncio en el periódico _____

10. servir la cena _____

11. conducir al centro comercial _____

12. poder ver a la dentista _____

# Forming and Using the Preterit Perfect

The preterit perfect is a compound tense, which means that it is made up of more than one part. The two elements that are needed to form the present perfect are:

1. The preterit tense of the helping verb *haber:* which expresses that something had taken place.

2. The past participle of the verb: which expresses what the action was.

The following diagram shows how the present perfect is formed:

Preterit Perfect of verb =      when + what

/ \

Preterit Perfect of verb =    (what) had   + happened

/ \

Preterit Perfect of verb =    helping verb + main verb

/ \

Preterit Perfect of verb = *haber* (to have) + past participle

The formula for the formation of the preterit perfect is:

> subject noun or pronoun + *haber* in preterit + past participle

The formation of past participles was explained in Chapter 1. Irregular past participles are listed in Table 1.3 and in Appendix H.

Note the following about the use of the preterit perfect:

◆ The preterit perfect is used mainly in literary and historic writings to show that the action or event had just ended:

En cuanto hubo llegado el teléfono sonó.
As soon as he had arrived the telephone rang.

◆ The preterit perfect generally follows expressions such as:

cuando (when)

apenas (hardly, scarcely)

después (de) que (after)

luego que (as soon as)

en cuanto (as soon as)

así que (as soon as)

tan pronto como (as soon as)

Tan pronto como me hube acostado, ella me llamó.
As soon as I had gone to bed, she called me.

◆ In conversation and informal writing, the preterit progressive is replaced by the pluperfect or the preterit tense.

### Práctica 9

Tell what had happened by completing each sentence with the correct form of the preterit perfect:

1. (abrir) Apenas nosotros _____ la puerta, él nos saludó.

2. (decir) Tan pronto él _____ la mentira, lo arrepintió.

3. (ver) En cuanto tú _____ la pregunta, supiste la respuesta correcta.

4. (escribir) Después de que yo _____ la carta, la destruí.

5. (volver) Tan pronto como Uds. _____, ella salió.

6. (poner) Luego que vosotros _____ la mesa, vosotros comisteis.

# Forming and Using the Past Progressive

The past progressive expresses what the subject was doing at a particular time: it speaks about an action that was in progress and was completed. As discussed in Chapter 1, the two elements that are needed to form the past perfect are:

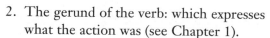

**¡Mira!**

Reflexive pronouns may precede *estar* or may be placed after and attached to the gerund. *Los niños se estuvieron bañando hasta las siete. Los niños estuvieron bañándose hasta las siete.* (The children were bathing until seven o'clock.)

1. The past tense of the verb *estar* (or *andar, continuar, entrar, ir, salir, seguir,* or *venir*): which expresses that something was taking place.

2. The gerund of the verb: which expresses what the action was (see Chapter 1).

The following diagram shows how the past progressive is formed:

Past Perfect of verb =     when + what

/     \

Past Perfect of verb =     (what) was + happening

/     \

Past Perfect of verb = *estar* (preterit) + main verb (present participle)

The formula for the formation of the past perfect is:

| subject noun or pronoun + *estar* in preterit + gerund |
| --- |

Yo estuve hablando.
I was speaking.

---

## Práctica 10

Express what each person was doing until midnight:

**Hasta el medianoche**

1. (trabajar) Vosotros _____.

2. (escribir) Ellos _____ sus tareas.

3. (vender) Tú _____ periódicos.

4. (leer) Yo _____.

5. (dormir) Nosotros _____ dormir.

6. (corregir) El profesor _____ papeles.

---

# Repaso

1. The preterit of regular *-ar* verbs is formed by dropping the infinitive ending and adding *-é, -aste, -ó, -amos, -asteis, -aron*.

2. The preterit of regular *-er* and *-ir* verbs is formed by dropping the infinitive ending and adding *-í, -iste, -ió, -imos, -isteis, -ieron*.

3. In the preterit tense, verbs ending in *-cer/-cir*, *-ger/-gir*, *-guir*, and *-quir* have no spelling changes and follow the regular rules of preterit formation.

4. All verbs ending in *-car, -gar, -guar*, and *-zar* change only in the *yo* form as follows: *c > qu, g > gu, gu > gü*, and *z > c*.

5. Verbs ending in vowel *er/ir* change the third person singular form (*el, ella, Ud.*) from *io* to *yó* and the third person plural form (*ellos, ellas, Uds.*) from *-ieron* to *yeron*. All other preterit forms have an accented *i: í*.

6. Verbs ending in *-uir* (but not *-guir*) change the third person singular form (*el, ella, Ud.*) from *io* to *yó* and the third person plural form (*ellos, ellas, Uds.*) from *-ieron* to *yeron*. All other preterit forms except *yo* remain without an accent on the *i*.

7. Verbs ending in *ñ* and *ll* before the infinitive ending drop the *i* of the preterit endings for the third person singular (*él, ella, Ud.*) and plural (*ellos, ellas, Uds.*) forms.

8. Verbs whose stems change from *e* to *ie* or from *e* to *i* in the present change their stems from *e* to *i* in the preterit in the third person singular (*él, ella, Ud.*) and in the third person plural (*ellos, ellas, Uds.*) forms.

9. Verbs whose stems change from *o* to *ue* in the present change their stems from *o* to *u* in the preterit in the third person singular (*él, ella, Ud.*) and in the third person plural.

10. In the preterit tense, the reflexive pronoun precedes the conjugated verb.

11. Verbs irregular in the preterit generally have the following endings: *-e, -iste, -o, -imos, -isteis,* and *-ieron* (or *-jeron* if the stem ends in *j* or *-ducir*).

12. Some irregular verbs change the vowel before the infinitive ending to *i*: *decir, venir, querer, hacer,* and *satisfacer.*

13. Some irregular verbs change the vowel before the infinitive ending to *u*: *caber, haber, saber, poner,* and *poder.*

14. Some irregular verbs have *j* in their stem: *traer* and verbs ending in *-ducir.*

15. *Dar* and *ver* have similar irregular preterit stems.

16. *Ser* and *ir* have the same preterit forms.

17. The preterit is used to express a completed past action.

18. The meanings of *conocer, poder, querer, saber,* and *tener* may change in the preterit.

19. The preterit perfect expresses what had occurred and is formed by conjugating *haber* in the preterit tense and adding a past participle (which remains the same for all subject pronouns).

20. The preterit perfect is usually found only in formal literary and historic writing and is used after the expressions *cuando, apenas, después (de) que, luego (de) que, en cuanto, así que,* and *tan pronto como.*

21. The past progressive expresses an action that was occurring and was completed. It is formed by conjugating the verb *estar* in the preterit tense and adding a gerund. Reflexive pronouns may precede *estar* or may be placed after and attached to the gerund.

## The Least You Need to Know

◆ The preterit endings of regular *-ar* verbs are *é, aste, ó, amos, asteis, aron*.

◆ The preterit endings of regular *-er* and *-ir* are *í, iste, ió, imos, isteis, ieron*.

◆ Spelling-change and stem-changing verbs require changes in the preterit.

◆ The preterit perfect is formed by taking the preterit of *haber* and adding a past participle.

◆ The past progressive is formed by taking the preterit of *estar* and adding a gerund.

# Chapter 5

# The Imperfect and the Pluperfect

## In This Chapter

- ◆ Forming the imperfect of regular, irregular, and reflexive verbs
- ◆ Forming the imperfect of stem-changing and spelling-change verbs
- ◆ When to use the preterit and the imperfect
- ◆ Using *hacía* with the imperfect

There are two different simple past tenses in Spanish: the preterit and the imperfect. This may tend to be confusing because the imperfect tense has no English grammatical equivalent. The imperfect is a past tense that shows an action that was continuous in the past—in other words, an action that was taking place or that used to happen repeatedly over an indefinite period of time. When the action started and when it ended is unclear. An imperfect past action is viewed as incomplete. Whereas the preterit relates specific actions that have occurred, the imperfect describes scenes, settings, situations, or states in the past.

The imperfect is a simple tense that expresses what the subject was or used to do: *I was leaving …*, *I used to leave …*. The pluperfect is the imperfect's compound equivalent that shows what the subject had been doing before another action took place, whether that other action is stated or implied. The past progressive using the imperfect describes an action that was taking place in the past without any indication of when that action ceased. In this chapter you'll learn how to use the imperfect and how to differentiate when it is more appropriate to use the preterit or the imperfect.

# The Imperfect of Regular and Reflexive Verbs

Although somewhat foreign to us in its application, the imperfect tense is delightfully easy because there are only three irregular verbs. There are no spelling or stem changes in verbs that have otherwise proven problematic. Once you've memorized the imperfect endings and the imperfect forms for *ir*, *ser*, and *ver* you will need to focus on when to correctly use this tense.

## Forming the Imperfect of Regular Verbs

To form the imperfect of regular verbs, drop the infinitive ending (*-ar*, *-er*, *-ir*) and add the imperfect endings shown in Table 5.1.

## Table 5.1    The Imperfect of Regular Verbs

| Subject | *-ar* verbs | *-er* verbs | *-ir* verbs |
|---|---|---|---|
| | **hablar** (*to speak*) | **beber** (*to drink*) | **abrir** (*to open*) |
| yo | habl**aba** | beb**ía** | abr**ía** |
| tú | habl**abas** | beb**ías** | abr**ías** |
| él, ella, Ud. | habl**aba** | beb**ía** | abr**ía** |
| nosotros | habl**ábamos** | beb**íamos** | abr**íamos** |
| vosotros | habl**abais** | beb**íais** | abr**íais** |
| ellos, ellas, Uds. | habl**aban** | beb**ían** | abr**ían** |

# The Imperfect of Spelling- and Stem-Changing Verbs

Since stem- and spelling-changing verbs are regular in the imperfect in all forms, they should be rather easy to conjugate, as illustrated in Table 5.2.

### Table 5.2 The Imperfect of Stem- and Spelling-Changing Verbs

| Verb | Imperfect Stem | Example |
|------|----------------|---------|
| *Spelling-Change Verbs* | | |
| **Group 1** | | |
| bus**car** | busc | yo buscaba |
| lle**gar** | lleg | tú llegabas |
| averi**guar** | averigu | él averiguaba |
| cru**zar** | cruz | nosotros cruzábamos |
| ven**cer** | venc | vosotros vencíais |
| frun**cir** | frunc | ellos fruncían |
| distin**guir** | distingu | yo distinguía |
| delin**quir** | delinqu | tú delinquías |
| **Group 2** | | |
| bu**ll**ir | bull | él bullía |
| ta**ñ**er | tañ | nosotros tañíamos |
| cr**eer** | cre | vosotros creíais |
| **oír** | oí | ellos oían |
| *Stem-Changing Verbs* | | |
| **Class 1** | | |
| c**e**rrar | cerr | yo cerraba |
| m**o**strar | mostr | tú mostrabas |
| p**e**rder | perd | él perdía |
| m**o**rder | mord | nosotros mordíamos |
| **Class 2** | | |
| m**e**ntir | ment | vosotros mentíais |
| d**o**rmir | dorm | ellos dormían |

*continues*

## Table 5.2   The Imperfect of Stem- and Spelling-Changing Verbs (continued)

| Verb | Imperfect Stem | Example |
|---|---|---|
| ***Stem-Changing Verbs*** | | |
| **Class 3** | | |
| pe**d**ir | ped | yo pedía |
| **Class 4** | | |
| reu**n**ir | reun | tú reunías |
| ***Other Verbs*** | | |
| var**iar** | var | él variaba |
| conti**nuar** | continu | nosotros continuábamos |
| conc**luir** | conclu | vosotros concluíais |
| distin**guir** | distingu | ellos distinguían |

In the imperfect tense, the reflexive pronoun precedes the conjugated verb:

Se acostaba cuando alguien llamó a la puerta.
He was going to bed when someone knocked on the door.

La muchacha se divertía mucho en la fiesta.
The girl was having a good time at the party.

## Práctica 1

Express what each person was doing right before a blackout:

1. (afeitarse) Él _____.

2. (beber) Nosotros _____ licuadas.

3. (escribir) Ellos _____ cartas.

4. (platicar) Vosotros _____ con sus amigos.

5. (pagar) Yo _____ mis cuentas.

6. (almorzar) Uds. _____.

7. (esquiar) Ella _____.

8. (volver) Tú _____ a casa.

9. (conducir) Ellas _____ al centro.

10. (estar) Ud. _____ en la escuela.

11. (venir) Yo _____ a casa.

12. (tener) Ellos _____ una pelea.

# The Imperfect of Irregular Verbs

You have already seen that verbs that are irregular in the present are not necessarily irregular in the preterit. All verbs in Spanish are regular in the imperfect except *ir* (*to go*), *ser* (*to be*), and *ver* (*to see*). These three irregular verbs are illustrated in Table 5.3.

## Table 5.3    The Imperfect of Irregular Verbs

|  | ir (*to go*) | ser (*to be*) | ver (*to see*) |
|---|---|---|---|
| yo | iba | era | veía |
| tú | ibas | eras | veías |
| él | iba | era | veía |
| nosotros | íbamos | éramos | veíamos |
| vosotros | ibais | erais | veíais |
| ellos | iban | eran | veían |

## Práctica 2

Express what happened in the restaurant by using the imperfect of the verbs indicated:

1. (ser) _____ martes.

2. (brillar) El sol _____.

3. (hacer) _____ frío.

4. (querer) Yo _____ entrar en un restaurante.

*continues*

*continued*

5. (estar) Un hombre guapo _____ sentado en una mesa.

6. (llevar) Él _____ pantalones negros y una camisa blanca.

7. (parecer) Él _____ tener unos veinte años.

8. (tener) Él _____ ojos azules y pelo rubio.

9. (pesar) Él _____ cien kilos más o menos.

10. (leer) Él _____ un periódico.

11. (temer) Yo _____ molestarlo.

12. (esperar) Yo _____ hablar con él.

## Práctica 3

Describe *la quinceañera* (Sweet 15 party) of Carmen Molina:

1. hacer/buen tiempo _____

2. los pájaros/cantar _____

3. todo el mundo/felicitar a Carmen _____

4. sus padres/llorar de alegría _____

5. Carmen/sonreír _____

6. yo/sacar fotografías _____

7. Uds./querer abrazar a Carmen _____

8. tú/esperar bailar con ella _____

## Práctica 4

Write what each person was in the habit of doing in the past by changing the sentences from the present to the imperfect:

1. Nosotros trabajamos todos los días. _____

2. Ellos comen hamburguesas en el café. _____

3. Tú interrumpes al profesor._____

4. Vosotros vais a la playa._____

5. Yo juego a los naipes._____

6. Ella escoje joyas caras._____

7. Él pierde cosas importantes._____

8. Uds. se visten con cuidado._____

9. Ellas se despiertan tarde._____

10. Ud. es romántico._____

# Using the Preterit and the Imperfect

It is sometimes difficult to choose whether to use the preterit or the imperfect in any given case. Very often, the mindset of the speaker determines whether he or she views the action as completed in the past at a particular time or taking place for an indefinite period in the past with no determined beginning or end.

To eliminate any confusion these two tenses may cause, think of a camera. The preterit represents an action that could be captured by a snapshot—the action happened and was completed and could be represented by a dot that indicates one moment in time. The imperfect, on the other hand, represents an action that could be captured by a video camera—the action continued to flow and could be represented by a wavy line. Another way of looking at this is that the preterit **states** what action took place while the imperfect **describes** the action that took place.

The following two lists provide a more in-depth look at the differences between these two tenses.

**The preterit ...**

◆ Expresses specific actions or events that were started or completed at a definite time in the past (even if the time isn't mentioned):

Anoche llamé a mi amiga.
Last night I called my friend.

Estuve contento de ver a mi amigo.
I was happy to see my friend.

◆ Expresses a specific action or event that occurred at a specific point in time:

Ayer yo me levanté a las ocho.
Yesterday I got up at eight o'clock.

◆ Expresses a specific action or event that was repeated a stated number of times:

Viajé a España dos veces.
I traveled to Spain two times.

◆ Expresses the beginning or end of a specific action:

Empecé a cocinar a la una y terminé a las cinco.
I started to cook at one o'clock and finished at five.

◆ Expresses a series of completed events:

Yo cené, miré la televisión y me acosté.
I ate dinner, I watched television and I went to bed.

**The imperfect …**

◆ Describes ongoing or continuous actions in the past (which might or might not have been completed):

Yo trabajaba con mi amigo.
I was working with my friend.

Estaba contento con mi trabajo.
I was happy with my work.

◆ Describes repeated or habitual actions that took place in the past:

Yo me levantaba a las ocho.
I used to get up at eight o'clock.

◆ Describes an action that continued for an unspecified period of time:

Viajaba a España a menudo.
I often traveled to Spain.

◆ Describes a person, place, thing, weather, time, day of the week, state of mind, and emotion:

Tenía miedo porque la calle estaba oscura.
I was afraid because the street was dark.

◆ Describes simultaneous actions taking place at the same time:

> Josefa bailaba mientras Jorge cantaba.
> Josefa was dancing while Jorge was singing.

**¡Mira!** _____

Verbs such as *creer* (to believe), *pensar* (to think), *querer* (to want), *preocuparse* (to worry), *poder* (to be able to), and *saber* (to know) show a state of mind.

## Práctica 5

Describe what the two friends did by choosing the correct form of the verb in the preterit or in the imperfect:

(Fue, Era) ___1___ un día magnífico de verano. (Hizo, Hacía) ___2___ buen tiempo. Yo no (tuve, tenía) ___3___ nada que hacer cuando de repente, el teléfono (sonó, sonaba) ___4___. Yo (contesté, contestaba) ___5___. (Fue, Era) ___6___ mi amiga Estela. Ella me (preguntó, preguntaba) ___7___ si yo (quise, quería) ___8___ ir a la playa con ella. Yo (respondí, respondía) ___9___: "¡Con mucho gusto!" Entonces yo (fui, iba) ___10___ a su casa a las once y nosotras (fuimos, íbamos) ___11___ a la playa en coche. El cielo (estuvo, estaba) ___12___ azul y el agua (estuvo, estaba) ___13___ muy clara. Nosotros (encontramos, encontrábamos) ___14___ un lugar muy tranquilo y (fuimos, íbamos) ___15___ al mar en seguida. (Pasamos, Pasábamos) ___16___ toda la tarde nadando, hablando de nuestros pasatiempos favoritos, y divirtiéndonos. (Estuvimos, Estábamos) ___17___ muy contentas. La tarde (fue, era) ___18___ muy agradable.

## Práctica 6

Complete Maribel's composition by using the correct form of the preterit or the imperfect:

Cuando (ser) ___1___ muy pequeña, (pasar) ___2___ todas las vacaciones en casa de mi tía Marta que (vivir) ___3___ en un pueblo pequeño cerca de San Juan. Los viernes yo (ir) ___4___ a la biblioteca para buscar libros. Siempre (escoger) ___5___ libros de ciencia ficción porque los (preferir) ___6___.

*continues*

*continued*

Un día, (aburrirse) ____7____ de este género. El viernes próximo, (tomar) ____8____ mi desayuno y (ir) ____9____ a la biblioteca. Cuando (entrar) ____10____, el bibliotecario (estar) ____11____ ocupado arreglando los libros. Le (preguntar) ____12____ cuales libros (poder) ____13____ recomendarme. Él (sugerir) ___14___ los libros de Isaac Asimov. Yo le (explicar) ____15____ que no (querer) ____16____ leer más libros de ciencia ficción. Él me (proponer) ____17____ historias de amor que yo (rechazar) ____18____. Los libros que me (mostrar) ____19____ después (ser) ____20____ demasiado intelectuales. Finalmente, él me (dar) ____21____ un libro de poemas aburridos. Así que yo (escoger) ____22____ otra vez un libro de ciencia ficción.

The imperfect describes a situation that was going on in the past when another action or event, expressed by the preterit, took place:

> Salía cuando ella me llamó.
> I was leaving when she called me.

## Práctica 7

Express what each person did by combining the two sentences and using the preterit and the imperfect to replace the present:

> Ejemplo:     Me quedo en casa. Estoy enfermo.
> Me quedé en casa porque estaba enfermo.

1. Arturo se cae. No presta atención. _____

2. Tu llamas a Miguel. Tu quieres ir al parque. _____

3. Ella compra un billete. Ella tiene ganas de ir al teatro. _____

4. Saco mi paraguas. Llueve mucho. _____

5. Nosotros le escribimos a nuestro amigo. Es su aniversario. _____

6. Uds. presentan sus excusas. Uds. se arrepienten de sus acciones. _____

### Práctica 8

Describe the bad luck of these people by completing the sentences with the preterit and the imperfect:

1. (conducir/detener) Pablo _____ muy rápidamente cuando un policía lo _____.

2. (salir/atacar) Los López _____ de su casa cuando un ladrón los _____.

3. (reñir/abrir) Marinela _____ a su hermano cuando su madre _____ la puerta.

4. (subir/llamar) Yo _____ a mi cuarto cuando alguien _____.

5. (comer/ver) Yo _____ en un restaurante elegante cuando yo _____ una mosca en mi sopa.

6. (viajar/desencadenarse) Mis primos _____ en Europa cuando una guerra _____

7. (correr/caerse) Ud. _____ cuando Ud. _____

8. (ir/perder) Tú _____ al centro cuando _____ tu cartera.

To express an event or action that began in the past and continued in the past use *hacía (que)* or *desde hacía*:

| | |
|---|---|
| ¿Cuánto tiempo hacía que estudiabas? | Hacía una hora (que estudiaba). |
| ¿Desde cuándo estudiabas? | Estudiaba desde hacía una hora. |
| How long had you been studying? | I'd been studying for an hour. |

### Práctica 9

Juanita wants to know how long her friends had been doing certain things. Give her questions by using *¿Cuánto tiempo hacía …?* and the answers by using *hacía … que*:

*continues*

*continued*

Ejemplo:

Jorge/trabajar/dos años

¿Cuánto tiempo hacía que Jorge trabajaba?

Hacía dos años que trabajaba.

1. Elena/ir a la universidad/un año _____

2. Esteban y José/ser amigos/diez años _____

3. nosotros/tocar la guitarra/dos meses _____

4. tú/tener tu propio carro/una semana _____

5. vosotros/vivir en los Estados Unidos/cinco años _____

6. Uds./estar a régimen/6 días _____

# Forming and Using the Pluperfect

The pluperfect is a compound tense, which means that it is made up of more than one part. The two elements that are needed to form the pluperfect are:

1. The imperfect tense of the helping verb *haber* (*había, habías, había, habíamos, habíais, habían*): which expresses that something had taken place.

2. The past participle of the verb: which expresses what the action was.

The following diagram shows how the pluperfect is formed:

Pluperfect of verb =   when + what

/   \

Pluperfect of verb =   (what) had + happened

/   \

Pluperfect of verb =   helping verb + main verb

/   \

Pluperfect of verb = *haber* (to have) + past participle

The formula for the formation of the pluperfect is:

| subject noun or pronoun + *haber* in imperfect + past participle |
| --- |

The formation of past participles was explained in Chapter 1. Irregular past participles appear in Table 1.3 and in Appendix H.

Note the following about the use of the pluperfect:

◆ The pluperfect describes an action or event that was completed in the past before another action took place and is usually expressed by the English "had" + past participle.

> Él había hablado antes de reflejar.
> He had spoken before thinking.

◆ Because the pluperfect is used in relation to another past action, that action is usually in the preterit or imperfect.

> Cuando el profesor llegó, los alumnos ya se habían sentado.
> When the teacher arrived, the students had already sat down.

> Cuando él iba a España, su familia ya había hecho planes para él.
> When he would go to Spain, his family had already made plans for him.

◆ When using the pluperfect, it is not always necessary to have the other past action expressed:

> Él había encontrado su libro en su cuarto.
> He had found his book in his room.

---

## Práctica 10

Give reasons for the situations that ensued by using the pluperfect:

Ejemplo:
Humberto estaba contento. (ir a una fiesta)
Él había ido a una fiesta.

1. Los niños lloraban. (perder su perro) _____

2. Carlota tuvo dolor de estómago. (comer demasiado) _____

3. Yo estaba triste. (recibir malas notas) _____

4. Nosotros estábamos despeinados. (salir sin nuestros sombreros) _____

5. Tú te acostaste temprano. (trabajar duro) _____

6. Vosotros sufríais. (caerse) _____

# Forming and Using the Past Progressive

The past progressive expresses what the subject was doing at a particular time; it speaks about an action that was in progress and was completed. As discussed in Chapter 1, the two elements that are needed to form the past progressive are:

1. The imperfect of the verb *estar* (or *andar, continuar, entrar, ir, salir, seguir* or *venir*): which expresses that something was taking place.

2. The gerund of the verb: which expresses what the action was (see Chapter 1).

The following diagram shows how the past progressive is formed:

Past Perfect of verb =      when + what

/    \

Past Perfect of verb =      (what) was + happening

/    \

Past Perfect of verb = *estar* (imperfect) + main verb (present participle)

The formula for the formation of the past perfect is:

subject noun or pronoun + *estar* in imperfect + gerund

Yo estaba cantando.
I was singing.

Note that reflexive pronouns may precede *estar* or may be placed after and attached to the gerund:

Los niños se estaban bañando.
Los niños estaban bañándose.
The children were bathing themselves.

## Práctica 11

Express what each person was doing when a sudden storm broke out:

1. yo/conducir al centro _____

2. nosotros/dormir al aire libre _____

3. los niños/jugar en el parque _____

4. tú/correr _____

5. vosotros/caminar _____

6. Mariana/plantar flores _____

# Repaso

1. The imperfect of regular *-ar* verbs is formed by dropping the infinitive ending and adding *-aba, -abas, -aba, -ábamos, -abais, -aban.*

2. The imperfect of regular *-er* and *-ir* verbs is formed by dropping the infinitive ending and adding *-ía, -ías, -ía, -íamos, -íais, -ieron.*

3. Stem- and spelling-change verbs are regular in the imperfect in all forms.

4. In the imperfect tense, the reflexive pronoun precedes the conjugated verb.

5. Only three verbs are irregular in the imperfect: *ir, ser,* and *ver.*

6. The preterit expresses a completed past action.

7. The imperfect describes an incomplete or habitual past action. The imperfect also expresses time of day, weather, states of mind, and emotions in the past.

8. The imperfect describes a situation that was going on in the past when another action or event, expressed by the preterit, took place.

9. To express an event or action that began in the past and continued in the past, use *hacía (que)* or *desde hacía.*

10. The pluperfect expresses what had occurred and is formed by conjugating *haber* in the imperfect tense and adding a past participle (which remains the same for all subject pronouns).

11. The past progressive expresses an action that was occurring and was completed. It is formed by conjugating the verb *estar* in the imperfect tense and adding a gerund. Reflexive pronouns may precede *estar* or may be placed after and attached to the gerund.

## The Least You Need to Know

- ◆ The imperfect endings for regular *-ar* verbs are *-aba, -abas, -aba, -ábamos, -abais, -aban*.

- ◆ The imperfect endings for regular *-er* and *-er* are *-ía, -ías, -ía, -íamos, -íais, -ieron*.

- ◆ The imperfect describes a continuous past action while the preterit expresses a completed past action.

- ◆ The pluperfect is formed by taking the imperfect of *haber* and adding a past participle.

- ◆ The past progressive is formed by taking the imperfect of *estar* and adding a gerund.

# Chapter 6

# The Future and the Future Perfect

## In This Chapter

- ◆ Using the present to express the future
- ◆ Using *ir* + infinitive to express the future
- ◆ Forming the future of regular and reflexive verbs
- ◆ Forming the future of stem-changing and spelling-change verbs
- ◆ Forming the future of irregular verbs
- ◆ When to use the future
- ◆ Forming and using the future perfect and the future progressive

In Spanish, the simple future can be expressed in one of three different ways: by using the present (as explained in Chapter 3), by using the irregular verb *ir* + *a* + an infinitive to say what the subject is *going to do* or what is *going to happen* soon, and by using the future tense to say what the subject *will do* or what *will happen* at a later date.

The future perfect is the compound equivalent of the future and it is used to express what the subject will have done or what will have happened before another future action will have occurred. The future progressive expresses an action that will be in progress at some time in the future. In this chapter you'll learn how to know whether to use the "near future" or the future tense and when to use the future perfect and the future progressive.

# Using the Present to Express the Future

The present tense may be used to express the future when the subject is asking for instructions or is referring to an action that will take place in the immediate future:

¿Lo hago ahora?          Te llamo pronto.
Shall I do it now?       I'll call you soon.

# Using *ir* + *a* + Infinitive to Express the Future

The irregular verb *ir* (to go) is used to express what is going to happen:

yo voy                   nosotros vamos

tú vas                   vosotros vais

él va                    ellos van

*Ir* is followed by the preposition *a*, which is followed by the infinitive of the verb expressing the action that the speaker is going to perform:

Voy a estudiar.          No vamos a trabajar.
I'm going to study.      We aren't going to work.

---

### Práctica 1

Express what the different people are going to do after work by using *ir* + *a* + *infinitive*:

1. yo/escuchar música _____

2. nosotros/leer _____

3. Uds./jugar al fútbol _____

4. tú/ir al centro comercial _____

5. vosotros/escribir mensajes por correo electrónico _____

6. ella/llamar a sus amigas _____

---

# The Future of Regular and Reflexive Verbs

The future tense in Spanish is really quite easy because all verbs, whether they have regular or irregular stems, have the same endings. Add to that that there are no spelling or stem changes in verbs that generally have these changes and you will understand that you will have very little trouble mastering this tense. Most Spanish verbs that are irregular in the future fit into one of three categories, and only two verbs are truly irregular and follow no rules.

# Forming the Future of Regular Verbs

To form the future of regular verbs, add the future endings in Table 6.1 to the infinitive (the "to" form) of the verb.

## Table 6.1    The Future of Regular Verbs

| Subject | -*ar* verbs | -*er* verbs | -*ir* verbs |
|---|---|---|---|
| | **mirar** (*to look at*) | **aprender** (*to learn*) | **subir** (*to go up*) |
| yo | mirar**é** | aprender**é** | subir**é** |
| tú | mirar**ás** | aprender**ás** | subir**ás** |
| él, ella, Ud. | mirar**á** | aprender**á** | subir**á** |
| nosotros | mirar**emos** | aprender**emos** | subir**emos** |
| vosotros | mirar**éis** | aprender**éis** | subir**éis** |
| ellos, ellas, Uds. | mirar**án** | aprender**án** | subir**án** |

Ellos viajarán al extranjero el año próximo.
They are going to travel abroad next year.

Yo te escribiré pronto.
I'll write to you soon.

**¡Mira!**

All future endings have an accent mark except the *nosotros -emos* ending.

# The Future of Spelling- and Stem-Changing Verbs

Because stem- and spelling-change verbs are regular in the future in all forms, they should be rather easy to conjugate, as illustrated in Table 6.2.

## Table 6.2  The Future of Stem- and Spelling-Change Verbs

| Verb | Future Stem | Example |
| --- | --- | --- |
| *Spelling-Change Verbs* | | |
| **Group 1** | | |
| bus**car** | buscar | yo buscaré |
| lle**gar** | llegar | tú llegarás |
| averi**guar** | averiguar | él averiguará |
| cru**zar** | cruzar | nosotros cruzaremos |
| ven**cer** | vencer | vosotros venceréis |
| espar**cir** | esparcir | ellos esparcirán |
| distin**guir** | distinguir | yo distinguiré |
| delin**quir** | delinquir | tú delinquirás |
| **Group 2** | | |
| bu**ll**ir | bullir | él bullirá |
| ta**ñ**er | tañer | nosotros tañeremos |
| cr**ee**r | creer | vosotros creeréis |
| **oír** | oir | ellos oirán |
| *Stem-Changing Verbs* | | |
| **Class 1** | | |
| c**e**rrar | cerrar | yo cerraré |
| m**o**strar | mostrar | tú mostrarás |
| p**e**rder | perder | él perderá |
| m**o**rder | morder | nosotros morderemos |
| **Class 2** | | |
| m**e**ntir | mentir | vosotros mentiréis |
| d**o**rmir | dormir | ellos dormirán |
| **Class 3** | | |
| p**e**dir | pedir | yo pediré |
| **Class 4** | | |
| re**u**nir | reunir | tú reunirás |

| Verb | Future Stem | Example |
|------|-------------|---------|
| *Other Verbs* | | |
| var**iar** | variar | él variará |
| contin**uar** | continuar | nosotros continuaremos |
| conc**luir** | concluir | vosotros concluiréis |
| distin**guir** | distinguir | ellos distinguirán |

In the future tense, the reflexive pronoun precedes the conjugated verb:

> Me acostaré después de trabajar.
> I'll go to bed after working.

> Ellos se vestirán rápidamente.
> They will get dressed quickly.

Note that verbs such as *oír*, and *reír*, whose infinitive contains an accent mark drop that accent in the future:

> Él no oirá las noticias.      Yo reiré.
> He won't hear the news.      I will laugh.

---

## Práctica 2

Express what each person will do tomorrow:

1. (celebrar) Yo _____ mi cumpleaños.

2. (asistir) Tú _____ a una conferencia.

3. (vender) Los niños _____ limonada a los transeúntes.

4. (anunciar) Ud. _____ su boda.

5. (correr) Nosotros _____ cinco kilómetros.

6. (acudir) Vosotros _____ a una cita.

7. (comunicarse) Uds. _____ con sus amigos.

8. (investigar) Él _____ un crimen.

9. (empezar) Nosotros _____ a estudiar francés.

10. (merendar) Vosotros _____ temprano.

*continues*

*continued*

11. (probarse) Ellas _____ vestidos nuevos.

12. (rociar) Vosotros _____ el jardín.

13. (continuar) Ellos _____ trabajando duro.

14. (dormir) Yo _____ mucho.

15. (mentir) Ella no _____ a sus padres.

16. (reír) Nosotros no _____ mucho.

17. (creer) Tú no _____ sus mentiras.

18. (vestirse) Ellos _____ con elegancia.

19. (cocer) Uds. _____ una comida sabrosa.

20. (corregir) Yo _____ mis tareas.

# The Future of Irregular Verbs

The verbs that are irregular in the future were also irregular in the present. Irregular verbs in the future fall into one of three categories:

♦ Those that drop *-e* from the infinitive ending before adding the future endings (*-e, -ás, -á, -emos, -éis, -án*):

| Infinitive | Meaning | Future Stem |
|------------|-------------|-------------|
| caber | to fit | cabr- |
| haber | to have | habr- |
| poder | to be able | podr- |
| querer | to want | querr- |
| saber | to know | sabr- |

♦ Those that drop *-e* or *-i* from the infinitive ending and replace the vowel with a *d* before adding the future endings:

| Infinitive | Meaning | Future Stem |
|------------|-------------|-------------|
| poner | to put | pon**dr**- |
| salir | to leave | sal**dr**- |
| tener | to have | ten**dr**- |

| Infinitive | Meaning | Future Stem |
|---|---|---|
| valer | to be worth | val**dr**- |
| venir | to come | ven**dr**- |

◆ Those that have a completely irregular stem to which are added the future endings:

| Infinitive | Meaning | Future Stem |
|---|---|---|
| decir | to say | dir- |
| hacer | to make, do | har- |

---

### Práctica 3

Complete the message left on your answering machine by filling in the correct form of the verb in the future.

¡Hola! Habla Roberto. Yo te (decir) ____1____ mis planes para mañana por la noche. Yo (poder) ____2____ estar en tu casa a las siete. Sé que tú y tu familia (querer) ____3____ ir conmigo al restaurante, pero todo el mundo no (caber) ____4____ en mi carro. Yo (tener) ____5____ que hacer dos viajes y los (hacer) ____6____ de buena gana. ¡No te preocupes! Yo (salir) ____7____ de mi casa a las seis y media e (ir) ____8____ a tu casa en seguida. ¿(saber) ____9____ Uds. como ir para allá? (valer) ____10____ la pena llegar a ese restaurante muy temprano porque yo estoy seguro de que no (haber) ____11____ mucha gente a esa hora. Este restaurante es muy famoso y yo (ponerse) ____12____ ropa elegante. Hasta mañana.

---

# Using the Future

The future is used in Spanish to express future time—what *will happen*.

> Vendrán la semana próxima.
> They will come next week.

The future may be used to predict a future action or event:

> Nevará mañana.
> It will snow tomorrow.

The future often expresses an expected action, event, or result caused by a current action or event:

>Si José trabaja mucho, ganará mucho dinero.
>If José works a lot, he will earn a lot of money.

**¡Mira!** _____

The expression *deber de* (in the present) + infinitive also expresses probability at the present time: *Debe de ser las tres.* (It is probably 3 o'clock.)

The future also expresses wonderment, probability, or speculation about actions or events occurring in the present and is equivalent to the English: I wonder, probably, must be, or can:

>¿Qué hora sera?              Serán las tres.
>What time can it be?         It must be 3 o'clock.
>I wonder what time it is.    It is probably 3 o'clock.

## Práctica 4

Describe what life will be like in 50 years:

1. (curar) Los científicos _____ todas las enfermedades.

2. (descubrir) Los astrónomos _____ la vida extraterrestre.

3. (desaparecer) La pobreza _____.

4. (enterarse) Los hombres _____ de una solución a los problemas ecológicos.

5. (establecer) Muchos países _____ colonias sobre la luna.

6. (eliminar) Nosotros _____ la violencia.

## Práctica 5

Express what is probable:

1. (ser) _____ la una.

2. (tener) ¿No pueden dormir? Uds. _____ hambre.

3. (llover) _____ mañana.

4. (estar) Él trabaja mucho. _____ cansado.

5. (recibir) ¿Cuántos regalos _____ ellos para su aniversario?

6. (tardar) ¿Cuánto tiempo _____ ella en venir?

# Forming and Using the Future Perfect

The future perfect is a compound tense, which means that it is made up of more than one part. The two elements that are needed to form the future perfect are:

1. The future tense of the helping verb *haber* (*habré, habrás, habrá, habremos, habréis, habrán*): which expresses that something will taken place.

2. The past participle of the verb: which expresses what the action was.

The following diagram shows how the future perfect is formed:

Future Perfect of verb =         when + what
                                  /        \

Future Perfect of verb =    (what) had  + happened
                                  /        \

Future Perfect of verb =    helping verb + main verb
                                  /        \

Future Perfect of verb = *haber* (to have) + past participle

The formula for the formation of the future perfect is:

| subject noun or pronoun + *haber* in future + past participle |
|---|

The formation of past participles was explained in Chapter 1. Irregular past participles appear in Table 1.3 and in Appendix H.

Note the following about the future perfect tense:

◆ The future perfect expresses an action or event that will have taken place or been completed in the future:

> No llame mañana porque todavía no habré recibido noticias.
> Don't call tomorrow because I will not have received news yet.

◆ The future perfect may be used to express probability or conjecture in the past:

¿Lo habrán visto?
I wonder if they have seen it?
(Can they have seen it?)

Habré perdido mi paraguas.
I (have) probably lost my umbrella.
(I must have lost my umbrella.)

◆ When expressing probability in past time, the future perfect may be replaced by *deber de* (in the present) + the perfect infinitive:

Debo de haber perdido mi paraguas.
I must have lost the keys.

---

### Práctica 6

Express what the following people will have done before 7 P.M.:

1. (comer) Nosotros _____ la cena.

2. (recibir) Ellos _____ un paquete.

3. (platicar) Yo _____ con mis amigos.

4. (poner) Manolo _____la mesa.

5. (resolver) Tú _____ un problema importante.

6. (abrir) Vosotros _____ una cuenta bancaria.

7. (ver) Uds. _____ una película.

8. (escribir) Ella _____ una carta.

---

# Forming and Using the Future Progressive

The future progressive expresses what the subject will be doing at a particular time: it speaks about an action that will be in progress and will be completed. As discussed in Chapter 1, the two elements that are needed to form the future progressive are:

1. The future of the verb *estar* (or *andar, continuar, entrar, ir, salir, seguir* or *venir*): which expresses that something was taking place.

2. The gerund of the verb: which expresses what the action was (see Chapter 1).

The following diagram shows how the future progressive is formed:

Future Perfect of verb =      when + what

                    /    \

Future Perfect of verb = (what) was + happening

                    /    \

Future Perfect of verb =      *estar* + main verb (present participle)

The formula for the formation of the past perfect is:

> subject noun or pronoun + *estar* in future + gerund

Uds. estarán bailando juntos antes de la tarde.
You will be dancing together before the afternoon.

Reflexive pronouns may precede *estar* or may be placed after and attached to the gerund.

Ellos se estarán enojando pronto.
Ellos estarán enojándose pronto.
They will be getting angry soon.

---

## Práctica 7

Express what each person will be doing by the end of the day:

1. (tocar) Nosotros _____ el piano.

2. (pilotar) Tú _____ un avión.

3. (ofrecer) Ella _____ consejos a todo el mundo.

4. (navegar) Uds. _____ por el internet.

5. (mandar) Yo _____ mensajes por correo electrónico.

6. (traducir) Vosotros _____ palabras en español.

# Repaso

1. The future of regular verbs is formed by keeping the infinitive ending and adding the future endings: *-é, -ás, -á, -emos, -éis, -án.*

2. Stem- and spelling-change verbs are regular in the future in all forms.

3. In the future tense, the reflexive pronoun precedes the conjugated verb.

4. *Caber* (to fit), *haber* (to have), *poder* (to be able to), *querer* (to want), and *saber* (to know) form the future by dropping the *-e* from the infinitive stem and adding the future endings.

5. *Poner* (to put), *salir* (to go out), *tener* (to have), *valer* (to be worth), and *venir* (to come) drop the *-e* or *-i* from the infinitive ending and replace it with a *-d* before adding the future endings.

6. *Decir* (to tell, say) and *hacer* (to make, do) are irregular in the future: *dir-* and *har-* respectively.

7. The future perfect expresses what will have occurred and is formed by conjugating *haber* in the future tense and adding a past participle (which remains the same for all subject pronouns).

8. The future progressive expresses an action that will be occurring. It is formed by conjugating the verb *estar* in the future tense and adding a gerund. Reflexive pronouns may precede *estar* or may be placed after and attached to the gerund.

## The Least You Need to Know

♦ The future endings: *-é, -ás, -á, -emos, -éis, -án* are added to the verb infinitive or to a special irregular stem.

♦ To form the future perfect, take the future of *haber* and add the past participle.

♦ To form the future progressive, take the future of *estar* and add a gerund.

**7**

# The Conditional and the Conditional Perfect

## In This Chapter

- Forming the conditional of regular and reflexive verbs
- Forming the conditional of stem-changing and spelling-change verbs
- Forming the conditional of irregular verbs
- When to use the conditional
- Forming and using the conditional perfect and the conditional progressive

In Spanish, the conditional mood is generally used in the same way it is used in English: to express what *would* happen under certain circumstances. Be careful not to confuse the conditional with the future, whose stem it borrows; or with the imperfect, whose endings it uses.

The conditional perfect is the compound equivalent of the conditional and it is used to express what the subject would have done or what would have happened in particular situations in the past. The conditional progressive expresses an action that would have been in progress at some time in the past had specific circumstances existed. In this chapter you'll learn when to form and use the conditional, the conditional perfect, and the conditional progressive.

# The Conditional of Regular and Reflexive Verbs

The conditional mood in Spanish is relatively simple to form once you've mastered the future and imperfect tenses, since it is a combination of the two. Because the stem of the conditional is identical to that of the future, verbs in the conditional have no spelling or stem changes. Just like verbs in the future, all verbs in the conditional, whether they have regular or irregular stems, have the same endings. Since it mirrors the future, most Spanish verbs that are irregular in the conditional fit into one of three categories and only two verbs are truly irregular and follow no rules.

# Forming the Conditional of Regular Verbs

To form the conditional of regular verbs, add the conditional endings in Table 7.1 to the infinitive (the "to" form) of the verb.

## Table 7.1 The Conditional of Regular Verbs

| Subject | -*ar* Verbs | -*er* Verbs | -*ir* Verbs |
|---|---|---|---|
| | **mirar** (*to look at*) | **aprender** (*to learn*) | **subir** (*to go up*) |
| yo | mirar**ía** | aprender**ía** | subir**ía** |
| tú | mirar**ías** | aprender**ías** | subir**ías** |
| él, ella, Ud. | mirar**ía** | aprender**ía** | subir**ía** |
| nosotros | mirar**íamos** | aprender**íamos** | subir**íamos** |
| vosotros | mirar**íais** | aprender**íais** | subir**íais** |
| ellos, ellas, Uds. | mirar**ían** | aprender**ían** | subir**ían** |

¿Qué necesitaríamos para viajar a España?
What would we need to travel to Spain?

¿Qué comerías en un restaurante español?
What would you eat in a Spanish restaurant?

# The Conditional of Spelling- and Stem-Changing Verbs

Since spelling and stem-changing verbs are regular in the conditional in all forms, they should be rather easy to conjugate, as illustrated in Table 7.2.

## Table 7.2   The Conditional of Spelling- and Stem-Changing Verbs

| Verb | Conditional Stem | Example |
|---|---|---|
| *Spelling-Change Verbs* | | |
| **Group 1** | | |
| bus**car** | buscar | yo buscaría |
| lle**gar** | llegar | tú llegarías |
| averi**guar** | averiguar | él averiguaría |
| cru**zar** | cruzar | nosotros cruzaríamos |
| ven**cer** | vencer | vosotros venceríais |
| frun**cir** | fruncir | ellos fruncirían |
| distin**guir** | distinguir | yo distinguiría |
| delin**quir** | delinquir | tú delinquirías |
| **Group 2** | | |
| bu**llir** | bullir | él bulliría |
| ta**ñer** | tañer | nosotros tañeríamos |
| cr**eer** | creer | vosotros creeríais |
| **oír** | oir | ellos oirían |
| *Stem-Changing Verbs* | | |
| **Class 1** | | |
| cerrar | cerrar | yo cerraría |
| mostrar | mostrar | tú mostrarías |
| perder | perder | él perdería |
| morder | morder | nosotros morderíamos |
| **Class 2** | | |
| mentir | mentir | vosotros mentiríais |
| dormir | dormir | ellos dormirían |

### Table 7.2    The Conditional of Stem- and Spelling-Change Verbs (continued)

| Verb | Conditional Stem | Example |
| --- | --- | --- |
| *Stem-Changing Verbs* | | |
| **Class 3** | | |
| pedir | pedir | yo pediría |
| **Class 4** | | |
| reunir | reunir | tú reunirías |
| *Other Verbs* | | |
| variar | variar | él variaría |
| continuar | continuar | nosotros continuaríamos |
| concluir | concluir | vosotros concluiríais |
| distinguir | distinguir | ellos distinguirían |

In the conditional, the reflexive pronoun precedes the conjugated verb:

Si hacía mal tiempo, nosotros nos quedaríamos en casa.
If the weather was bad, we would stay home.

Si estudiaras, sacarías mejores notas.
If you studied, you would get better grades.

Note: Verbs such as *oír*, and *reír*, whose infinitive contains an accent mark drop that accent in the conditional: *Ella no me oiría.* (She wouldn't hear me.) *Tú reirías.* (You would laugh.)

### Práctica 1

Express what each of these people would do if they could do anything they wanted:

1. (comprar) Nosotros _____ una casa grande.

2. (vivir) Yo _____ en Europa.

3. (aprender) Tú _____ a hablar portugués.

4. (publicar) Ellos _____ sus poemas.

5. (jugar) Vosotros _____ muchos deportes.

6. (comenzar) Él _____ a estudiar arte.

7. (despertarse) Uds. _____ tarde todos los días.

8. (continuar) Ud. _____ trabajando.

9. (conducir) Ella _____ un coche deportivo.

10. (sonreír) Yo _____ todo el tiempo.

11. (leer) Nosotros _____ muchos libros.

12. (proteger) Ellas _____ a sus amigas.

# The Conditional of Irregular Verbs

The verbs that are irregular in the conditional were also irregular in the future and in the present. Irregular verbs in the conditional fall into one of three categories:

◆ Those that drop -e from the infinitive ending before adding the conditional endings (-e, -ás, -á, -emos, -éis, -án):

| Infinitive | Meaning | Conditional Stem |
| --- | --- | --- |
| caber | to fit | cabr- |
| haber | to have | habr- |
| poder | to be able | podr- |
| querer | to want | querr- |
| saber | to know | sabr- |

◆ Those that drop -e or -i from the infinitive ending and replace the vowel with a d before adding the conditional endings:

| Infinitive | Meaning | Conditional Stem |
| --- | --- | --- |
| poner | to put | pon**dr**- |
| salir | to leave | sal**dr**- |
| tener | to have | ten**dr**- |
| valer | to be worth | val**dr**- |
| venir | to come | ven**dr**- |

◆ Those that have a completely irregular stem to which are added the conditional endings:

| Infinitive | Meaning | Conditional Stem |
|---|---|---|
| decir | to say | dir- |
| hacer | to make, do | har- |

---

## Práctica 2

Express what might happen at the office if there were a big snow storm:

1. no haber citas este día _____

2. los empleados/poder salir temprano _____

3. los directores/tener que esperar hasta las cinco _____

4. los clientes/no venir _____

5. el gerente/no decir nada _____

6. yo/salir con los otros _____

7. Ricardo y yo/querer completar nuestro trabajo _____

8. valer la pena no tomar el autobús _____

9. tú/hacer todo lo necesario para ayudarnos _____

10. todo el mundo/no caber en el café de la oficina _____

11. Uds./no saber como ir a casa _____

12. vosotros/poner música en la oficina _____

---

# Using the Conditional

The conditional is used in Spanish to express an action or event that would happen under certain circumstances:

Me gustaría hablarte.
I would like to speak to you.

Paco no diría eso.
Paco wouldn't say that.

¿Podría Ud. explicármelo?
Could you explain it to me?

The conditional may be used to express an action that would take place after a past event occurred:

> Él me dijo que vendría temprano.
> He told me he would come early.

> Yo sabía que él no me diría la verdad.
> I knew he wouldn't tell me the truth.

The conditional often expresses probability or speculation in the past and may be the English equivalent of: I wonder, probably, must have, could, etc.:

> ¿Que hora sería cuando ellos llegaron?
> I wonder what time they arrived?
> What time could it have been when they arrived?

> Serían las dos.
> It must have been two o'clock.
> It was probably two o'clock.

**¡Cuidado!**

When would means "used to," the imperfect is used in Spanish: *Visitaba a mi abuela el sábado.* (I used to [would] visit my grandmother on Saturdays.) When would means "to be willing (to want)," *querer* is used in the preterit: *No quise trabajar el domingo.* (I wasn't willing to [wouldn't] work on Sundays.)

Note that the expression *deber de* (in the imperfect) + infinitive also expresses probability at the present time:

> Debía de ser las dos.
> It was probably two o'clock.

## Práctica 3

Express what these people would do if they won the lottery:

1. (comprar) Vosotros _____ un coche deportivo.

2. (ayudar) Nosotros _____ a los pobres.

3. (tener) Yo _____ un castillo magnífico.

4. (dar) Uds. _____ la vuelta al mundo.

5. (hacer) Tú _____un viaje a los países hispanohablantes.

6. (vivir) Ella _____ en una isla tropical.

---

**Práctica 4**

Use the verb indicated to express wonderment or probability:

1. (hacer) ¿Qué tiempo _____?

2. (nevar) ¿_____?

3. (ser) ¿Qué hora _____ cuando los niños se acostaron?

4. (tener) Ella _____ treinta años cuando el la conoció.

5. (pasar) ¿_____ ellos un buen rato?

6. (ir) ¿_____ Ud. a España?

---

# Forming and Using the Conditional Perfect

The conditional perfect is a compound tense, which means that it is made up of more than one part. The two elements that are needed to form the conditional perfect are:

1. The conditional tense of the helping verb *haber* (*habría, habrías, habría, habríamos, habríais, habrían*): which expresses that something will take place.

2. The past participle of the verb: which expresses what the action was.

The following diagram shows how the conditional perfect is formed:

Conditional perfect of verb =          when + what

                                                      /      \

Conditional perfect of verb =     (what) had    + happened

                                                      /      \

Conditional perfect of verb =     helping verb + main verb

                                                      /      \

Conditional perfect of verb = *haber* (to have) + past participle

The formula for the formation of the conditional perfect is:

| subject noun or pronoun + haber in conditional + past participle |
| --- |

The formation of past participles was explained in Chapter 1. Irregular past participles appear in Table 1.3 and in Appendix H.

Note the following about the conditional perfect tense:

♦ The conditional perfect expresses an action or event that would have taken place or been completed in the past:

> Yo les habría dicho todo.
> I would have told them everything.

♦ The conditional perfect may be used to express probability or conjecture in the past:

> ¿Lo habrían visto?
> I wonder if they had seen it?
> (Could they have seen it?)

> Habría dejado mi paraguas en la tienda.
> I (had) probably left my umbrella in the store.
> (I must have left my umbrella in the store.)

> Habrían sido las siete cuando él llegó.
> It was probably six o'clock when he arrived.
> (It must have been six o'clock when he arrived.)

---

### Práctica 5

Express what the following people would have done had they had the time:

1. (mirar) Yo _____ la televisión.

2. (salir) Ellos _____.

3. (cocinar) Ella _____ su plato favorito.

4. (ir) Nosotros _____ al centro comercial.

5. (jugar) Vosotros _____ tenis.

6. (escribir) Tú _____ un poema.

---

# Forming and Using the Conditional Progressive

The conditional progressive expresses what the subject would be doing at a particular time: it speaks about an action that would be in progress under certain conditions. As discussed in Chapter 1, the two elements that are needed to form the conditional perfect are:

1. The conditional of the verb *estar* (or *andar, continuar, entrar, ir, salir, seguir* or *venir*): which expresses that something was taking place.

2. The gerund of the verb: which expresses what the action was (see Chapter 1).

The following diagram shows how the conditional progressive is formed.

Conditional Perfect of verb =    when + what

/    \

Conditional Perfect of verb = (what) was + happening

/    \

Conditional Perfect of verb =    *estar*  + main verb (present participle)

The formula for the formation of the past perfect is:

| subject noun or pronoun + *estar* in conditional + gerund |
| --- |

Ellos estarían viajando si pudieran.
They would be traveling if they could.

**¡Mira!** _____

Reflexive pronouns may precede *estar* or may be placed after and attached to the gerund.

*Generalmente ellos se estarían levantando ahora.*
*Generalmente ellos estarán levantándose ahora.*
Generally they would be getting up now.

## Práctica 6

Express what each person would be doing if he/she were available to help with the chores:

1. (cocinar) Vosotros _____ una paella.

2. (limpiar) Ella _____ su cuarto.

3. (ir) Ellos _____ al supermercado.

4. (lavar) Tú _____ los platos.

5. (servir) Nosotros _____ la cena.

6. (llevar) Yo _____ la ropa a la lavandería.

# Repaso

1. The conditional of regular verbs is formed by keeping the infinitive ending and adding the conditional endings: *-ía, -ías, -ía, -íamos, -íais, -ían.*

2. Stem- and spelling-change verbs are regular in the conditional in all forms.

3. In the conditional, the reflexive pronoun precedes the conjugated verb.

4. *Caber* (to fit), *haber* (to have), *poder* (to be able to), *querer* (to want), and *saber* (to know) form the conditional by dropping the *-e* from the infinitive stem and adding the conditional endings.

5. *Poner* (to put), *salir* (to go out), *tener* (to have), *valer* (to be worth), and *venir* (to come) drop the *-e* or *-i* from the infinitive ending and replace it with a *-d* before adding the conditional endings.

6. *Decir* (to tell, say) and *hacer* (to make, do) are irregular in the conditional: *dir-* and *har-* respectively.

7. The conditional perfect expresses what would have occurred under certain conditions and is formed by conjugating *haber* in the conditional and adding a past participle (which remains the same for all subject pronouns).

8. The conditional progressive expresses an action that would be occurring under certain conditions. It is formed by conjugating the verb *estar* in the conditional and adding a gerund. Reflexive pronouns may precede *estar* or may be placed after and attached to the gerund.

## The Least You Need to Know

◆ The conditional endings: *-ía, -ías, -ía, -íamos, -íais, -ían* are added to the verb infinitive or to a special irregular stem.

◆ To form the conditional perfect, take the conditional of *haber* and add the past participle.

◆ To form the conditional progressive, take the conditional of *estar* and add a gerund.

# The Present and the Present Perfect Subjunctive

## In This Chapter

- ◆ Forming the subjunctive of regular and reflexive verbs
- ◆ Forming the subjunctive of stem-changing and spelling-change verbs
- ◆ Forming the subjunctive of irregular verbs
- ◆ When to use the subjunctive
- ◆ Forming and using the past subjunctive

The subjunctive is a mood that is used far more frequently in Spanish than it is in English. The subjunctive mood allows Spanish-speakers to express and describe various attitudes through the use of different verb forms and constructions.

Whereas the indicative mood states a factual condition or situation and expresses certainty or reality, the subjunctive mood expresses unreal, hypothetical, or unsubstantiated conditions or situations resulting from doubt, wishes, needs, desires, speculation, and supposition.

The past subjunctive is also referred to as the present perfect subjunctive and is the compound equivalent of the present subjunctive. The past subjunctive is used to express an action that has already taken place.

In this chapter you'll learn how to form and when to use the present and the past subjunctive and how to avoid using the subjunctive when possible.

# The Present Subjunctive of Regular and Reflexive Verbs

The present subjunctive of regular verbs, unlike the tenses studied so far, is not formed by dropping the infinitive ending (-*ar*, -*er*, -*ir*), but rather by going to the first person singular form of the verb (*yo*) in the present indicative, dropping the final -*o*, and adding appropriate endings.

**¡Mira!**

Note that -*er* verbs and -*ir* verbs have the exact same endings in the subjunctive.

## The Present Subjunctive of Regular Verbs

To form the present subjunctive of regular verbs, drop the -*o* from the *yo* form of the present indicative and add the endings shown in Table 8.1.

## Table 8.1 The Present Subjunctive of Regular Verbs

| Subject | -*ar* Verbs | -*er* Verbs | -*ir* Verbs |
|---|---|---|---|
| *yo* form of present | hablo (*I speak*) | bebo (*I drink*) | abro (*I open*) |
| yo | hable | beba | abra |
| tú | hables | bebas | abras |
| él, ella, Ud. | hable | beba | abra |
| nosotros | hablemos | bebamos | abramos |
| vosotros | habléis | bebáis | abráis |
| ellos, ellas, Uds. | hablen | beban | abran |

Es necesario que yo le ayude.
It is necessary that I help him.

Es importante que tú comas legumbres.
It is important for you to eat vegetables.

Es posible que ellos insistan en venir.
It is possible that they will insist on coming.

Because the subjunctive is not a tense (a verb form indicating time), the present subjunctive can be used to refer to actions in the present or in the future:

Es posible que ella compre ese coche.
It is possible that she will buy that car.

In the subjunctive, the reflexive pronoun precedes the conjugated verb:

Dudo que Pedro se despierte temprano.
I doubt that Pedro will get up early.

---

## Práctica 1

Express what it is necessary for each person to do to be a good citizen:

Ejemplo:
Ud./trabajar con conciencia
Es necesario que Ud. trabaje con conciencia.

1. los ciudadanos/respetar las leyes _____

2. yo/votar _____

3. vosotros/no quejarse de todo _____

4. tú/aceptar tus responsabilidades humanitarias _____

5. nosotros/no abusar del ambiente _____

6. la gente/evitar cometer infracciones _____

---

## Práctica 2

Express what it is important for each person to do to stay healthy:

Ejemplo:
Uds./beber bastante agua
Es importante que Uds. beban bastante agua.

*continues*

*continued*

1. vosotros/correr una milla cada día _____

2. tú/asumir la responsabilidad de tu salud _____

3. yo/prometer adelgazar _____

4. ellos/combatir la fatiga _____

5. ella/emprender el entrenamiento _____

6. nosotros/consumir menos calorías _____

## Irregular Verbs in the Present-Tense *yo* Form

Some verbs that are irregular in the *yo* form of the present indicative, form the subjunctive in the same manner as regular verbs: drop the final *-o* from the irregular *yo* form and add appropriate subjunctive endings, as shown in Table 8.2:

## Table 8.2 The Subjunctive Irregular *yo* Verbs

| Verb | Meaning | *yo* Form | Subjunctive Forms |
|------|---------|-----------|-------------------|
| caber | to fit | quepo | quepa, quepas, quepa, quepamos, quepáis, quepan |
| caer | to fall | caigo | caiga, caigas, caiga, caigamos, caigáis, caigan |
| decir | to say, tell | digo | diga, digas, diga, digamos, digáis, digan |
| hacer | to make, do | hago | haga, hagas, haga, hagamos, hagáis, hagan |
| oír | to hear | oigo | oiga, oigas, oiga, oigamos, oigáis, oigan |
| poner | to put | pongo | ponga, pongas, ponga, pongamos, pongáis, pongan |
| salir | to go out | salgo | salga, salgas, salga, salgamos, salgáis, salgan |
| tener | to have | tengo | tenga, tengas, tenga, tengamos, tengáis, tengan |
| traer | to bring | traigo | traiga, traigas, traiga, traigamos, traigáis, traigan |

| Verb | Meaning | *yo* Form | Subjunctive Forms |
|------|---------|-----------|-------------------|
| valer | to be worth | valgo | valga, valgas, valga, valgamos, valgáis, valgan |
| venir | to come | vengo | venga, vengas, venga, vengamos, vengáis, vengan |
| ver | to see | veo | vea, veas, vea, veamos, veáis, vean |

## Práctica 3

Express what is possible for each person:

Ejemplo:
el niño/caerse
Es posible que el niño se caiga.

1. nosotros/venir mañana _____

2. él/ponerse enfermo _____

3. tú/tener buena suerte _____

4. yo/traer los documentos importantes _____

5. vosotros/hacer el trabajo _____

6. ellos/decir la verdad _____

7. Ud./salir con su familia _____

8. ella/no oír bien _____

# The Present Subjunctive of Spelling-Change Verbs

In the present subjunctive, verbs ending in *-car*, *-gar*, *-guar*, and *-zar* undergo the same change that occurred in the *yo* form of the **preterit:** *c* to *qu*, *g* to *gu*, *gu* to *gü*, and *z* to *c* respectively, as shown in Table 8.3.

## Table 8.3    Present Subjunctive of -car, -gar, -guar, and -zar Verbs

|  | Pret. *yo* | Pret. *yo* | Pret. *yo* | Pret. *yo* |
|---|---|---|---|---|
|  | busqué | llegué | averigüé | crucé |

*Subjunctive*

| Subject | *-car* verbs | *-gar* verbs | *-guar* verbs | *-zar* verbs |
|---|---|---|---|---|
|  | buscar<br>(*to look for*) | llegar<br>(*to arrive*) | averiguar<br>(*to ascertain*) | cruzar<br>(*to cross*) |
| yo | busque | llegue | averigüe | cruce |
| tú | busques | llegues | averigües | cruces |
| él | busque | llegue | averigüe | cruce |
| nosotros | busquemos | lleguemos | averigüemos | crucemos |
| vosotros | busquéis | lleguéis | averigüéis | crucéis |
| ellos | busquen | lleguen | averigüen | crucen |

### Práctica 4

Express what is necessary for each person to do:

Ejemplo:
yo/buscar a mi perro
Es preciso que yo busque a mi perro.

1. nosotros/pagar la cuenta _____

2. tú/gozar de buena salud _____

3. vosotros/memorizar todo _____

4. Uds./verificar toda la información _____

5. yo/castigar a mi niño _____

6. ella/practicar sus verbos _____

Those verbs ending in *-cer/-cir*, *-ger/-gir*, *-guir* (not *-uir*), and *-quir* undergo the same change that occurred in the *yo* form of the **present indicative:** consonant + *-cer* and *-cir*, *c* to *z*; vowel + *cer* or *cir*, *c* to *zc*; *-ger* and *-gir*, *g* to *j*; *-guir*, *gu* to *g*; and *-quir* *qu* to *c* respectively, as shown in Table 8.4.

Note that verbs whose stems end in *-ñ, -ll + -er* or *-ir*, and those whose endings are *-eer* are regular in the present subjunctive: drop the *-o* from the *yo* form of the present indicative and add the appropriate subjunctive endings.

## Table 8.4    The Subjunctive of Spelling-Change Verbs

| | Pres. yo | Pres. yo | Pres. yo | Pres. yo | Pres. yo | Pres. yo |
|---|---|---|---|---|---|---|
| | venzo | frunzo | | | | |
| | conozco | conduzco | escoja | dirijo | distingo | delinco |

*Subjunctive*

| Subject | -cer verbs | -cir verbs | -ger verbs | -gir verbs | -guir verbs | -quir verbs |
|---|---|---|---|---|---|---|
| | **vencer** *(to conquer)* | **fruncir** *(to frown)* | **escoger** *(to choose)* | **dirigir** *(to direct)* | **distinguir** *(to distinguish)* | **delinquir** *(to offend)* |
| | **conocer** *(to know)* | **conducir** *(to drive)* | | | | |
| yo | venza conozca | frunza conduzca | escoja | dirija | distinga | delinca |
| tú | venzas conozcas | frunzas conduzcas | escojas | dirijas | distingas | delincas |
| él | venza conozca | frunza conduzca | escoja | dirija | distinga | delinca |
| nosotros | venzamos conozcamos | frunzamos conduzcamos | escojamos | dirijamos | distingamos | delincamos |
| vosotros | venzáis conozcáis | frunzáis conduzcáis | escojáis | dirijáis | distingáis | delincáis |
| ellos | venzan conozcan | frunzan conduzcan | escojan | dirijan | distingan | delincan |

## Práctica 5

Express what it is necessary for these people to do:

Ejemplo:
ella/escoger el más interesante.
Es menester que ella escoja el más interesante.

*continues*

*continued*

1. Ud./complacer a sus clientes _____

2. yo/conducir con cuidado _____

3. nosotros/zurcir estos vestidos _____

4. ellos/me convencer de la verdad _____

5. vosotros/erigir un monumento en su honor _____

6. tú/acoger a estas muchachas _____

7. Ud./extinguir el fuego _____

8. ellas/no delinquir _____

# The Present Subjunctive of Stem-Changing Verbs

Just like in the present tense, all stem changes in the present subjunctive occur in the "shoe" formation, or in the *yo, tú, él, ella, Ud., ellos, ellas, Uds.* forms.

For verbs ending in *-ar* and *-er*, the same change occurs in the stem vowel in the subjunctive that occurs in the stem vowel of the present tense as shown in Table 8.5.

$\left.\begin{array}{l} e \text{ to } ie \\ o \text{ to } ue \end{array}\right\}$ in all present subjunctive forms except *nosotros* and *vosotros*

## Table 8.5   The Present Subjunctive of *-ar/-er* Stem-Changing Verbs

| Verb | Change | Present Subjunctive |
|---|---|---|
| **Class 1** | | |
| *-ar* verbs | *e* to *ie* | cerrar (*to close*) <br> yo **cie**rre <br> tú **cie**rres <br> él **cie**rre <br> nosotros cerremos <br> vosotros cerréis <br> ellos **cie**rren |
| *-ar* verbs | *o* to *ue* | mostrar (*to show*) <br> yo m**ue**stre <br> tú m**ue**stres <br> él m**ue**stre <br> nosotros mostremos |

| Verb | Change | Present Subjunctive |
|------|--------|---------------------|
| | | vosotros mostréis |
| | | ellos muestren |
| -er verbs | e to ie | perder (*to lose*) |
| | | yo pierda |
| | | tú pierdas |
| | | él pierda |
| | | nosotros perdamos |
| | | vosotros perdáis |
| | | ellos pierdan |
| -er verbs | o to ue | morder (*to bite*) |
| | | yo muerda |
| | | tú muerdas |
| | | él muerda |
| | | nosotros mordamos |
| | | vosotros mordáis |
| | | ellos muerdan |

For verbs ending in -*ir*, the same change occurs in the stem vowel in the subjunctive that occurs in the stem vowel in the present tense. Additionally, the stem vowel changes from *e* to *i* or from *o* to *u* in the *nosotros* and *vosotros* forms as shown in Table 8.6.

e to ie
i to ie  } in all present subjunctive *yo, tú, el, ellos* forms
e to i

o to ue
e to i  } in present subjunctive *nosotros* and *vosotros* forms
o to u

## Table 8.6   The Present Subjunctive of -*ir* Stem-Changing Verbs

| Verb | Change | Present Subjunctive |
|------|--------|---------------------|
| **Class 2** | | |
| -ir verbs | stressed e to ie | mentir (*to lie*) |
| | | yo mienta |
| | | tú mientas |
| | | él mienta |

*continues*

## Table 8.6    The Present Subjunctive of *-ir* Stem-Changing Verbs (continued)

| Verb | Change | Present Subjunctive |
|------|--------|---------------------|
| **Class 2** | | |
| *-ir* verbs | | nosotros mintamos<br>vosotros mintáis<br>ellos mientan |
| | stressed<br>*o* to *ue* | dormir (*to sleep*)<br>yo duerma<br>tú duermas<br>él duerma<br>nosotros durmamos<br>vosotros durmáis<br>ellos duerman |
| **Class 3** | | |
| *-ir* verbs | stressed<br>*e* to *i* | pedir (*to ask*)<br>yo pida<br>tú pidas<br>él pida<br>nosotros pidamos<br>vosotros pidáis<br>ellos pidan |
| **Class 4 (There are very few verbs in this class.)** | | |
| | Stressed | reunir (*to join*) |
| *-ar* verbs | *ai* to *aí* | yo reúna |
| *-er* verbs | *au* to *aú* | tú reúnas |
| *-ir* verbs | *eu* to *eú* | él reúna<br>nosotros reunamos<br>vosotros reunáis<br>ellos reúnan |

# Verbs Ending in *-iar* and *-uar*

For some verbs ending in *-iar* and for all verbs ending in *-uar* (except those ending in *-cuar* and *-guar* listed in Appendix D), *i* changes to *í* and *u* changes to *ú* in the *yo*, *tú*, *él*, and *ellos* forms of the present subjunctive, as shown in Table 8.7.

### Table 8.7    Present Subjunctive of Verbs Ending in -*iar* and -*uar*

| Subject | variar (*to vary*) | continuar (*to continue*) |
| --- | --- | --- |
| yo | varíe | continúe |
| tú | varíes | continúes |
| él | varíe | continúe |
| nosotros | variemos | continuemos |
| vosotros | variéis | continuéis |
| ellos | varíen | continúen |

## Verbs Ending in -*uir*

For verbs ending in -*uir* (except for those ending in -*guir*, listed in Appendix F), a *y* is inserted after the *u* in all forms of the present subjunctive, as shown in Table 8.8.

### Table 8.8    The Present Subjunctive of Verbs Ending in -*uir* (but not -*guir*)

| Subject | incluir (*to include*) |
| --- | --- |
| yo | incluya |
| tú | incluyas |
| él | incluya |
| nosotros | incluyamos |
| vosotros | incluyáis |
| ellos | incluyan |

### Práctica 6

Express what it is better for each person to do:

Ejemplo:
él/enviar las cartas
Más vale que él envíe las cartas.

1. Ud./concluir pronto su trabajo _____

2. ellos/despertarse temprano _____

3. nosotros/dormir en nuestra propio casa _____

*continues*

*continued*

4. ella/variar el enfoque de su discurso _____

5. yo/acostarme a las diez en punto _____

6. vosotros/perder cinco kilos _____

7. Uds./volver a buscar sus libros _____

8. tú/medir tu cuarto _____

9. él/poder ayudarme _____

10. ellas/encerrar sus joyas _____

11. yo/contribuir con cincuenta dólares _____

12. nosotros/continuar nuestros estudios _____

## Práctica 7

Express what is doubtful by making the necessary spelling and stem changes:

Ejemplo:
ella/empezar el trabajo
Es dudoso que ella empiece el trabajo.

1. Ud./volcar el vaso _____

2. nosotros/colgar el cuadro hoy _____

3. yo/tropezar con el escalón _____

4. vosotros/torcer el dedo jugando al tenis _____

5. ellos/jugar bien al golf _____

6. tú/almorzar con Julio _____

7. ella/conseguir su objetivo _____

8. Uds./corregir el error _____

# The Subjunctive of Irregular Verbs

A few high-frequency verbs that are irregular in the present (including the helping verb, *haber*) also have irregular subjunctive forms, as shown in Table 8.9.

### Table 8.9    The Subjunctive of Irregular Verbs

| Subject | dar (*to give*) | estar (*to be*) | haber (*to have*) | ir (*to go*) | saber (*to know*) | ser (*to be*) |
|---------|------|-------|-------|------|-------|------|
| yo | dé | esté | haya | vaya | sepa | sea |
| tú | des | estés | hayas | vayas | sepas | seas |
| él | dé | esté | haya | vaya | sepa | sea |
| nosotros | demos | estemos | hayamos | vayamos | sepamos | seamos |
| vosotros | deis | estéis | hayáis | vayáis | sepáis | seáis |
| ellos | den | estén | hayan | vayan | sepan | sean |

## Práctica 8

Express what is probable:

Ejemplo:
ellos/ir a la escuela.
Es probable que ellos vayan a la escuela.

1. yo/dar un paseo _____

2. tú/saber cocinar _____

3. vosotros/estar cansados _____

4. Uds./ir al centro _____

5. él/ser profesor _____

6. nosotros/haber recibido el anuncio _____

# Using the Subjunctive

The subjunctive is used when the following conditions are met:

◆ Two different clauses exist with two different subjects.

◆ The two clauses are joined by *que* (that), which is followed by the clause in the subjunctive.

◆ One of the clauses must show, among other things, wishing, wanting, need, necessity, emotion, or doubt.

| ¿Qué quiere decir...? |
| --- |
| A clause is a group of words that contains a verb and its subject and is used as a part of a sentence. A clause may be main or independent, which means that it can stand by itself as a simple sentence. A clause may also be subordinate or dependent, which means that it cannot stand alone and is used as a noun, an adjective, or an adverb. |

## The Subjunctive After Impersonal Expressions

The subjunctive is used in Spanish after impersonal expressions that show need, necessity, doubt, uncertainty, possibility, probability, and emotion, among others, as shown in Table 8.10.

## Table 8.10    Impersonal Expressions Taking the Subjunctive

| Expression | Spanish |
| --- | --- |
| it could be that | puede ser que |
| it is a pity that | es una lástima que |
| it is absurd that | es absurdo que |
| it is advisable that | es aconsejable que |
| it is amazing that | es asombroso que |
| it is amusing that | es divertido que |
| it is bad that | es malo que |
| it is better that | es mejor que<br>más vale que |
| it is curious that | es curioso que |
| it is difficult that | es difícil que |

| Expression | Spanish |
| --- | --- |
| it is doubtful that | es dudoso que |
| it is easy that | es fácil que |
| it is enough that | es suficiente que |
| it is essential that | es esencial que |
| it is fair that | es justo que |
| it is fitting that | es conveniente que |
| it is good that | es bueno que |
| it is imperative that | es imperativo que |
| it is important that | es importante que |
| it is impossible that | es imposible que |
| it is improbable that | es improbable que |
| it is incredible that | es increíble que |
| it is indispensable that | es indispensable que |
| it is interesting that | es interesante que |
| it is ironic that | es irónico que |
| it is natural that | es natural que |
| it is necessary that | es necesario que |
|  | es preciso que |
|  | es menester que |
| it is nice that | es bueno que |
| it is normal that | es normal que |
| it is possible that | es posible que |
| it is preferable that | es preferible que |
| it is probable that | es probable que |
| it is rare that | es raro que |
| it is regrettable that | es lamentable que |
| it is strange that | es extraño que |
| it is surprising that | es sorprendente que |
| it is unfair that | es injusto que |
| it is urgent that | es urgente que |
| it is useful that | es útil que |
| it seems that | parece que |

Note how the subjunctive is used in the clause following an impersonal expression:

Es preferible que Ud. llegue temprano.
It is preferable that you arrive early.

Es extraño que tú no quieras salir.
It is strange that you don't want to go out.

These expressions take the subjunctive even when preceded by no:

No es bueno que él esté ausente.
It is not good that he is absent.

No es posible que yo esté allá.
It is not possible that I will be there.

**¡Cuidado!**

The subjunctive is used after *tal vez* (perhaps) and *quizás* (perhaps) when doubt or uncertainty are implied. When certainty is expressed, the indicative is used:

*Tal vez (Quizás) pase por su casa mañana.*
Perhaps I'll come by your house tomorrow.

*Tiene la pier na rota. Quizás (Tal vez) tuvo un accidente.*
He has a broken leg. Perhaps he had an accident.

The following impersonal expressions show certainty and, therefore, require the indicative:

| | |
|---|---|
| it is certain (sure) | es cierto |
| it is clear | es claro |
| it is evident | es evidente |
| it is exact | es exacto |
| it is sure | es seguro |
| it is true | es verdad |

Es verdad que él está ausente.
It is true that he is absent.

Es cierto que yo estaré allá.
It is certain that I'll be there.

In the negative or in a question, however, these expressions show doubt or denial and require the subjunctive:

> ¿No es verdad que él esté ausente?
> Isn't it true that he is absent?

> No es cierto que yo estaré allá.
> It is uncertain that I'll be there.

---

### Práctica 9

Express opinions about a party that you and a friend are planning by using the correct form of the indicative or the subjunctive:

1. (venir) No es seguro que José _____.

2. (comprar) Está claro que nosotros _____ bastantes cosas de comer.

3. (divertirse) Es probable que Uds. _____ mucho.

4. (traer) Puede ser que Ana y Luisa _____ CDs.

5. (tocar) Es posible que yo _____ la guitarra.

6. (estar) Es evidente que tú _____ contento.

---

**¡Cuidado!** _____

   Although we often omit the word "that" when using the subjunctive in English, in Spanish *que* must always be used to join the two clauses:

*Es importante que Ud. me ayude.*
It's important (that) you help me.

*Quiero que tú me despiertes a las siete.*
I want you to wake me at 7 o'clock.

## Using the Subjunctive After Certain Verbs

The subjunctive is used in the dependent clause introduced by *que* when the main clause expresses advice, command, demand, desire, emotion, hope, permission, preference, prohibition, request, suggestion, wishing, and wanting, as shown in Table 8.11.

## Table 8.11   Verbs of Wishing, Emotion, and Doubt

| Spanish Verb | Meaning |
| --- | --- |
| aconsejar | to advise |
| agradecer | to be grateful |
| alegrarse (de) | to be glad, happy (about) |
| decir | to tell, say |
| dejar | to allow, let |
| desear | to desire, wish, want |
| dudar | to doubt |
| enfadarse | to become angry |
| enojarse | to become angry |
| esperar | to hope |
| exigir | to require, demand |
| hacer | to make, cause |
| insistir | to insist |
| lamentar | to regret |
| mandar | to command, order |
| necesitar | to need |
| negar | to deny |
| ojalá (que) | if only … |
| ordenar | to order |
| pedir | to ask for, request |
| permitir | to permit |
| preferir | to prefer |
| prohibir | to forbid |
| querer | to wish, want |
| reclamar | to demand |
| recomendar | to recommend |
| requerir | to require |
| rogar | to beg, request |
| sentir | to be sorry, to regret |
| solicitar | to request |
| sorprenderse (de) | to be surprised |
| sugerir | to suggest |
| suplicar | to beg, plead |

| Spanish Verb | Meaning |
|---|---|
| temer | to fear |
| tener miedo (de) | to fear |
| tener vergüenza (de) | to be ashamed (of) |

Yo les pido que salgan.
I ask them to leave.

¡Ojalá que Ud. gane!
I hope that you win!

## When There's No Doubt About It

When an event or an opinion is questioned, doubt exists and the subjunctive is used. When doubt is negated, certainty or probability exists and the indicative is used, as shown in Table 8.12.

**¡Cuidado!**

The verb *decir* is followed by the subjunctive only when it is used to give an order: *Dígale que venga.* (Tell him to come.) *Les diré que salgan.* (I will tell them to leave.)

## Table 8.12    Doubt and the Indicative Versus the Subjunctive

| Indicative (Certainty) | Subjunctive (Uncertainty) |
|---|---|
| yo creo<br>*I believe* | ¿Cree Ud. …?<br>*Do you believe …?* |
| | yo no creo<br>*I don't believe* |
| yo estoy seguro/a<br>*I'm sure* | ¿Está Ud. seguro/a …?<br>*Are you sure?* |
| | yo no estoy seguro/-a<br>*I'm not sure* |
| yo no dudo<br>*I don't doubt* | ¿Duda Ud. …?<br>*Do you doubt …?* |
| | yo dudo<br>*I doubt* |
| yo no niego<br>*I don't deny* | ¿Niega Ud. …?<br>*Do you deny …?* |
| | yo niego<br>*I deny* |

*continues*

## Table 8.12   Doubt and the Indicative Versus the Subjunctive (continued)

| Indicative (Certainty) | Subjunctive (Uncertainty) |
| --- | --- |
| yo opino<br>*I'm of the opinion* | ¿Opina Ud. …?<br>*Is it your opinion?* |
| | yo no opino<br>*I'm not of the opinion* |
| yo pienso<br>*I think* | ¿Piensa Ud. …?<br>*Do you think …?* |
| | yo no pienso<br>*I don't think* |
| yo sé<br>*I know* | ¿Sabe Ud. …?<br>*Do you know …?* |
| | yo no sé<br>*I don't know* |

¿Cree Ud. que ella lo haga?
*Do you believe she will do it?*

No creo que ella lo haga.
*I don't believe she will do it.*

Creo que ella lo hará.
*I believe she will do it.*

**¡Cuidado!**

In many instances the use of the subjunctive or the infinitive has to do with the intended meaning of the speaker. If the speaker wishes to imply doubt, the subjunctive is used. If the speaker wishes to imply certainty, the indicative is used. Sometimes there are no hard and fast rules.

### Práctica 10

Express how each person feels by completing the sentence with the correct form of the subjunctive or the infinitive:

1. (hacer) Los padres prefieren que su niño no _____ tanto ruido.

2. (saber) El profesor insiste en que los alumnos _____ la respuesta correcta.

3. (ir) Mi madre teme que yo _____ sola al centro.

4. (decir) Yo no niego que tú _____ la verdad.

5. (ser) Él se sorprende de que nosotros _____ tan responsables.

6. (pagar) Mi amigo defiende que yo _____ la cuenta.

7. (salir) Vuestros padres exigen que vosotros no _____.

8. (dar) Yo pienso que él _____ un paseo con sus amigos cada noche.

## Using the Subjunctive After Certain Adjectives

The subjunctive is also used after adjectives (that follow the verb *estar*) that express feelings, as shown in Table 8.13:

## Table 8.13   Adjectives Expressing Feelings

| Spanish | Adjective |
| --- | --- |
| alegre | happy |
| asombrado/a | astonished, surprised |
| asustado/a | afraid |
| avergonzado/a | embarrassed |
| contento/a | happy |
| encantado/a | delighted |
| enfadado/a | displeased |
| enojado/a | angry |
| fastidiado/a | bothered |
| feliz | happy |
| furioso/a | furious |
| infeliz | unhappy |
| irritado/a | irritated |
| lisonjeado/a | flattered |
| orgulloso/a | proud |
| triste | sad |

Note how the subjunctive is used after these adjectives:

Estoy contenta de que ella comprenda el problema.
I'm happy that she understands the problem.

Estamos furiosos de que él no nos preste dinero.
We are furious that he doesn't lend us money.

---

### Práctica 11

Express how these people feel:

1. (salir) Estoy furioso de que mis amigos no _____ conmigo.

2. (dar) Ella está feliz de que él siempre le _____ flores.

3. (recibir) Él está orgulloso de que Ud. _____ el premio.

4. (seguir) Tú estás avergonzado de que yo no _____ tus consejos.

5. (irse) Estamos tristes de que tu _____.

6. (estudiar) Estáis alegres de que nosotros _____ el español.

---

## The Subjunctive After Conjunctions

The subjunctive is used after certain conjunctions when uncertainty, doubt, purpose, anticipation, or indefiniteness is implied.

The subjunctive is used with the following conjunctions. Those with an asterisk (*) always take the subjunctive because doubt, uncertainty, and purpose are implied:

◆ Conjunctions that express time:

hasta que (until)

antes (de) que* (before)

Expresses doubt—he may not come:
Él esperará hasta que venga su amigo.
He'll wait until his friend comes.

Expresses certainty—he showed up:
Él esperó hasta que vino.
He waited until he came.

---

A conjunction is a part of speech that connects and relates words, phrases, or clauses. Coordinating conjunctions, such as *and, but, or, nor,* and *for,* connect words, phrases, and clauses of equal importance. Subordinating conjunctions, *such as if, although, since, in order that, as, because, unless, after, before, until, when, whenever, where, while, wherever,* etc., connect dependent clauses with independent clauses.

---

◆ Conjunctions that express purpose:

   a fin de que* (in order that)

   para que* (in order that)

   de modo que (so that)

   de manera que (so that)

   Expresses purpose—so that you may study:
       Yo no hablaré a fin de que Ud. pueda trabajar.
       I won't talk so that you can work.

◆ Conjunctions that express condition:

   con tal (de) que* (provided that)

   a menos que* (unless)

   en caso de que* (in case [that])

   a condición (de) que (on condition that)

   Expresses doubt—Maybe they serve fish and maybe they don't:
       Comeré en este restaurante con tal de que sirvan pescado.
       I'll eat in this restaurant provided that they serve fish.

◆ Conjunctions that express concession:

   although (aunque)

   Expresses doubt—Maybe they pay well and maybe they don't:
       Aceptaré este puesto aunque no paguen bien.
       I'll take this job although they may not pay well.

   Expresses certainty—They don't pay well:
       Aceptaré este puesto aunque no pague bien.
       I'll take this job although they don't pay well.

**¡Mira!** _____

The present subjunctive is often translated with "may" as a part of its meaning: *Es posible que ella venga.* (It is possible that she may come.)

◆ Conjunctions that express negation:

without (sin que*)

Expresses purpose—in such a way that I don't notice:
Mi amigo miente sin que yo lo sepa.
My friend lies without my knowing it.

◆ Conjunctions that express fear:

for fear that (por miedo [a] que)

Expresses emotion—shows fear:
Telefoneo por miedo a que Ud. no venga.
I'm calling for fear that you aren't coming.

The following conjunctions use the indicative to refer to past or present actions or events and the subjunctive to refer to future events that are considered uncertain:

cuando (when)

después (de) que (after)

en cuanto como (as soon as)

hasta que (until)

luego que (as soon as)

mientras que (while)

tan pronto como (as soon as)

La criada limpió su casa mientras que ellos trabajaban.
The maid cleaned their house while they were working.

but

Ella limpiará su casa mientras que ellos trabajen.
She will clean their house while they are (will be) working. (It is unsure how long they will be working.)

Use the infinitive after these conjunctions when the subject does not change:

para (in order to)

sin (without)

antes de (before)

Llamé para reservar una mesa.
I called to reserve a table.

Ella salío sin decir adiós.
She left without saying good-bye.

Te llamaré antes de venir.
I'll call you before coming.

## Práctica 12

Express that the members of the Hidalgo family do the following things:

Exemplo:
mamá trabaja/de modo que/los niños/ir a la universidad
Mamá trabaja de modo que los niños vayan a la universidad.

1. papá le da dinero a Carlos/para que/él/comprar un carro

   _____

2. Rosa no hace mucho ruido/de manera que/nosotros/poder dormir

   _____

3. yo escucharé la radio/mientras que/mi hermana/hacer sus tareas

   _____

4. Tomás fregará los platos/a condición de que/yo/ordenar/la sala

   _____

5. yo no te presto mi libro/a menos que/tú/me lo devolver

   _____

6. mamá prepara sándwiches/en caso de que/mis hermanos/tener hambre

   _____

# The Subjunctive After Indefinites

The subjunctive is used after indefinites or compounds of *-quiera + que*:

dondequiera (wherever)

cualquier/a (whatever, any)

quienquiera (whoever)

cuando quiera (whenever)

por + adj./adv. + que (however)

Cualquiera que sea tu problema, te ayudaré.
Whatever your problem, I'll help you.

Él castigará a quienquiera que sea responsable.
He'll punish whoever is responsible.

# The Subjunctive in Relative Clauses

The subjunctive is used in relative clauses if the person or thing in the main clause is indefinite, desired but not yet attained, or is nonexistent or whose existence is doubtful:

Busco a alguien que pueda ayudarme.
I'm looking for someone who can help me.
(Does such a person exist?)

Encontré a una mujer que puede ayudarme.
I found a woman who can help me.
(Such a person exists.)

# The Subjunctive in Third Person Commands

The subjunctive is used in third person singular or plural commands:

Que entren.                    ¡Viva el presidente!
Let them come in.              Long live the president!

Que sea feliz.
Let him/her be happy.

# The Subjunctive After Superlative Expressions

The superlative is used after superlative expressions to show an opinion, a feeling, or an emotion:

Ella es la única persona que sepa hacerlo.
She's the only person who knows how to do it.

Es el mejor chocolate que Ud. pueda comprar.
It's the best chocolate you can buy.

The indicative is used after a superlative to state a fact when no opinion is stated:

> Es su mejor amigo que viene.
> It's his best friend who is coming.

The indicative is used after the superlative of an adverb:

> Trabajo tan rápido como puedo.
> I'm working as fast as I can.

---

### Práctica 13

Complete each person's thought with the correct form of the indicative or the superlative:

1. (ir) Dondequiera que yo _____, me divierto.

2. (poder) Él camina lo más despacio que _____.

3. (ser) Busco un carro que _____ barato.

4. (tener) Es la camisa más bonita que tú _____.

5. (saber) Conozco a alguien que _____ bailar el tango.

6. (vivir) ¡_____ la princesa!

---

# Forming and Using the Past (Present Perfect) Subjunctive

The past subjunctive is a compound tense, which means that it is made up of more than one part. The two elements that are needed to form the past subjunctive are:

1. The present subjunctive of the helping verb *haber* (*haya, hayas, haya, hayamos, hayáis, hayan*): which expresses that something took place in the past.

2. The past participle of the verb: which expresses what the action was.

The following diagram shows how the past subjunctive is formed:

Past Subjunctive of verb =       when + what

                              /    \

Past Subjunctive of verb =   (what) had + happened

                              /    \

Past Subjunctive of verb =   helping verb + main verb

                              /    \

Past Subjunctive of verb = *haber* (to have) + past participle

The formula for the formation of the past subjunctive is:

> subject noun or pronoun + haber in present subjunctive + past participle

The formation of past participles was explained in Chapter 1. Irregular past participles appear in Table 1.3 and in Appendix H.

Lo siento que tú hayas estado enfermo.
I'm sorry that you have been ill.

Me alegro de que Susana haya venido a mi fiesta.
I'm glad that Susana came to my party.

---

### Práctica 14

Express what happened by using the past subjunctive:

1. (perderse) Yo temo que él _____.

2. (ganar) Nosotros nos alegramos de que tú _____el campeonato.

3. (olvidarse) Es dudoso que Uds. _____ el dinero en casa.

4. (hacer) Es imposible que yo _____ un error.

5. (ver) Él no cree que vosotros _____ esta película.

6. (venir) Es una lástima que nosotros _____ con retraso.

---

# Sequence of Tenses in the Subjunctive

When it is necessary to use the subjunctive, the tense (time) of the subjunctive in the dependent clause depends on the tense of the verb used in the main clause. It is important to keep in mind the time to which you are referring when choosing the tenses you use. For example, if the main clause is in the present, present perfect, future, or if it is a command, you may use either the present or present perfect subjunctive in the dependent clause, depending on the meaning you wish to convey. If the main clause is in the imperfect, preterit, conditional, or pluperfect tenses, you must use either the imperfect or pluperfect subjunctive, which will be explained in Chapter 9.

| Main Clause | | Dependent Clause |
| --- | --- | --- |
| Present | | Present Subjunctive |
| Present Perfect | *que* | or |
| Future | | Present Perfect Subjunctive |
| Command | | |

- Present/Present Subjunctive

    The teacher demands that the students speak Spanish.
    El profesor exige que los alumnos hablen español.

- Present Perfect/Present Subjunctive

    The teacher has demanded that the students speak Spanish.
    El profesor ha exigido que los alumnos hablen español.

- Future/Present Subjunctive

    The teacher will demand that the students speak Spanish.
    El profesor exigirá que los alumnos hablen español.

- Command/Present Subjunctive

    Demand that the students speak Spanish!
    ¡Exija Ud. que los alumnos hablen español!

- Present/Present Perfect Subjunctive

    I'm glad that you have come.
    Me alegro de que Ud. haya venido.

- Present Perfect/Present Perfect Subjunctive

    They have been afraid that she may have told a lie.
    Ellos han tenido miedo de que ella haya dicho una mentira.

- Future/Present Perfect Subjunctive

    I will hope that he has done it.
    Yo esperaré que él lo haya hecho.

◆ Command/Present Perfect Subjunctive

Advise him that he hasn't given it to me.
Aconséjele que no me lo haya dado.

# Avoiding the Subjunctive

It is generally preferable to avoid the subjunctive whenever possible. Until this point, the verbs in the dependent clause (where the subjunctive is used) and the verbs in the main clause (need, necessity, wishing, wanting, etc.) have different subjects. If the subjects in both clauses are the same, *que* is omitted and the infinitive replaces the subjunctive:

Ella prefiere que yo la conduzca al centro.
She prefers me to drive her to the city.

Ella prefiere conducir al centro.
She prefers driving to the city.

The verbs *dejar* (to allow), *hacer* (to make, do), *mandar* (to order), *permitir* (to permit), and *prohibir* (to forbid) may be followed by either the subjunctive or the infinitive:

Te manda que te quedes en casa.
Te manda quedarte en casa.
He orders you to stay home.

Me prohiben que beba alcohol.
Me prohiben beber alcohol.
They forbid me to drink alcohol.

---

### Práctica 15

Express what the teacher allows certain students to do by combining the thoughts to avoid the subjunctive:

Ejemplo:
Nos manda que leamos este libro.
Nos manda leer este libro.

1. Le manda que trabaje. _____

2. Me deja que escriba en la pizarra. _____

3. Te hace que leas. _____

4. Nos prohibe que fumemos. _____

5. Me permite que salga de la clase. _____

6. Te deja que hables en inglés. _____

## Práctica 16

For each sentence decide whether to use the subjunctive or the indicative to describe what happens in school:

1. (traducir) El profesor de español quiere que nosotros _____ las frases.

2. (llegar) El director no cree que yo _____ a la escuela a tiempo.

3. (escoger) Ojalá que los alumnos _____ las respuestas correctas.

4. (traer) Es cierto que vosotros _____ vuestras tareas a clase.

5. (tener) Busco un libro que _____ buenas explicaciones.

6. (perder) Es necesario que tú no _____ tu libro de español.

7. (dormir) Es seguro que nosotros no _____ en clase.

8. (estudiar) Los profesores nos mandan _____.

9. (estar) Estoy contenta de que el profesor de ciencia no _____ ausente hoy.

10. (ir) Más vale que ellos _____ a la biblioteca.

11. (ser) ¿Creen ellos que yo _____ inteligente.

12. (conocer) Susana es la muchacha más bonita que mi amigo _____.

13. (explicar) Tengo un profesor que no _____ bien la gramática.

14. (saber) Es probable que Julio _____ todas las palabras del vocabulario.

15. (venir) El profesor siempre espera hasta que todos los alumnos _____.

16. (hacer) No está claro que todos los alumnos _____ el trabajo escolar.

# Repaso

1. The subjunctive of most verbs is formed by dropping the *-o* from the *yo* form of the present indicative and adding the appropriate subjunctive ending.

2. The subjunctive endings for verbs ending in *-ar* are *-e, -es, -e, -emos, -éis, -en*.

3. The subjunctive endings for verbs ending in *-er* or *ir* are *-a, -as, -a, -amos, -áis, -an*.

4. Verbs with irregular *yo* forms in the present tense are:

| | | |
|---|---|---|
| caber | to fit | quepo |
| caer | to fall | caigo |
| decir | to say, tell | digo |
| hacer | to make, do | hago |
| oír | to hear | oigo |
| poner | to put | pongo |
| salir | to go out | salgo |
| tener | to have | tengo |
| traer | to bring | traigo |
| valer | to be worth | valgo |
| venir | to come | vengo |
| ver | to see | veo |

5. For verbs ending in *-car, -gar, -guar,* and *-zar*, drop the *-o* from the *yo* form of the present indicative and add the subjunctive endings for *-ar* verbs. The following changes will occur: *c* to *qu, g* to *gu, gu* to *gü,* and *z* to *c* respectively.

6. For verbs ending in *-cer/-cir, -ger/-gir, -guir,* and *-quir*, drop the *-o* from the *yo* form of the present indicative and add the subjunctive endings for *-er* and *-ir* verbs. The following changes will occur: *consonant + -cer* and *-cir, c* to *z; vowel + cer* or *cir, c* to *zc; -ger* and *-gir, g* to *j; -guir, gu* to *g;* and *-quir, qu* to *c* respectively.

7. Verbs whose stem ends in *-ñ, -ll + -er or -ir,* and *-eer* are regular in the present subjunctive

8. For spelling-change verbs, those ending in *-ar* and *-er* have the same change in the stem vowel in the subjunctive that occurs in the stem vowel of the present

tense *e* to *ie* and *o* to *ue* in all present subjunctive forms except *nosotros* and *vosotros*.

9. For verbs ending in *-ir*, the same change occurs in the stem vowel in the subjunctive that occurs in the stem vowel in the present tense. Additionally, the stem vowel changes from *e* to *i* or from *o* to *u* in the *nosotros* and *vosotros* forms. The following changes will occur: *e* to *ie*, *i* to *ie*, *e* to *i*, and *o* to *ue* in all present subjunctive *yo, tú, el, ellos* forms, and *e* to *i* and *o* to *u* in present subjunctive *nosotros* and *vosotros* forms.

10. Class 4 verbs have an accented vowel in the *yo, tú, él,* and *ellos* forms of the present subjunctive. The following changes will occur: stressed *ai* to *aí*, *au* to *aú*, and *eu* to *eú*.

11. For some verbs ending in *-iar* and for all ending in *-uar* (except those ending in *-cuar* and *-guar*), i changes to *í* and u changes to *ú* in the *yo, tú, él,* and *ellos* forms of the present subjunctive.

12. For verbs ending in *-uir* (except for those ending in *-guir*), a *y* is inserted after the *u* in all forms of the present subjunctive.

13. The following verbs are irregular in the subjunctive and must be memorized:

| | | |
|---|---|---|
| dar | to give | dé, des, dé, demos, deis, den |
| estar | to be | esté, estés, esté, estemos, estéis, estén |
| haber | to have | haya, hayas, haya, hayamos, hayáis, hayan |
| ir | to go | vaya, vayas, vaya, vayamos, vayáis, vayan |
| saber | to know | sepa, sepas, sepa, sepamos, sepáis, sepan |
| ser | to be | sea, seas, sea, seamos, seáis, sean |

14. In the subjunctive, the reflexive pronoun precedes the conjugated verb.

15. The subjunctive is used to express the present and the future.

16. The subjunctive is used in sentences where there are two clauses with different subjects and that are joined by *que*. One of the clauses must express need, necessity, doubt, uncertainty, possibility, probability, emotion, advice, command, demand, desire, emotion, hope, permission, preference, prohibition, request, suggestion, wishing, or wanting.

17. The subjunctive is used after certain conjunctions when uncertainty, doubt, purpose, anticipation, or indefiniteness is implied.

18. The subjunctive is used after indefinites or compounds of *-quiera* + *que*.

19. The subjunctive is used in relative clauses if the person or thing in the main clause is indefinite, desired but not yet attained, or is nonexistent or whose existence is doubtful.

20. The subjunctive is used in third person singular or plural commands.

21. The superlative is used after superlative expressions to show an opinion, a feeling, or an emotion.

22. The present perfect (past) subjunctive expresses what has occurred in the past and is formed by conjugating *haber* in the subjunctive and adding a past participle (which remains the same for all subject pronouns).

23. If the main clause of a sentence is in the present, present perfect, future, or if it is a command, either the present or present perfect subjunctive may be used in the dependent clause.

24. The subjunctive may be avoided if the subjects in both clauses are the same. *Que* is omitted and the infinitive replaces the subjunctive.

25. The verbs *dejar* (to allow), *hacer* (to make, do), *mandar* (to order), *permitir* (to permit), and *prohibir* (to forbid) may be followed by either the subjunctive or the infinitive.

## The Least You Need to Know

- To form the present subjunctive, take the present-tense *yo* form of the indicative, drop the *-o*, and add *-e, -es, -e, -emos, -éis, -en* for *-ar* verbs and *-a, -as, -a, -amos, -áis, -an* for *-er* and *-ir* verbs.

- Spelling-change and stem-changing verbs require changes in the subjunctive based on their *yo* present-tense indicative forms.

- The present perfect (past) subjunctive is formed by taking the subjunctive of *haber* and adding a past participle.

- The subjunctive is used after certain verbs and expressions showing wishing, wanting, need, necessity, emotion, doubt, and the like.

- The subjunctive is also used after certain conjunctions, in relative clauses, in third person commands, and in superlative sentences when there is wishing, emotion, or doubt.

# The Imperfect and the Pluperfect Subjunctive

## In This Chapter

◆ Forming the imperfect subjunctive

◆ Forming the pluperfect subjunctive

◆ Using the imperfect and pluperfect subjunctive

◆ Conditional sentences

Like the present subjunctive, the imperfect subjunctive is a mood that expresses attitudes and is used after certain adjectives, verbs, and expressions showing wishing, need, emotion, doubt, and the like.

The major difference between the present subjunctive and the imperfect subjunctive is the time frame in which the action of the main verb is taking place. When the main verb is in the present, present perfect, or future tense, or is in the imperative (command) mode, then the present or present perfect subjunctive is required in the dependent clause. When the main verb is in the preterit, imperfect, conditional, or pluperfect tense, then the imperfect or, in certain cases, the pluperfect subjunctive is used.

Conditional sentences or *"si"* clauses express conditions that are real or contrary-to-fact. Different tenses are used depending upon the type of condition being expressed.

In this chapter you'll learn the two ways to form the imperfect subjunctive, how to form the pluperfect subjunctive, and when to use each. You'll also learn the correct sequence of tenses in conditional sentences.

# The Imperfect Subjunctive of All Verbs

In Spanish, the imperfect subjunctive has two forms, often referred to as the *-ra* and the *-se* forms. The same two sets of endings are used for all verbs. To form the imperfect subjunctive of all verbs, drop *-ron* from the third person plural preterit indicative (*ellos* form) and add either of the endings shown in Table 9.1.

## Table 9.1    *-ra* and *-se* Forms of the Imperfect Subjunctive

| Subject | *-ra* endings | *-se* endings |
| --- | --- | --- |
| yo | -ra | -se |
| tú | -ras | -ses |
| él, ella, Ud. | -ra | -se |
| nosotros | -ramos* | -semos* |
| vosotros | -rais | -seis |
| ellos, ellas, Uds. | -ran | -sen |

*Note: An acute accent (´) goes over whatever vowel happens to precede* -ramos *or* -semos.

## The Imperfect Subjunctive of Regular Verbs *-ra* Form

For the imperfect subjunctive of regular verbs, simply drop the *-ron* from the *ellos* form of the preterit and add the *-ra* endings, as shown in Table 9.2.

## Table 9.2   The Imperfect Subjunctive of Regular Verbs -*ra* Form

|  | -*ar* verbs | -*er* verbs | -*ir* verbs |
|---|---|---|---|
|  | **hablar** (*to speak*) | **beber** (*to drink*) | **abrir** (*to open*) |
| ellos/preterit | habla**ron** | bebie**ron** | abrie**ron** |
| yo | hablara | bebiera | abriera |
| tú | hablaras | bebieras | abrieras |
| él | hablara | bebiera | abriera |
| nosotros | habláramos | bebiéramos | abriéramos |
| vosotros | hablarais | bebierais | abrierais |
| ellos | hablaran | bebieran | abrieran |

El doctor insistió en que yo bebiera mucha agua.
The doctor insisted that I drink a lot of water.

Only the *nosotros* form of the imperfect subjunctive requires an accent mark on the vowel immediately preceding the ending.

## The Imperfect Subjunctive of Regular Verbs -*se* Form

For the imperfect subjunctive of regular verbs, simply drop the -*ron* from the *ellos* form of the preterit and add the -*ra* endings, as shown in Table 9.3.

## Table 9.3  The Imperfect Subjunctive of Regular Verbs -*se* Form

|  | -*ar* verbs | -*er* verbs | -*ir* verbs |
|---|---|---|---|
|  | **hablar** (*to speak*) | **beber** (*to drink*) | **abrir** (*to open*) |
| ellos/preterit | habla**ron** | bebie**ron** | abrie**ron** |
| yo | hablase | bebiese | abriese |
| tú | hablases | bebieses | abrieses |
| él | hablase | bebiese | abriese |
| nosotros | hablásemos | bebiésemos | abriésemos |
| vosotros | hablaseis | bebieseis | abrieseis |
| ellos | hablasen | bebiesen | abriesen |

El doctor insistió en que yo bebiese mucha agua.
The doctor insisted that I drink a lot of water.

---

### Práctica 1

Express what each person told the other to do by giving both forms of the imperfect subjunctive:

1. (acompañar) Nuestros primos insistieron en que nosotros los _____ al cine.

2. (vender) Roberto me aconsejó que yo _____ mi carro.

3. (abrir) Tus padres sugirieron que tú _____ una cuenta bancaria.

4. (descansar) Sus amigos les dijeron que ellos _____ más después de trabajar.

5. (escribir) Su madre le pidió que ella _____una carta a sus abuelas.

6. (aprender) Vuestros abuelos os suplicaron que vosotros _____ el español.

---

# The Imperfect Subjunctive of Spelling-Change Verbs

Because verbs ending in *-car*, *-gar*, *-guar*, and *-zar* do not require a spelling change in the *ellos* form of the preterit and do not, therefore, require a spelling change in the imperfect subjunctive, as shown in Table 9.4.

## Table 9.4   The Imperfect Subjunctive of *-ar* Spelling Change Verbs

| Verb | ellos/preterit | *-ra* endings | *-se* endings |
|---|---|---|---|
| buscar<br>(*to look for*) | busca**ron** | buscara<br>buscaras<br>buscara<br>buscáramos<br>buscarais<br>buscaran | buscase<br>buscases<br>buscase<br>buscásemos<br>buscaseis<br>buscasen |
| llegar<br>(*to arrive*) | llega**ron** | llegara<br>llegaras<br>llegara<br>llegáramos<br>llegarais<br>llegaran | llegase<br>llegases<br>llegase<br>llegásemos<br>llegaseis<br>llegasen |
| averiguar<br>(*to ascertain*) | averigua**ron** | averiguara<br>averiguaras<br>averiguara<br>averiguáramos<br>averiguarais<br>averiguaran | averiguase<br>averiguases<br>averiguase<br>averiguásemos<br>averiguaseis<br>averiguasen |
| lanzar<br>(*to throw*) | lanza**ron** | lanzara<br>lanzaras<br>lanzara<br>lanzáramos<br>lanzarais<br>lanzaran | lanzase<br>lanzases<br>lanzase<br>lanzásemos<br>lanzaseis<br>lanzasen |

Likewise, verbs ending in *-cer/-cir* (except those ending in *-ducir*), *-ger/-gir*, *-guir*, and *-quir* have no spelling changes in the preterit, they follow the regular rules for the formation of the imperfect subjunctive, as shown in Table 9.5. Spelling-change verbs with stem changes will require changes in the subjunctive, as shown in the following table.

## Table 9.5  The Imperfect Subjunctive of -*er*/-*ir* Spelling Change Verbs

| Verb | ellos/preterit | -*ra* endings | -*se* endings |
|---|---|---|---|
| cono**cer**<br>(*to know*) | conocie**ron** | conociera<br>conocieras<br>conociera<br>conociéramos<br>conocierais<br>conocieran | conociese<br>conocieses<br>conociese<br>conociésemos<br>conocieseis<br>conociesen |
| espar**cir**<br>(*to scatter*) | esparcie**ron** | esparciera<br>esparcieras<br>esparciera<br>esparciéramos<br>esparcierais<br>esparcieran | esparciese<br>esparcieses<br>esparciese<br>esparciésemos<br>esparcieseis<br>esparciesen |
| esco**ger**<br>(*to choose*) | escogie**ron** | escogiera<br>escogieras<br>escogiera<br>escogiéramos<br>escogierais<br>escogieran | escogiese<br>escogieses<br>escogiese<br>escogiésemos<br>escogieseis<br>escogiesen |
| diri**gir**<br>(*to direct*) | dirigie**ron** | dirigiera<br>dirigieras<br>dirigiera<br>dirigiéramos<br>dirigierais<br>dirigieran | dirigiese<br>dirigieses<br>dirigiese<br>dirigiésemos<br>dirigieseis<br>dirigiesen |
| distin**guir**<br>(*to distinguish*) | distinguie**ron** | distinguiera<br>distinguieras<br>distinguiera<br>distinguiéramos<br>distinguierais<br>distinguieran | distinguiese<br>distinguieses<br>distinguiese<br>distinguiésemos<br>distinguieseis<br>distinguiesen |
| delin**quir**<br>(*to offend*) | delinquie**ron** | delinquiera<br>delinquieras<br>delinquiera<br>delinquiéramos<br>delinquierais<br>delinquieran | delinquiese<br>delinquieses<br>delinquiese<br>delinquiésemos<br>delinquieseis<br>delinquiesen |

### Práctica 2

Express what was important for each person by giving the correct form of the imperfect subjunctive in both forms:

Ejemplo:
él/buscar su perro
Era importante que él buscara (buscase) su perro.

1. nosotros/almorzar temprano _____

2. ella/parecer contenta _____

3. vosotros/apaciguar a los niños _____

4. tú/no equivocarse _____

5. Uds./proteger a sus amigos _____

6. yo/investigar el problema _____

7. el conductor/dirigir la orquesta _____

8. nosotros/distinguirse _____

## The Imperfect Subjunctive of Verbs Ending in Vowel + -er/-ir

Verbs ending in vowel + -er/-ir (see Appendixes E and F) change the third person plural form (*ellos*) from -*ieron* to -*yeron* in the preterit, and therefore, in the imperfect subjunctive, as shown in Table 9.6.

## Table 9.6   Spelling Changes in Vowel + -er/-ir Verbs

| Verb | ellos/preterit | -ra endings | -se endings |
|------|---------------|-------------|-------------|
| caer (to fall) | cayeron | cayera | cayese |
| | | cayeras | cayeses |
| | | cayera | cayese |
| | | cayéramos | cayésemos |
| | | cayerais | cayeseis |
| | | cayeran | cayesen |
| leer (to read) | leyeron | leyera | leyese |
| | | leyeras | leyeses |
| | | leyera | leyese |
| | | leyéramos | leyésemos |
| | | leyerais | leyeseis |
| | | leyeran | leyesen |
| oír (to hear) | oyeron | oyera | oyese |
| | | oyeras | oyeses |
| | | oyera | oyese |
| | | oyéramos | oyésemos |
| | | oyerais | oyeseis |
| | | oyeran | oyesen |

## The Imperfect Subjunctive of Verbs Ending in -uir

Verbs ending in -uir (but not -guir) change the third person plural form (ellos, ellas, Uds.) from -ieron to yeron: ellos distribuyeron (they distributed):

| -ra form | -se form |
|----------|----------|
| distribuyera | distribuyese |
| distribuyeras | distribuyeses |
| distribuyera | distribuyese |
| distribuyerámos | distribuyésemos |
| distribuyerais | distribuyeseis |
| distribuyera | distribuyesen |

## The Imperfect Subjunctive of Verb Stems Ending in ñ and ll

Verbs ending in ñ and ll before the infinitive ending drop the i of the preterit endings for the third person plural (ellos) form, as shown in Table 9.7.

## Table 9.7     The Imperfect Subjunctive of Verb Stems Ending in *ñ* and *ll*

| Verb | ellos/preterit | -*ra* endings | -*se* endings |
|---|---|---|---|
| teñ**ir** (*to dye*) | teñe**ron** | teñera | teñese |
| | | teñeras | teñeses |
| | | teñera | teñese |
| | | teñéramos | teñésemos |
| | | teñerais | teñeseis |
| | | teñeran | teñesen |
| tañ**er** (*to ring*) | tañe**ron** | tañera | tañese |
| | | tañeras | tañeses |
| | | tañera | tañese |
| | | tañéramos | tañésemos |
| | | tañerais | tañeseis |
| | | tañeran | tañesen |
| bull**ir** (*to boil*) | bulle**ron** | bullera | bullese |
| | | bulleras | bulleses |
| | | bullera | bullese |
| | | bulléramos | bullésemos |
| | | bullerais | bulleseis |
| | | bulleran | bullesen |

## Práctica 3

Express what was possible by giving both forms of the imperfect subjunctive:

Ejemplo:
el profesor/no creer a los alumnos
Era posible que el profesor no creyera (creyese) a los alumnos.

1. el cerdo/gruñir _____

2. el agua/bullir _____

3. los alumnos/no oír el timbre _____

4. el paquete/no incluir las mercancías correctas _____

5. estos muchachos/poseer mucho talento _____

6. el coche/caer por un barranco _____

# The Imperfect Subjunctive of Stem-Changing Verbs

Since the only verbs with stem changes in the preterit are those whose infinitive ends in *-ir*, these are the only verbs with stem changes in the imperfect subjunctive.

## *-ir* Verbs with *e* to *ie* or *e* to *i* Stem Changes

Verbs whose stems change from *e* to *ie* or from *e* to *i* in the present (see Appendix F), change their stems from *e* to *i* in the preterit in the third person plural (*ellos*) form, as well as in the imperfect subjunctive, as shown in Table 9.8.

### Table 9.8   The Imperfect Subjunctive of Verbs with *e* to *ie* or *e* to *i* Stem Changes

| Verb | ellos/preterit | *-ra* endings | *-se* endings |
| --- | --- | --- | --- |
| preferir (*to prefer*) | prefirieron | prefiriera prefirieras prefiriera prefiriéramos prefirierais prefirieran | prefiriese prefirieses prefiriese prefiriésemos prefirieseis prefiriesen |
| servir (*to serve*) | sirvieron | sirviera sirvieras sirviera sirviéramos sirvierais sirvieran | sirviese sirvieses sirviese sirviésemos sirvieseis sirviesen |

The verb *reír* (to laugh) and *sonreír* (to smile) both have the same changes but drop *i* in the stem of the third person plural (*ellos*) form:

| | |
| --- | --- |
| yo (son)riera | yo (son)riese |
| tú (son)rieras | tú (son)rieses |
| él (son)riera | él (son)riese |
| nosotros (son)riéramos | nosotros (son)riésemos |
| vosotros (son)rierais | vosotros (son)rieseis |
| ellos (son)rieran | ellos (son)riesen |

## Verbs with *o* to *ue* Changes

Verbs whose stem changes from *o* to *ue* in the present (see Appendix F), change their stems from *o* to *u* in the preterit in the third person plural, as well as in the imperfect subjunctive: *ellos durmieron* (they slept):

| -*ra* form | -*se* form |
|---|---|
| durmiera | durmiese |
| durmieras | durmieses |
| durmiera | durmiese |
| durmiéramos | durmiésemos |
| durmierais | durmieseis |
| durmieran | durmiesen |

---

### Práctica 4

Express what was a pity by using both forms of the imperfect subjunctive:

Ejemplo:
él/dormir hasta tarde
Era una lástima que él durmiera (durmiese) hasta tarde.

1. vosotros/mentir _____

2. ella/morir _____

3. nosotros/no referirse al diccionario _____

4. tú/no vestirse a la moda _____

5. yo/no sonreír _____

6. Uds./repetir un curso _____

---

# The Imperfect Subjunctive of Irregular Verbs

Those high-frequency verbs that are irregular in the preterit are also irregular in the imperfect subjunctive. Once again, these verbs can be grouped by the changes they undergo.

## Verbs with *i* in the Preterit Stem

Some verbs change the vowel before the infinitive ending (*e* or *a*) to *i* and may or may not use a different consonant in the stem, as shown in Table 9.9.

## Table 9.9   Verbs with *i* in the Preterit Stem

| Verb | ellos/preterit | *-ra* endings | *-se* endings |
|---|---|---|---|
| decir<br>(*to say, tell*) | dije**ron** | dijera<br>dijeras<br>dijera<br>dijéramos<br>dijerais<br>dijeran | dijese<br>dijeses<br>dijese<br>dijésemos<br>dijeseis<br>dijesen |
| venir<br>(*to come*) | vinie**ron** | viniera<br>vinieras<br>viniera<br>viniéramos<br>vinierais<br>vinieran | viniese<br>vinieses<br>viniese<br>viniésemos<br>vinieseis<br>viniesen |
| querer<br>(*to want*) | quisie**ron** | quisiera<br>quisieras<br>quisiera<br>quisiéramos<br>quisierais<br>quisieran | quisiese<br>quisieses<br>quisiese<br>quisiésemos<br>quisieseis<br>quisiesen |
| hacer<br>(*to make, do*) | hicie**ron** | hiciera<br>hicieras<br>hiciera<br>hiciéramos<br>hicierais<br>hicieran | hiciese<br>hicieses<br>hiciese<br>hiciésemos<br>hicieseis<br>hiciesen |
| satisfacer<br>(*to satisfy*) | satisficie**ron** | satisficiera<br>satisficieras<br>satisficiera<br>satisficiéramos<br>satisficierais<br>satisficieran | satisficiese<br>satisficieses<br>satisficiese<br>satisficiésemos<br>satisficieseis<br>satisficiesen |

# Verbs with *u* in the Preterit Stem

Some verbs change the vowel before the infinitive ending (*a* or *o*) to *u* and may or may not use a different consonant in the stem, as shown in Table 9.10.

**Table 9.10    Verbs with *u* in the Preterit Stem**

| Verb | ellos/preterit | *-ra* endings | *-se* endings |
|---|---|---|---|
| caber<br>(*to fit*) | cupie**ron** | cupiera<br>cupieras<br>cupiera<br>cupiéramos<br>cupierais<br>cupieran | cupiese<br>cupieses<br>cupiese<br>cupiésemos<br>cupieseis<br>cupiesen |
| haber<br>(*to have*) | hubie**ron** | hubiera<br>hubieras<br>hubiera<br>hubiéramos<br>hubierais<br>hubieran | hubiese<br>hubieses<br>hubiese<br>hubiésemos<br>hubieseis<br>hubiesen |
| saber<br>(*to know*) | supie**ron** | supiera<br>supieras<br>supiera<br>supiéramos<br>supierais<br>supieran | supiese<br>supieses<br>supiese<br>supiésemos<br>supieseis<br>supiesen |
| poner<br>(*to put*) | pusie**ron** | pusiera<br>pusieras<br>pusiera<br>pusiéramos<br>pusierais<br>pusieran | pusiese<br>pusieses<br>pusiese<br>pusiésemos<br>pusieseis<br>pusiesen |
| poder<br>(*to be able*) | pudie**ron** | pudiera<br>pudieras<br>pudiera<br>pudiéramos<br>pudierais<br>pudieran | pudiese<br>pudieses<br>pudiese<br>pudiésemos<br>pudieseis<br>pudiesen |

## Verbs with *uv* in the Preterit Stem

Some verbs drop the infinitive ending (*-ar* or *-er*) and add *uv* before the preterit ending, and therefore, before the imperfect subjunctive ending, as shown in Table 9.11. Note that *tener* also drops *en*.

## Table 9.11 Verbs with *uv* in the Preterit Stem

| Verb | ellos/preterit | *-ra* endings | *-se* endings |
|------|----------------|---------------|---------------|
| andar (*to walk*) | and**uvie**r**on** | anduviera anduvieras anduviera anduviéramos anduvierais anduvieran | anduviese anduvieses anduviese anduviésemos anduvieseis anduviesen |
| estar (*to be*) | est**uvie**r**on** | estuviera estuvieras estuviera estuviéramos estuvierais estuvieran | estuviese estuvieses estuviese estuviésemos estuvieseis estuviesen |
| tener (*to have*) | t**uvie**r**on** | tuviera tuvieras tuviera tuviéramos tuvierais tuvieran | tuviese tuvieses tuviese tuviésemos tuvieseis tuviesen |

## Verbs with *j* in the Preterit Stem

Some verbs have *-j* in their preterit stem. These verbs include all those that end in *-ducir* (see Appendix F), as shown in Table 9.12. Note that this occurs in the verb *decir*, shown in Table 9.9.

## Table 9.12    Verbs with *j* in the Preterit Stem

| Verb | ellos/preterit | -*ra* endings | -*se* endings |
|---|---|---|---|
| traer (*to bring*) | traje**ron** | trajera<br>trajeras<br>trajera<br>trajéramos<br>trajerais<br>trajeran | trajese<br>trajeses<br>trajese<br>trajésemos<br>trajeseis<br>trajesen |
| conducir (*to drive*) | conduje**ron** | condujera<br>condujeras<br>condujera<br>condujéramos<br>condujerais<br>condujeran | condujese<br>condujeses<br>condujese<br>condujésemos<br>condujeseis<br>condujesen |

## Dar and Ver

The verbs *dar* (to give) and *ver* (to see) are similar in the third person plural preterit and, therefore, in the imperfect subjunctive, as shown in Table 9.13.

## Table 9.13    *Dar* and *Ver* in the Imperfect Subjunctive

| Verb | ellos/preterit | -*ra* endings | -*se* endings |
|---|---|---|---|
| dar (*to give*) | die**ron** | diera<br>dieras<br>diera<br>diéramos<br>dierais<br>dieran | diese<br>dieses<br>diese<br>diésemos<br>dieseis<br>diesen |
| ver (*to see*) | vie**ron** | viera<br>vieras<br>viera<br>viéramos<br>vierais<br>vieran | viese<br>vieses<br>viese<br>viésemos<br>vieseis<br>viesen |

# Ser and Ir

*Ser* (to be) and *ir* (to go) have the exact same preterit forms, and therefore, the same exact imperfect subjunctive forms. You must understand the context of the sentence in order to distinguish which verb is being used. The highly irregular forms of these two verbs are:

| | |
|---|---|
| yo fuera | yo fuese |
| tú fueras | tú fueses |
| él fuera | él fuese |
| nosotros fuéramos | nosotros fuésemos |
| vosotros fuerais | vosotros fueseis |
| ellos fueran | ellos fuesen |

## Práctica 5

Complete each sentence with the correct form of the imperfect subjunctive in both forms:

1. Era necesario que él

   a. traducir una carta al español _____

   b. ir al supermercado _____

   c. satisfacer a todos los requisitos del puesto _____

   d. decir la verdad _____

   e. hacer planes para su futuro _____

   f. poner dinero en el banco _____

2. Era menester que tú

   a. traer estos papeles a la oficina _____

   b. ver a tu profesora _____

   c. poder ir a la biblioteca _____

   d. querer su ayuda _____

   e. tener razón _____

   f. no le dar pena _____

3. Era improbable que ellos

   a. andar por el parque a esta hora _____

   b. estar de retraso _____

   c. no saben jugar al fútbol _____

   d. caber en ese carro _____

   e. venir en tren _____

   f. ser culpables de ese crimen _____

# The Pluperfect Subjunctive of All Verbs

The pluperfect subjunctive is a compound tense, which means that it is made up of more than one part. The two elements that are needed to form the pluperfect subjunctive are:

1. The imperfect subjunctive of the helping verb *haber* (*hubiera, hubieras, hubiera, hubiéramos, hubierais, hubieran* or *hubiese, hubieses, hubiese, hubiésemos, hubieseis, hubiesen*): which expresses that something has taken place in the past.

2. The past participle of the verb: which expresses what the action was.

The following diagram shows how the past subjunctive is formed:

Pluperfect Subjunctive of verb =     when + what

/ \

Pluperfect Subjunctive of verb =   (what) had + happened

/ \

Pluperfect Subjunctive of verb =   helping verb + main verb

/ \

Pluperfect Subjunctive of verb = haber (to have) + past participle

The formula for the formation of the pluperfect subjunctive is:

subject noun or pronoun + *haber* in imperfect subjunctive + past participle

The formation of past participles was explained in Chapter 1. Irregular past participles are listed in Table 1.3 and in Appendix H.

Yo dudaba que ellos lo hubieran (hubiesen) comprendido.
I doubted that they had understood it.

Ella temía que Ud. no lo hubiera (hubiese) recibido.
She was afraid that you hadn't received it.

### Práctica 6

Express how each person felt by using both forms of the pluperfect subjunctive:

1. (tener) Mis amigos se alegraban de que yo _____ éxito.

2. (hacer) Ellos dudaban que nosotros _____ nuestro trabajo.

3. (decir) Ud. temía que ella _____ mentiras.

4. (ponerse) Él negó que Uds. _____ furiosos.

5. (escribir) Me sorprendió que tú _____ esta carta.

6. (volver) Nosotros nos alegrábamos de que vosotros _____ muy pronto.

# Sequence of Tenses in the Subjunctive

In sentences requiring the subjunctive, the tense (time) of the subjunctive in the dependent clause depends on the tense of the verb used in the main clause. If the main clause is in the imperfect, preterit, conditional, or pluperfect, you *must* use either the imperfect or the pluperfect subjunctive in the dependent clause, depending on the meaning you wish to convey. The imperfect subjunctive tenses are generally interchangeable in Spanish.

| Main Clause | Dependent Clause |
|---|---|
| Imperfect | Imperfect Subjunctive |
| Preterit | que or |
| Conditional Pluperfect | Pluperfect Subjunctive |

◆ Imperfect/Imperfect Subjunctive

  Ella dudaba que él lo hiciera (hiciese).
  She doubted that he might do it.

◆ Preterit/Imperfect Subjunctive

  Ella dijó que él lo hiciera (hiciese).
  She said that he might do it.

◆ Conditional/Imperfect Subjunctive

  Preferería que él lo hiciera (hiciese).
  She would prefer that he might do it.

◆ Pluperfect/Imperfect Subjunctive

> Había preferido que él lo hiciera (hiciese).
> She would have preferred that he might do it.

Although the imperfect subjunctive is normally used when the main verb is in the imperfect, preterit, conditional, or pluperfect, the pluperfect subjunctive is used in Spanish when English uses the past perfect tense (had + past participle):

◆ Imperfect/Pluperfect Subjunctive

> Lo sentíamos que Ud. no lo hubiera (hubiese) hecho.
> We were sorry that you hadn't done it.

◆ Preterit/Pluperfect Subjunctive

> Insistió en que ellos lo hubieran (hubiesen) hecho.
> He insisted that they had done it.

◆ Conditional/Pluperfect Subjunctive

> ¿Creerían Uds. que yo lo hubiera (hubiese) hecho?
> Would you believe that I had done it?

◆ Pluperfect/Pluperfect Subjunctive

> Yo había preferido que tú lo hubieras (hubieses) hecho.
> I would have preferred that you had done it.

The imperfect subjunctive may follow a main clause verb in the present, future, or present perfect tense when the action of the dependent clause takes place in the past:

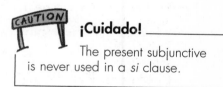

**¡Cuidado!**

The present subjunctive is never used in a *si* clause.

> ¡Es una lástima que Uds. no pudieran acompañarnos!
> It's a pity that you couldn't accompany us!

In Spanish, it is considered more polite to soften a request by using the *-ra* subjunctive form of *querer:*

> Quiero salir.          Quisiera salir.
> I want to go out.      I would like to go out.

The *-ra* forms of *deber* and *poder* are also used to form a polite or softened statement:

Debes insistir.
You must insist.

Debieras insistir.
You should insist.

Puede hablar.
You can speak.

Pudiera hablar.
You may speak.

**¡Mira!**

Whereas the present subjunctive may be translated with "may" as part of its meaning, the imperfect subjunctive can be translated with "might": *La llevé al centro para que ella comprara (comprase) algo.* (I took her to the city so that she might buy something.)

# Conditional Sentences

A conditional sentence consists of a condition, an "if" clause (*si* clause) and a result (result or main clause). Two basic conditions exist: "real" conditions and "unreal" or "contrary-to-fact" conditions.

## Real Conditions

Real conditions address situations that exist, that are certain, or that are likely to occur. The indicative is used after *si* to express a real condition:

Si me ayudas, te pagaré.
If you help me, I will pay you.

Si Ud. me llamó ayer, yo no estaba en la oficina.
If you called me yesterday, I wasn't in the office.

### Práctica 7

Express what each person does under certain circumstances:

Ejemplo:
Ud./tener calor/quitar el abrigo
Si Ud. tiene calor, tú te quitas el abrigo.

1. tú/tener sueño/dormir _____

2. nosotros/tener hambre/comer un sándwich _____

3. ellos/tener frío/ponerse un suéter _____

4. yo/tener sed/beber agua _____

5. Ud./tener vergüenza/ruborizarse _____

6. vosotros/tener dolor de cabeza/tomar una aspirina _____

# Contrary-to-Fact Conditions

Contrary-to-fact conditions address situations that do not actually exist or that have not occurred. To express something that is contrary to fact (not true) at the present time, or something that was contrary-to-fact in the past, Spanish uses the imperfect or pluperfect subjunctive. The result or main clause is usually, but not always, expressed by the conditional or the conditional perfect, as shown in Table 9.14.

Note: Never use the present subjunctive in a *si* clause.

## Table 9.14   Contrary-to-Fact Conditions

| When? | Tense of *si* Clause | Tense of Result Clause |
|---|---|---|
| Present | Imperfect Subjunctive (*-ra* or *-se* form) | Conditional (preferred in simple tenses) or Imperfect Subjunctive (*-ra* form) |
| Past | Pluperfect Subjunctive (*-ra* or *-se* form) | Conditional Perfect or Pluperfect Subjunctive (*-ra* form) |

Si Ud. trabajara (trabajase) más, ganaría más dinero.
If you worked more, you would earn more money.
(You don't earn much money.)

Si Ud. hubiera (hubiese) trabajado más, habría (hubiera) ganado más dinero.
If you had worked more, you would have earned more money.
(You didn't earn much money.)

The imperfect subjunctive is used after *si* to express that something is not expected to happen but might happen in the future. If the English sentence expresses "should" or "were to" in the "if" clause, the imperfect subjunctive is used in Spanish.

Si él viniera (viniese) mañana, él repararía el carro.
If he should (were to) come tomorrow, he would repair the car.

The expression *como si* (as if) also expresses a contrary-to-fact condition and is followed by the imperfect subjunctive to express the present and by the pluperfect subjunctive to express the past:

Hablan como si no tuvieran (tuviesen) nada que hacer.
They speak as if they have nothing to do.

Hablaron como si no hubieran (hubiesen) tenido nada que hacer.
They spoke as if they had nothing to do.

---

### Práctica 8

Complete the sentence expressing what each person would do in the following situations by filling in the correct form of the verb:

1. (olvidar) Si Ud. _____ su cita conmigo, yo le llamaría.

2. (estar) Yo te habría visitado, si tú _____ enfermo.

3. (tener) Si ellos _____ hambre, ella les habría preparado un sándwich.

4. (ir) Si nosotros ganáramos la lotería, _____ a España.

5. (hacer) Yo _____ este trabajo si hubiera tenido el tiempo.

6. (caerse) Si un viejo _____ en la calle, nosotros lo habríamos ayudado.

---

# Repaso

1. The imperfect subjunctive has two forms: the *-ra* and the *-se* forms.

2. The same two sets of endings are used for all verbs.

3. To form *-ra* imperfect subjunctive of all verbs, drop *-ron* from the third person plural preterit indicative (*ellos* form) and add *-ra, -ras, -ra, -ramos, -rais, -ran*.

4. To form *-se* imperfect subjunctive of all verbs, drop *-ron* from the third person plural preterit indicative (*ellos* form) and add *-se, -ses, -se, -semos, -seis, -sen*.

5. Because verbs ending in *-car, -gar, -guar,* and *-zar* do not require a spelling change in the *ellos* form of the preterit and do not, therefore, require a spelling change in the imperfect subjunctive.

6. Verbs ending in *-cer/-cir* (except those ending in *-ducir*), *-ger/-gir, -guir,* and *-quir* have no spelling changes in the preterit; they follow the regular rules for the formation of the imperfect subjunctive.

7. Verbs ending in *vowel + -er/-ir* change the third person plural form (*ellos*) from -*ieron* to *yeron* in the preterit, and therefore, in the imperfect subjunctive.

8. Verbs ending in -*uir* (but not -*guir*) change the third person plural form (*ellos*) from -*ieron* to -*yeron*.

9. Verbs ending in -*ñ* and -*ll* before the infinitive ending drop the *i* of the preterit endings for the third person plural (*ellos*) form.

10. Verbs whose stems change from *e* to *ie* or from *e* to *i* in the present change their stems from *e* to *i* in the preterit in the third person plural (*ellos*) form, as well as in the imperfect subjunctive.

11. The verb *reír* (to laugh) and *sonreír* (to smile) both have the same changes but drop *i* in the stem of the third person plural (*ellos*) form.

12. Verbs whose stem changes from *o* to *ue* in the present change their stems from *o* to *u* in the preterit in the third person plural, as well as in the imperfect subjunctive.

13. Some irregular verbs change the vowel before the infinitive ending to *i*: *decir*, *venir*, *querer*, *hacer*, and *satisfacer*.

14. Some irregular verbs change the vowel before the infinitive ending to *u*: *caber*, *haber*, *saber*, *poner*, and *poder*.

15. Some irregular verbs have *j* in their stem: *traer* and verbs ending in -*ducir*.

16. *Dar* and *ver* have similar irregular imperfect subjunctive stems.

17. *Ser* and *ir* have the same imperfect subjunctive forms.

18. The pluperfect subjunctive expresses what had occurred in the past and is formed by conjugating *haber* in the imperfect subjunctive and adding a past participle (which remains the same for all subject pronouns).

19. If the main clause of a sentence is in the imperfect, preterit, conditional, or pluperfect, either the imperfect or pluperfect subjunctive must be used in the dependent clause.

20. A conditional sentence consists of a condition, an "if" clause (*si* clause) and a result (result or main clause).

21. Real conditions address situations that exist, that are certain, or that are likely to occur and require the indicative after *si*.

22. Contrary-to-fact conditions address situations that do not actually exist or that have not occurred. The imperfect subjunctive or the pluperfect subjunctive is used after *si* while the result or main clause is usually, but not always, expressed by the conditional or the conditional perfect.

23. The imperfect subjunctive is used after *si* to express that something is not expected to happen but might happen in the future.

24. The expression *como si* (as if) also expresses a contrary-to-fact condition and is followed by the imperfect subjunctive to express the present and by the pluperfect subjunctive to express the past.

## The Least You Need to Know

◆ To form the imperfect subjunctive, take the preterit tense *ellos* form, drop *-ron*, and add either *-ra, -ras, -ra, -ramos, -rais, -ran*, or *-se, -ses, -se, -semos, -seis, -sen*.

◆ Spelling-change and stem-changing verbs require changes in the imperfect subjunctive based on their *ellos* preterit forms.

◆ The pluperfect subjunctive is formed by taking the imperfect subjunctive of *haber* and adding a past participle.

◆ The imperfect subjunctive is used to express past actions in the same way that the present subjunctive is used to express present actions.

# Chapter 10

# The Imperative

## In This Chapter

- ◆ Forming and using formal commands
- ◆ Forming and using indirect commands
- ◆ Forming and using familiar commands

The imperative is a mood whereby the speaker gives a command. Issuing a command does not generally mean that the speaker is being bossy or nasty. Commands are given to request items or actions, to offer directions, to issue warnings, to give advice, to provide instructions, to tell people what to do, and to make suggestions.

Just like in English, the subject of most commands is understood to be "you," because you are being asked to do something by the speaker. Because there are four ways to express "you" in Spanish, forming the imperative in Spanish becomes quite a bit more complicated than it is in English. Compound that with the fact that some negative commands are formed in a different manner than their affirmative counterparts and it becomes clear that the imperative in Spanish is something that has to be studied in depth.

In this chapter you'll learn how to use the imperative in both the affirmative and the negative for all four Spanish "you" subjects. You'll also learn how to make suggestions and issue indirect commands using "Let's" and how to use *que* + the subjunctive to form third person commands.

# Formal Commands with *Ud.* and *Uds.*

Formal or polite commands are ones you'd give to or receive from someone you don't know very well. When addressing the person, or when being addressed by the person, the subject of the command is *Ud.* or *Uds.* depending upon whether the subject is one person (*Ud.*) or many (*Uds.*).

## Forming Formal Commands

When forming a command in Spanish, the speaker has the option of using or omitting the subject pronoun, since the subject is easily understood by listening to the verb form being used.

To form an affirmative or negative command with any verb, when *Ud.* or *Uds.* is the subject, use the present subjunctive of the *Ud.* or *Uds.* form of that verb. Remember that opposite vowel endings are added to form the subjunctive: *-ar* verb subjunctive endings contain an *-e: -e, -es, -e, -emos, -éis, -en*; and *-er* and *-ir* verb subjunctive endings contain an *-a: -a, -as, -a, -amos, -áis, -an*, as shown in Table 10.1.

**¡Mira!**

To form the present subjunctive of a verb, drop the *-o* ending from the *yo* form of the present indicative of the verb you are using and add the appropriate subjunctive ending.

## Table 10.1　Forming Commands with *Ud.* and *Uds.*

| *-ar* verbs<br>hablar | *-er* verbs<br>comer | *-ir* verbs<br>subir |
|---|---|---|
| (no) hable (Ud.)<br>*(don't) speak* | (no) coma (Ud.)<br>*(don't) eat* | (no) suba (Ud.)<br>*(don't) go up* |
| (no) hablen (Uds.)<br>*(don't) speak* | (no) coman (Uds.)<br>*(don't) eat* | (no) suban (Uds.)<br>*(don't) go up* |

### Práctica 1

Express what the teacher says to his class:

Ejemplo:
abrir los libros
Abran (Uds.) los libros.

1. escribir el ejercicio _____

2. aprender las palabras _____

3. trabajar con un compañero de clase _____

4. leer en voz alta _____

5. mirar la pizarra _____

6. asistir a la escuela todos los días _____

Spelling-change, stem-changing, and all irregular verbs follow this same pattern for formation of the formal affirmative and negative imperative. Table 10.2 gives representative examples of verbs that fall into this category.

## Table 10.2    The Imperative of Verbs with Changes

| Verb | Imperative | Meaning |
|------|------------|---------|
| | *Verbs with irregular* **yo** *forms* | |
| decir | (no) diga(n) Ud(s). | (don't) tell |
| hacer | (no) haga(n) Ud(s). | (don't) do |
| oír | (no) oiga(n) Ud(s). | (don't) hear |
| poner | (no) ponga(n) Ud(s). | (don't) put |
| salir | (no) salga(n) Ud(s). | (don't) leave |
| tener | (no) tenga(n) Ud(s). | (don't) have (be) |
| traer | (no) traiga(n) Ud(s). | (don't) bring |
| valer | (no) valga(n) | (don't) be worth |
| venir | (no) venga(n) Ud(s). | (don't) come |

*continues*

## Table 10.2  The Imperative of Verbs with Changes (continued)

| Verb | Imperative | Meaning |
|---|---|---|
| *Spelling-change verbs* | | |
| bus**car** | (no) bus**que**(n) Ud(s). | (don't) look for |
| lle**gar** | (no) lle**gue**(n) Ud(s). | (don't) arrive |
| averi**guar** | (no) averi**güe**(n) Ud(s). | (don't) ascertain |
| cru**zar** | (no) cru**ce**(n) Ud(s). | (don't) cross |
| ven**cer** | (no) ven**za**(n) Ud(s). | (don't) conquer |
| ofre**cer** | (no) ofre**zca**(n) Ud(s). | (don't) offer |
| frun**cir** | (no) frun**za**(n) Ud(s). | (don't) frown |
| condu**cir** | (no) condu**zca**(n) Ud(s). | (don't) drive |
| esco**ger** | (no) esco**ja**(n) Ud(s). | (don't) choose |
| diri**gir** | (no) diri**ja**(n) Ud(s). | (don't) direct |
| distin**guir** | (no) distin**ga**(n) Ud(s). | (don't) distinguish |
| delin**quir** | (no) delin**ca**(n) Ud(s). | (don't) offend |
| *Stem-changing verbs* | | |
| cerrar | (no) c**ie**rre(n) Ud(s). | (don't) close |
| mostrar | (no) m**ue**stre(n) Ud(s). | (don't) show |
| perder | (no) p**ie**rda(n) Ud(s). | (don't) lose |
| morder | (no) m**ue**rda(n) Ud(s). | (don't) bite |
| mentir | (no) m**ie**nta(n) Ud(s). | (don't) lie |
| dormir | (no) d**ue**rma(n) Ud(s). | (don't) sleep |
| pedir | (no) p**i**da(n) Ud(s). | (don't) ask for |
| reunir | (no) re**ú**na(n) Ud(s). | (don't) join |
| enviar | (no) env**í**e(n) Ud(s). | (don't) send |
| continuar | (no) contin**ú**e(n) Ud(s). | (don't) continue |
| incluir | (no) inclu**ya**(n) Ud(s). | (don't) include |
| *Irregular verbs* | | |
| dar | (no) dé (den) Ud(s). | (don't) give |
| estar | (no) esté(n) Ud(s). | (don't) be |
| ir | (no) vaya(n) Ud(s). | (don't) go |
| saber | (no) sepa(n) Ud(s). | (don't) know |
| ser | (no) sea(n) Ud(s). | (don't) be |

## Adding Emphasis

In Spanish, an upside down exclamation mark (¡) is placed at the beginning of an emphasized command and a regular exclamation mark (!) is placed at the end:

¡CAUTION!

**¡Cuidado!**

The singular command form of *dar* (*dé*) has an accent, while the plural form does not.

¡Siga Ud. trabajando!  ¡No me molesten!
Continue working!  Don't bother me!

---

### Práctica 2

Express the advice that *la señora* López gives to one of her students who is going on a job interview.

Ejemplo:
no llegar tarde
No llegue tarde.

1. no masticar chicle _____

2. no pedir permiso para hablar _____

3. no ir al baño durante la entrevista _____

4. no tener miedo _____

5. no mentir _____

6. no ofrecer consejos _____

7. no contar chistes _____

8. no hacer mucho ruido _____

9. no interrogar el jefe _____

10. no estar nervioso _____

---

# Informal Commands with *tú*

An informal command with *tú* (also referred to as a familiar command) is used when the speaker is talking to one individual: a friend, a peer, a family member, or a pet. There are only a few irregular commands and they occur in the affirmative singular *tú* form. All other informal or familiar commands, whether singular or plural, affirmative or negative, are regular.

## Forming Informal Commands with *tú*

The affirmative imperative *tú* form is the same as the *él* form of the present indicative or it is the same as the *tú* form of the indicative without the final -*s*.

The negative imperative *tú* form is the same as the present subjunctive *tú* form, which means that -*ar* verbs will use an -*e* before the final -*s*, and -*er* and -*ir* verbs, will use an -*a* before the final -*s*. These same rules hold true for all verbs with spelling and stem changes except for a few irregular verbs as shown in Table 10.3.

## Table 10.3   The Singular Informal Imperative

| Verb | Affirmative | Negative | Meaning |
|------|-------------|----------|---------|
| | | *Regular verbs* | |
| hablar | habla (tú) | no hables (tú) | (don't) speak |
| comer | come (tú) | no comas (tú) | (don't) eat |
| subir | sube (tú) | no subas (tú) | (don't) go up |
| | | *Verbs with irregular* **yo** *forms* | |
| oír | oye (tú) | no oigas | (don't) hear |
| traer | trae (tú) | no traigas | (don't) bring |
| | | *Spelling-change verbs* | |
| bus**car** | bus**c**a (tú) | no bus**qu**es | (don't) look for |
| lle**gar** | lle**g**a (tú) | no lle**gu**es | (don't) arrive |
| averi**guar** | averi**gu**a (tú) | no averi**gü**es | (don't) ascertain |
| cru**zar** | cru**z**a (tú) | no cru**c**es | (don't) cross |
| ven**cer** | ven**c**e (tú) | no ven**z**as | (don't) conquer |
| ofre**cer** | ofre**c**e (tú) | no ofre**zc**as | (don't) offer |
| condu**cir** | condu**c**e (tú) | no condu**zc**as | (don't) drive |
| esco**ger** | esco**g**e (tú) | no esco**j**as | (don't) choose |
| diri**gir** | diri**g**e (tú) | no diri**j**as | (don't) direct |
| distin**guir** | distin**gu**e (tú) | no distin**g**as | (don't) distinguish |
| delin**quir** | delin**qu**e (tú) | no delin**c**as | (don't) offend |

| Verb | Affirmative | Negative | Meaning |
|------|-------------|----------|---------|
| *Stem-changing verbs* | | | |
| cerrar | cierra (tú) | no cierres (tú) | (don't) close |
| mostrar | muestra (tú) | no muestres (tú) | (don't) show |
| perder | pierde (tú) | no pierdas (tú) | (don't) lose |
| morder | muerde (tú) | no muerdas (tú) | (don't) bite |
| mentir | miente (tú) | no mientas (tú) | (don't) lie |
| dormir | duerme (tú) | no duermas (tú) | (don't) sleep |
| pedir | pide (tú) | no pidas (tú) | (don't) ask for |
| reunir | reúne (tú) | no reúnas (tú) | (don't) gather |
| enviar | envía (tú) | no envíes (tú) | (don't) send |
| continuar | continúa (tú) | no continúes (tú) | (don't) continue |
| incluir | incluye (tú) | no incluyas (tú) | (don't) include |
| *Irregular verbs* | | | |
| decir | di (tú) | no digas (tú) | (don't) tell |
| hacer | haz (tú) | no hagas (tú) | (don't) do |
| ir | ve (tú) | no vayas (tú) | (don't) go |
| poner | pon (tú) | no pongas (tú) | (don't) put |
| salir | sal (tú) | no salgas (tú) | (don't) leave |
| ser | sé (tú) | no seas (tú) | (don't) be |
| tener | ten (tú) | no tengas (tú) | (don't) have |
| valer | val or vale (tú) | no valgas (tú) | (don't) be worth |
| venir | ven (tú) | no vengas (tú) | (don't) come |

## Práctica 3

Express the positive and negative advice a mother gives to her child.

1. hacer tus tareas en la sala/
   en tu cuarto _____

2. almorzar en una confitería/
   un restaurante elegante _____

3. decir mentiras/la verdad _____

*continues*

*continued*

4. obedecer a tus amigos/
   a tus profesores

   _____

5. salir a la escuela tarde/temprano

   _____

6. exigir demasiado/poco

   _____

7. ir a casa de Felipe/a la escuela

   _____

8. seguir los consejos de tus amigos/
   de tus profesores

   _____

# Informal Commands with *vosotros (vosotras)*

An informal command with *vosotros (vosotras)* (also referred to as a familiar command) is used when the speaker is talking to more than one individual: friends, peers, family members, or pets. The *vosotros (vosotras)* subject is generally omitted. In most Spanish American countries, the *Uds.* command is generally substituted for the *vosotros (vosotras)* command in familiar plural address.

## Forming Informal Commands with *vosotros*

The affirmative imperative *vosotros* form for all verbs is formed by dropping the final -*r* of the infinitive and adding a -*d*.

The negative imperative *vosotros* form is the same as the present subjunctive *vosotros* form, which means that -*ar* verbs will use an -*e* in the ending and -*er* and -*ir* verbs, will use an -*a* in the ending, as shown in Table 10.4.

## Table 10.4 The Plural Informal Imperative

| Verb | Affirmative | Negative | Meaning |
| --- | --- | --- | --- |
| *Regular verbs* | | | |
| hablar | hablad | no habléis | (don't) speak |
| comer | comed | no comáis | (don't) eat |
| subir | subid | no subáis | (don't) go up |
| *Verbs with irregular* **yo** *forms* | | | |
| oír | oíd | no oigáis | (don't) hear |
| traer | traed | no traigáis | (don't) bring |

| Verb | Affirmative | Negative | Meaning |
|------|-------------|----------|---------|
| *Spelling-change verbs* | | | |
| bus**car** | bus**c**ad | no bus**qu**éis | (don't) look for |
| lle**gar** | lle**g**ad | no lle**gu**éis | (don't) arrive |
| averi**guar** | averi**gu**ad | no averi**gü**éis | (don't) ascertain |
| cru**zar** | cru**z**ad | no cru**c**éis | (don't) cross |
| ven**cer** | ven**c**ed | no ven**z**áis | (don't) conquer |
| ofre**cer** | ofre**c**ed | no ofre**zc**áis | (don't) offer |
| frun**cir** | frun**c**id | no frun**z**áis | (don't) frown |
| condu**cir** | condu**c**id | no condu**zc**áis | (don't) drive |
| esco**ger** | esco**g**ed | no esco**j**áis | (don't) choose |
| diri**gir** | diri**g**id | no diri**j**áis | (don't) direct |
| distin**guir** | distin**gu**id | no distin**g**áis | (don't) distinguish |
| delin**quir** | delin**qu**id | no delin**c**áis | (don't) offend |
| *Stem-changing verbs* | | | |
| c**e**rrar | c**e**rrad | no c**e**rréis | (don't) close |
| m**o**strar | m**o**strad | no m**o**stréis | (don't) show |
| p**e**rder | p**e**rded | no p**e**rdáis | (don't) lose |
| m**o**rder | m**o**rded | no m**o**rdáis | (don't) bite |
| m**e**ntir | m**e**ntid | no m**i**ntáis | (don't) lie |
| d**o**rmir | d**o**rmid | no d**u**rmáis | (don't) sleep |
| p**e**dir | p**e**did | no p**i**dáis | (don't) ask for |
| re**u**nir | re**ú**nid | no reunáis | (don't) gather |
| env**iar** | enviad | no enviéis | (don't) send |
| contin**uar** | continuad | no continuéis | (don't) continue |
| incl**uir** | incluid | no incluyáis | (don't) include |
| *Irregular verbs* | | | |
| decir | decid | no digáis | (don't) tell |
| hacer | haced | no hagáis | (don't) do |
| ir | id | no vayáis | (don't) go |
| poner | poned | no pongáis | (don't) put |
| salir | salid | no salgáis | (don't) leave |

*continues*

## Table 10.4    The Plural Informal Imperative  (continued)

| Verb | Affirmative | Negative | Meaning |
|---|---|---|---|
| | | *Irregular verbs* | |
| ser | sed | no seáis | (don't) be |
| tener | tened | no tengáis | (don't) have be |
| valer | valed | no valgáis | (don't) be worth |
| venir | venid | no vengáis | (don't) come |

### Práctica 4

You're having a day where you are constantly changing your mind. Tell your children what to do and what not to do.

Ejemplo:
comer
Comed. No comáis.

1. abrir las ventanas _____

2. cerrar la puerta _____

3. apagar la televisión _____

4. sacar la basura _____

5. comenzar a estudiar _____

6. subir _____

7. seguir jugando _____

8. encender la luz _____

# Indirect Commands

♦ The indirect command "Let's + verb" is expressed by using the first person plural (*nosotros*) subjunctive form:

Salgamos de la tienda.          Miremos la televisión.
Let's leave the store.          Let's watch TV.

◆ "Let's + verb" may also be expressed by using *vamos a* + an infinitive in an affirmative sentence, if the action is going to be performed in the very near future:

> Vamos a salir de la tienda.    Vamos a mirar la televisión.
> Let's leave the store (now).    Let's watch TV (soon).

◆ "Let's go" may be expressed by *vamos a* + noun. In a negative sentence, the present subjunctive *nosotros* form, *vayamos* must be used:

> Vamos al cine.    Let's go to the movies.
>
> No vayamos al cine.    Let's not go to the movies.

**¡Mira!**

*Vamos a* + infinitive (we are going to …) may also indicate that the subject plans on performing the action at a later time: *Vamos a jugar a los naipes.* (We're going to play cards [later].)

◆ Third person (*él*, *ella*, *ellos*, *ellas*) indirect commands are expressed by the present subjunctive as follows:

> *que* + present subjunctive + subject (if used)

In this construction, a verb of volition requiring the subjunctive, such as *quiero*, is understood to precede que:

> ¡Que hablen (los niños)!
> May (Have, Let) the children speak!

**¡Cuidado!**

The suggestion: "Let's not go" may only be expressed by *no vayamos* + noun. *No vamos* + noun can only mean "we are not going." *No vayamos al centro.* (Let's not go to the city.) *No vamos al centro.* (We aren't going to the city.)

---

## Práctica 5

Express suggestions made about a camping trip in two ways.

Ejemplo:
comer mucho
Comamos mucho. Vamos a comer mucho.

1. jugar al fútbol _____

2. ir al campo _____

*continues*

*continued*

   3. dar un paseo por el bosque _____

   4. dormir al aire libre _____

   5. encender un gran fuego _____

   6. contar cuentos espantosos _____

---

## Práctica 6

Express what each person should do.

   Ejemplo:
   (Julio)/trabajar menos
   ¡Que trabaje menos!

   1. (Felipe)/decir la verdad _____

   2. (María y Marta)/venir a la oficina _____

   3. (José y Ricardo)/tener cuidado _____

   4. (Luz)/hacer caso de sus consejos _____

   5. (los niños)/volver temprano _____

   6. (el doctor)/llegar en seguida _____

---

# Object Pronouns with Commands

In Spanish direct object, indirect object, and reflexive pronouns precede negative commands and follow and are attached to affirmative commands.

| | |
|---|---|
| Hágalo Ud. | No lo haga Ud. |
| Do it. | Don't do it. |
| Hazlo (tú). | No lo hagas. |
| Do it. | Don't do it. |
| Hácedlo (vosotros). | No lo hagáis. |
| Do it. | Don't do it. |

In Spanish, direct objects, indirect objects, and reflexive pronouns precede negative commands and follow and are attached to affirmative commands.

No te pongas el sombrero. (Don't put on your hat.)

Ponte el abrigo. (Put on your coat.)

The stressed vowel normally requires an accent mark when the command form (without any attached pronouns) has more than one syllable. When one pronoun is attached, count back three vowels and add an accent:

Quítate el sombrero. (Take off your hat.)

When two pronouns are attached, count back four vowels and add an accent:

Quítatelo. (Take it off.)

Note the following about reflexive verbs:

- When forming the singular familiar command (*tú*), an accent mark must be added when *te* is added to a singular command form containing more than one syllable. For verbs with only one syllable, no accent is required:

    sentarse (to sit down)    siéntate

    but

    irse (to go away)        vete

- When forming the plural familiar command (*vosotros*), the final -*d* is dropped before adding *os* for all verbs except *ir*:

    levantarse: levantad + *os* = ¡Levantaos! (Get up!)

    bañarse: bañad + *os* = ¡bañaos! (Bathe!)

    but

    Irse: ir + *os* = ¡Iros! (Go away!)

- When forming the plural familiar command (*vosotros*), when *os* is added to an -*ir* reflexive verb, an accent mark must be added:

    divertirse: divertid + *os* = ¡Divertíos! (Have fun!)

- In an affirmative "let's" command, the final -*s* of the *nosotros* form is dropped before adding the reflexive pronoun *nos* and an accent is placed on the stressed syllable (usually determined by counting back three vowels):

levantarse: levantemos + *nos* = ¡Levantémonos! (Let's get up!)

Irse: vamos + *nos* = ¡Vámonos! (Let's go!)

---

## Práctica 7

Elena can't decide what she wants. Express what she tells her sister to do and then not to do.

Ejemplo:
hablar
Háblame. No me hables.

1. ayudar _____

2. traer el libro _____

3. escribir una lista de compras _____

4. escuchar _____

5. decir tus problemas _____

6. pedir permiso para salir _____

---

## Práctica 8

Express what the parents tell their children to do and not to do.

Ejemplo:
levantarse temprano/tarde
Levantaos temprano. No os levantéis tarde.

1. ponerse contentos/tristes _____

2. despertarse a las nueve/a las ocho _____

3. acostarse temprano/tarde _____

4. divertirse en el parque/en la escuela _____

5. irse más tarde/en seguida _____

6. negarse a fumar/comer legumbres _____

**Práctica 9**

Make commands to a friend that express "let's."

Ejemplo:
levantarse
Levantémonos.

1. apresurarse _____

2. desayunarse _____

3. irse _____

4. sentarse _____

5. peinarse _____

6. divertirse _____

# Repaso

1. When forming a command in Spanish, the speaker has the option of using or omitting the subject pronoun.

2. To form an affirmative or negative command with any verb, when *Ud.* or *Uds* is the subject, use the present subjunctive of the *Ud.* or *Uds.* form of that verb.

3. Opposite vowel endings are added to form the subjunctive: *-ar* verb subjunctive endings contain an *-e: -e, -es, -e, -emos, -éis, -en*; and *-er* and *-ir* verb subjunctive endings contain an *-a: -a, -as, -a, -amos, -áis, -an*.

4. Spelling-change, stem-changing, and all irregular verbs follow this same pattern for formation of the formal affirmative and negative imperative with *Ud.* and *Uds.*

5. In Spanish, an upside down exclamation mark (¡) is placed at the beginning of an emphasized command and a regular exclamation mark (!) is placed at the end.

6. The affirmative imperative *tú* form is the same as the *él* form of the present indicative or it is the same as the *tú* form of the indicative without the final *-s*.

7. The negative imperative *tú* form is the same as the present subjunctive *tú* form.

8. These same rules hold true for all verbs with spelling and stem changes except for the irregular verbs *decir* (to tell), *hacer* (to make, do), *ir* (to go), *poner* (to put), *salir* (to go out), *ser* (to be), *tener* (to have), *valer* (to be worth), and *venir* (to come).

9. The affirmative imperative *vosotros* form for all verbs is formed by dropping the final *-r* of the infinitive and adding a *-d*.

10. The negative imperative *vosotros* form is the same as the present subjunctive *vosotros* form.

11. The indirect command "Let's + verb" is expressed by using the first person plural (*nosotros*) subjunctive form.

12. "Let's + verb" may also be expressed by using *vamos a* + an infinitive in an affirmative sentence, if the action is going to be performed in the very near future.

13. *Vamos a* + infinitive (we are going to ...) may also indicate that the subject plans on performing the action at a later time.

14. Third person (*él, ella, ellos, ellas*) indirect commands are expressed by the present subjunctive: *que* + present subjunctive + subject (if used).

15. In Spanish direct object, indirect object, and reflexive pronouns precede negative commands and follow and are attached to affirmative commands.

16. An accent mark is added if the original stress on the verb (without the attached pronoun) was on the next-to-last syllable.

17. For reflexive verbs: an accent mark must be added when *te* is added to a singular command form containing more than one syllable. For verbs with only one syllable, no accent is required.

18. For reflexive verbs: When forming the plural familiar command (*vosotros*), the final *-d* is dropped before adding *os* for all verbs except *ir*.

19. For reflexive verbs: When forming the plural familiar command (*vosotros*), when *os* is added to an *-ir* reflexive verb, an accent mark must be added.

20. For reflexive verbs: in an affirmative "let's" command, the final *-s* of the *nosotros* form is dropped before adding the reflexive pronoun *nos* and an accent is placed on the stressed syllable.

## The Least You Need to Know

◆ When *Ud.* or *Uds.* is the subject of an affirmative or negative command, use the present subjunctive of the *Ud.* or *Uds.* form of that verb.

◆ The affirmative imperative *tú* form is the same as the *él* form of the present indicative or it is the same as the *tú* form of the indicative without the final -*s*. The negative imperative *tú* form is the same as the present subjunctive *tú* form.

◆ The affirmative imperative *vosotros* form for all verbs is formed by dropping the final -*r* of the infinitive and adding a *d*. The negative imperative *vosotros* form is the same as the present subjunctive *vosotros* form.

◆ In Spanish direct object, indirect object, and reflexive pronouns precede negative commands and follow and are attached to affirmative commands.

# Part 3

# Verbal Distinctions and Expressions

In English, sometimes all we need is one verb to express a thought. In Spanish, however, different connotations require the use of completely different verbs with different conjugations. Chapter 11 shows you these distinctions to ensure that you use each verb correctly.

It is very important to use any language idiomatically so that your speech or writing patterns mirror the way native speakers use their language. In Spanish, the knowledge of a few irregular verbs helps you accomplish this task. Chapter 12 provides a list of verbal idioms and expressions that will have you speaking excellent Spanish in no time.

The two chapters in this part give you a very large foundation for effective, idiomatic communication as well as an understanding of the differences between active and passive voice. By the time you've finished this section, if you've worked seriously and conscientiously, you'll be well equipped and ready to use Spanish verbs proficiently.

# Chapter 11

# Common Verbal Distinctions

## In This Chapter

- ◆ Verbs with different meanings with prepositions
- ◆ Verbs with different meanings when reflexive
- ◆ Verbs with different connotations

In Spanish there are a few verbs whose meanings change depending upon whether they are used alone or in conjunction with a preposition or another word. In order to speak and write good, colloquial Spanish, it is essential to know how to use the verbs correctly.

There are other verbs whose meaning changes when they are made reflexive. It is equally important to know when to use these verbs alone and when to make them reflexive so that their proper meaning is conveyed. When used incorrectly, they could prove embarrassing, and you'd certainly want to avoid that.

Finally, there are verbs that have the same meanings but connote different ideas. Although we use only one verb in English to get our meaning across, Spanish requires different verbs to express these concepts.

This chapter explains when to use verbs with or without prepositions, when it's necessary to make a verb reflexive, and when different verbs are required to make yourself properly understood.

# Using Verbs Alone and with Prepositions

The following high-frequency verbs may be used with or without a preposition depending upon the meaning that you wish to convey:

## Acabar

This verb may be used alone or with the prepositions *de*, *con*, or *por* as follows:

◆ *acabar*   to finish, in the sense of to terminate an activity:

> Le falta poco para acabar el suéter.
> She's nearly finished the sweater.

◆ *acabar*   to finish using something:

> Ya he acabado el azúcar.
> I've used up the sugar.

◆ *acabar de*   to have just finished performing a task

> Él acaba de leer el periódico.
> He (has) just finished reading the newspaper.

*Acabar de* may be used in the imperfect to express what the subject "had just" done. Note that in Spanish *acabar de* is followed by an infinitive whereas in English we use a past participle:

> Él acababa de leer el periódico cuando ella llegó.
> He had just finished reading the newspaper when she arrived.

◆ *acabar con*   to finish off, to put a stop to, to finish with, to end a relationship:

> Él acaba con la comida.
> He finishes off the meal.

> ¿Cuándo vamos a acabar con el prejuicio?
> When are we going to put a stop to prejudice?

> ¡Acabemos con ellos!
> Let's do away with them!

> Yo acabé con él.
> I split up with him.

◆ *acabar por*   to end up by doing something, to finally …:

> Ella comenzó por llorar pero acabó por reír.
> She began by crying but ended up laughing.

# Dar

This verb may be used by itself or with the prepositions *a, con, contra, de, en, para,* or *por*, as follows:

**¡Mira!**

The verb *dar* is often used with an indirect object noun or pronoun expressing that something is being given "to" a person: *Le doy un abrazo a mi amigo.* (I give a hug to my friend.)

♦ *dar*   to give:

> Cuando ganaron, ellos dieron gritos.
> When they won, they shouted (gave shouts).

♦ *dar a*   to overlook, face:

> Esta habitación da al mar.
> This room faces the sea.

♦ *dar con*   to find, come up with:

> Finalmente ellos dieron con una buena idea.
> They finally came up with a good idea.

♦ *dar contra*   to hit:

> El carro dio contra el edificio.
> The car hit the building.

♦ *dar de*   to give somebody something:

> La mujer les dió de beber.
> The woman gave them something to drink.

♦ *dar en*   to hit (upon), to come up with:

> El sol me da en la cara.
> The sun is in my eyes.

♦ *dar para*   to be enough for:

> Con eso da para tres personas.
> This is enough for three people.

♦ *dar por*   to consider:

> Él dio el asunto por concluido.
> He considered the matter settled.

# Deber

*Deber* may be used alone or with the preposition *de*:

◆ *deber*   to owe, to have to:

> Te debo veinte dólares.
> I owe you twenty dollars.
>
> Debes estudiar más.
> You have to study more.

**¡Mira!** _____

*Deber* may or may not be used with *de* to express supposition.

◆ *deber de* + infinitive   to suppose, must be:

> Debe (de) ser americana.
> She must be American.

# Dejar

*Dejar* may be used alone or with the preposition *de*:

◆ *dejar*   to leave:

> ¡Déjame en paz!
> *Leave me alone.*

◆ *dejar de* + infinitive   to stop doing something:

> Ella no dejó de fumar.
> *She didn't stop smoking.*

**¡Mira!** _____

*Dejar* may be followed by *que* + subjunctive to express "to allow to" or "to wait for": *Ellos dejaron que las cosas vayan de mal en peor.* (They allowed things to go from bad to worse.) *Deja que acabe de nevar.* (Wait for it to stop snowing.)

# Estar

*Estar* may be used alone or with *a, con, de, en, para,* and *por* (+ infinitive):

Estoy alegre.
I'm happy.

Estamos con él.
We're with him.

En eso está la respuesta.
That's where the idea is.

No estoy aquí para nadie.
I'm not here for anybody.

Estamos a siete de octubre.
It's October seventh.

Estás de mal humor.
You're in a bad mood.

Estoy por esa idea.
I'm for that idea.

Estoy por estudiarlo.
I'm for studying it.

# Haber

Haber is used as an auxiliary verb to form compound tenses or it may be followed by de:

◆ *haber*   to have:

> Han llegado.
> They have arrived.

◆ *haber de* + infinitive   must, should (shows obligation and supposition):

> Han de tener paciencia.
> They must be patient.

> Han de ser las once.
> It must be eleven o'clock.

# Hacer

Hacer may be used alone or with de or por:

◆ *hacer*   to make or to do:

> Yo hago el trabajo.
> I do the work.

◆ *hacer de*   to play the part of, to act as:

> El alumno hace de profesor en la sátira.
> The student plays the part of the teacher in the skit.

◆ *hacer por*   to try to:

> Ella hizo por verlo.
> She tried to see him.

**¡Mira!**

Hacer may be followed by que + subjunctive to express "to make sure": Ellos harán que él no venga. (They will make sure that he doesn't come.)

# Ir

*Ir* can be followed by *a, con, él de, para, por,* and *tras*:

- ◆ *ir*   to go:

    Los sábados yo voy al cine.
    On Saturdays, I go to the movies.

- ◆ *ir a* + infinitive   to be going to:

    Vamos a jugar a los naipes.
    We're going to play cards.

- ◆ *ir con*   to go (belong) with:

    Este anuncio debe ir con la carta.
    This announcement has to go (in) with the letter.

- ◆ *ir de*   to be about:

    ¿De qué va la película?
    What's the film about?

- ◆ *ir para*   to be going on for:

    Va para treinta años que soy profesora.
    It's going on thirty years that I'm a teacher.

- ◆ *ir por*   to intend:

    Eso no va por ella.
    That wasn't meant (intended) for her.

- ◆ *ir tras*   to go after:

    Iban tras ellos.
    They were going after them.

# Pensar

*Pensar* may be used alone (when it is normally followed by an infinitive), but is usually followed by *de* or *en*:

- ◆ *pensar*   to think, to intend:

    No pensaban volver.
    They didn't intend to return.

Ella tomó medidas sin pensar.
She acted without thinking.

◆ *pensar de*   to think of (to have an opinion of):

¿Qué piensas de este libro?
What do you think of this book?

◆ *pensar en*   to think about something or somebody:

Pensamos en las vacaciones.
We're thinking about our vacation.

Pienso en él.
I'm thinking about him.

# Tener

*Tener* may be used alone or with *por*, when referring to a person. *Tener* also has many idiomatic uses, which are discussed in Chapter 12.

◆ *tener*   to have:

Tengo una hermana.
I have a sister.

◆ *tener por*   to consider:

La tengo por persona honrada.
I consider her an honest person.

 **¡Mira!** _____

*Tener que* + infinitive means to have to and expresses a sense of obligation: (*Yo tengo que ir al supermercado.*) I have to go to the supermarket.

# Volver

*Volver* may be used alone or with *a* or *en sí*:

◆ *volver*   to return:

No volvemos hasta las nueve.
We aren't returning until nine o'clock.

◆ *volver a* + infinitive   to do something again:

> Él volvió a casarse.
> He got remarried.

◆ *volver en sí*   to come around, to come to:

> Ella se enfermó y nunca volvió en sí.
> She became ill and never came around.

---

## Práctica 1

Select the word that best completes each sentence:

| de | por | trás |
|----|-----|------|
| a | para | en |
| con | contra | que |

1. Él acaba _____ llegar a casa.          _____

2. ¿Vuelve Ud. _____ empezar?          _____

3. Yo tengo _____ ayudar a mis padres.          _____

4. ¿Qué piensas _____ mis consejos?          _____

5. El iba _____ su madre a la tienda.          _____

6. ¿Dejó Ud. _____ mentir?          _____

7. Ella dió _____ el cesto.          _____

8. Hay _____ estudiar para tener éxito.          _____

9. ¿Piensas _____ mí algunas veces?          _____

10. Nosotros vamos _____ viajar.          _____

---

# Verbs with Special Reflexive Meanings

Some Spanish verbs change meanings when used reflexively, so be careful to choose the verb that best expresses exactly what you would like to say. Use the following list as a guide:

| Basic Meaning | Reflexive Meaning |
|---|---|
| aburrir (to bore) | aburrirse (to become bored) |
| acostar (to put to bed) | acostarse (to go to bed) |
| bañar (to bathe [someone]) | bañarse (to bathe oneself) |
| cansar (to tire) | cansarse (to become tired) |
| cepillar (to brush) | cepillarse (to brush [part of body hair, teeth, and so on]) |
| dar (to give) | darse (to give in, to hit oneself, to happen, to grow) |
| dormir (to sleep) | dormirse (to go [fall] to sleep) |
| engañar (to deceive) | engañarse (to be mistaken) |
| esconder (to hide [something]) | esconderse (to hide oneself) |
| hacer (to make, do) | hacerse (to become) |
| ir (to go) | irse (to go away) |
| levantar (to raise [something]) | levantarse (to get up) |
| parar (to stop [something]) | pararse (to stop [oneself]) |
| poner (to put [something]) | ponerse (to put [something on], to become, to place oneself) |
| sentar (ie) (to seat) | sentarse (to sit down) |

Note the difference in meaning in the following examples:

Este libro me aburre.
This book bores me.

Me aburro de leer.
I'm bored with reading.

Acuesto a los niños.
I put the children to bed.

Me acuesto a las diez.
I go to bed at ten o'clock.

Baño al perro.
I bathe the dog.

Me baño.
I bathe myself.

Le cansa mucho trabajar.
Working really tires him out.

Él se cansó de ella.
He got tired of her.

Cepilla su perro.
He brushes his dog.

Se cepilla el pelo.
He brushes his dog.

Él me ha dado un regalo.
He gave me a present.

Yo me he dado contra la mesa.
I bumped into the table.

Sólo ha dormido una hora.
He only slept for an hour.

Se durmió tarde.
He fell asleep late.

| | |
|---|---|
| Ella engaña a su amiga. | Ella se engañó. |
| She deceives her friend. | She was wrong. |
| Escondí la carta de él. | Me escondí en mi cuarto. |
| I hid the letter from him. | I hid in my room. |
| Hizo el trabajo. | Se hizo rico. |
| He did the work. | He made himself rich. |
| Voy al centro comercial. | Me voy a las nueve. |
| I'm going to the mall. | I'm leaving at nine o'clock. |
| El alumno levanta la mano. | Se levanta. |
| The student raises his hand. | He gets up. |
| Nos paró el director. | El coche se paró. |
| The principal stopped us. | The car stopped. |
| Pone el papel en su cartera. | Se pone un sombrero. |
| He puts the paper in his briefcase. | He puts on a hat. |
| La azafata sienta a los pasajeros. | Los pasajeros se sientan. |
| The stewardess seats the passengers. | The passengers sit down. |

## Práctica 2

Use the correct form of the present tense to complete each sentence:

1. (sentar/sentarse) El profesor _____ a los alumnos y después _____ él.

2. (dormir/dormirse) Cuando yo _____ en mi silla, yo no _____ bien.

3. (engañar/engañarse) Tú _____, yo no _____ a mis amigos.

4. (bañar/bañarse) Ella _____ y entonces _____ a los niños.

5. (levantar/levantarse) Él _____ la mano y _____ para contestar las preguntas.

6. (ir/irse) Yo _____ a las siete porque _____ al cine con mis amigos.

7. (poner/ponerse) La madre _____ un delantal y después ella _____ la mesa.

8. (parar/pararse) El trabajo _____ porque ella no _____ de quejarse.

# Different Verbs with Different Connotations

In Spanish, sometimes it's necessary to use different verbs where English connotations differ. Contextually it is important to use these verbs correctly to get the proper meaning across.

## Conocer and Saber

Both *conocer* and *saber* mean "to know." Selecting the correct word to use is really quite simple:

◆ *Conocer* means "to know" in the sense of being acquainted with a person, place, or thing. If you can substitute the words "acquainted with" for the word "know," then use *conocer*:

Yo conozco a ese hombre.
I know (I am acquainted with) that man.

Ellos conocen bien Madrid.
They know (are well aquainted with) Madrid well.

Ella conoce la canción.
She knows (is acquainted with) the song.
(She's heard of it but doesn't know the words!)

◆ *Saber* means "to know a fact" or "to know how to do something" when followed by an infinitive:

Yo sé su nombre.          Ella sabe cocinar.
I know your name.         She knows how to cook.

Note the difference in connotation between *conocer* and *saber* in the following sentences:

Nosotros conocemos el poema.          Nosotros sabemos el poema.
We know the poem.                      We know the poem.
(We are acquainted with it.)           (We have memorized it and can recite it.)

## Deber and Tener Que

*Deber* is generally used to express a moral obligation while *tener* que is used to express something that the subject has to do:

Debo intentar hablar con él.
I must try to speak to him.

Tengo que hablarle con él porque tengo un problema.
I have to speak to him because I have a problem.

## Dejar and Salir

*Dejar* expresses to leave something behind while *salir* expresses to leave a place:

Él dejó sus llaves en su cuarto.
He left his keys in his room.

Ella sale de su oficina ahora.
She's leaving (from) her office now.

Él salió a las nueve.
He left at nine o'clock.

## Estar and Ser

These two verbs mean "to be" and often create confusion among students of Spanish. Pay careful attention to the rules governing the use of each of these verbs:

Use *estar* to express:

◆ Health

¿Cómo estás?
How are you?

Estoy bien.
I'm well.

◆ Location, position, or situation:

Barcelona está en España.
Barcelona is in Spain.

Su carro está allá.
His car is over there.

¿Dónde están mis cuadernos?
Where are my notebooks?

◆ A temporary state or condition of the subject (person, place or thing):

Yo estoy contenta.
I'm happy.

La tienda está cerrada.
The store is closed.

El vaso está sucio.
The glass is dirty.

◆ A progressive tense:

Estaba mirando la televisión.
He was watching television.

Estoy leyendo.
I'm reading.

Use *ser*:

◆ To express a quality or characteristic inherent to the subject:

Julia es inteligente.　　　　El carro es azul.
Julia is intelligent.　　　　The car is blue.

Mi reloj es de oro.
My watch is gold.

◆ To describe or identify the subject:

Juan es alto.　　　　　　　El señor Rueda es profesor.
Juan is tall.　　　　　　　Mr. Rueda is a teacher.

◆ To give the time, date, and place of an event:

Es la una.　　　　　　　　Es jueves.
It's one o'clock.　　　　　It's Thursday.

¿Dónde es la fiesta?
Where is the party?

◆ In impersonal expressions:

Es importante leer.
It's important to read.

◆ In passive constructions:

La tienda fue cerrada por el empleado.
The store was closed by the employee.

# Gastar and Pasar

Use *gastar* when you are spending money and *pasar* when you are spending time:

Gasto mucho dinero cuando viajo.
I spend a lot of money when I travel.

Paso mucho tiempo visitando los monumentos importantes.
I spend a lot of time visiting the important monuments.

# Jugar and Tocar

Use *jugar* + *a* when you are playing a sport or game and *tocar* when you are playing a musical instrument:

Juego al tenis.
I play tennis.

¿Juegas a los naipes?
Do you play cards?

Ellos tocan la guitarra.
They play the guitar.

## Llevar and Tomar

Both *llevar* and *tomar* mean "to take." Use *llevar* when you can carry or transport the item or person in your hands, or when you are leading someone to a place. Use *tomar* when you pick something up and can hold it in your hands:

Él toma una botella de agua y la lleva a la mesa.
He takes a bottle of water and carries it to the table.

## Pedir and Preguntar

Both of these verbs mean "to ask." While *pedir* means to request or ask for something, *preguntar* means to ask a question or to inquire about something or someone:

¿Pidió Ud. la cuenta?
Did you ask for the bill?

¿Le preguntó si quería venir?
Did you ask him if he wanted to come?

## Poder and Saber

These verbs both express "can." *Poder* shows that the subject possesses the ability to perform an action and saber shows that the subject actually knows how to perform the action:

No puedo hacerlo ahora.
I can't do it now.

No sé hacerlo.
I can't do it.
(I don't know how to do it.)

## Volver and Devolver

*Volver* means "to return" in the sense of "to come back." *Devolver* also means "to return," but in the sense of giving something back to its owner:

Yo voy a volver a eso de las tres.
I'm going to return around three o'clock.

Yo voy a devolver su libro mañana.
I'm going to return your book tomorrow.

### Práctica 3

Complete each sentence with the correct form of the proper verb in the present tense:

1. (conocer/saber) Ella _____ que yo _____ a su primo.

2. (estar/ser) _____ las dos y ellos _____ en la escuela.

3. (dejar/salir) Cuando él _____ de mi casa siempre _____ algo en mi cuarto.

4. (deber/tener que) Tú _____ estudiar porque _____ recibir buenas notas.

5. (jugar/tocar) Julio _____ el piano mientras su hermano _____ al fútbol.

6. (devolver/volver) Yo te _____ tu suéter cuando tú _____ a casa.

7. (pedir/preguntar) Papá siempre me _____ si tú _____ mucho dinero a Carlos.

8. (llevar/tomar) Él _____ un sándwich y lo _____ a la mesa.

# Repaso

1. *Acabar* may be used alone to express "to finish" or with the prepositions *de, con,* or *por.*

2. *Dar* expresses "to give" or may be used with *a, con, contra, de, en, para,* or *por.*

3. *Deber* expresses "to have to" or "to owe" and may be used with *de* + infinitive to show supposition.

4. *Dejar* expresses "to leave" and may be used with *de* + infinitive to express "to stop doing something."

5. *Haber* is used as an auxiliary verb or with or with *de* + infinitive to show obligation.

6. *Hay que* + infinitive means to be necessary.

7. *Hacer* expresses "to make" or to do" and may be used with *de* or *por.*

8. *Ir* "to go" can be followed by *a, con, él de, para, por,* and *tras.*

9. *Pensar* is usually followed by *de* or *en.*

10. *Tener* expresses "to have." *Tener que* + infinitive shows obligation.

11. *Volver* generally expresses "to return."

12. *Conocer* means "to know" or "to be acquainted with." *Saber* means "to know a fact" or "to know how to do something."

13. *Dejar* means to leave something behind while *salir* means to leave a place.

14. *Estar* and *ser* mean "to be." Use *estar* to express: health; location, position, or situation; and a progressive tense. Use *ser:* to express a quality or characteristic inherent to the subject.

15. Use *gastar* when you are spending money and *pasar* when you are spending time.

16. Use *jugar* + *a* when playing a sport or game and *tocar* when playing a musical instrument.

17. Use *llevar* when you can carry something and *tomar* when you pick something up.

18. *Pedir* means to request something and *preguntar* means to ask a question.

19. *Poder* shows that the subject possesses an ability and *saber* shows that the subject knows how to perform the action.

20. *Volver* means "to come back." *Devolver* also means "to return" something to its owner.

## The Least You Need to Know

◆ Certain Spanish verbs have different meanings when they are followed by prepositions.

◆ Certain Spanish verbs have different meanings when they are used reflexively.

◆ Although English may use only one word to connote a meaning, distinctions are made in Spanish and these verbs must be learned to avoid confusion.

# Common Verbal Expressions

## In This Chapter

- ◆ Using idioms
- ◆ Recognizing verbs frequently used idiomatically
- ◆ Using other verbal expressions
- ◆ Verbs such as *gustar*
- ◆ The passive voice

It is important to acquire a good working knowledge of Spanish idioms if you want to speak and understand the language as if you were a native. Idioms add life and color to any language and are an integral part of its own very special beauty. Without them, languages would be lifeless.

In Spanish, certain verbs, especially some high-frequency irregular verbs, lend themselves to being used idiomatically. That is why it is so very essential to focus on learning these verbs in particular. Their recurrent, everyday use in a wide variety of situations forces you to pause and commit them to memory. In no time, you will use them with ease and confidence in every tense you've studied.

Some Spanish verbs are less frequently used idiomatically, but they still add their own special flavor to the language. A quick look at some of them is worth the time spent.

A few verbs such as *gustar* follow special rules for conjugation and are worth a quick review.

Although only occasionally used, the passive voice appears from time to time and it is important to recognize it and understand how it is used.

In this chapter you will learn how to use idioms effectively, how to recognize the Spanish verbs most commonly used in everyday idioms and expressions, and how to use the passive voice.

# What Is an Idiom?

An idiom (referred to as *un modismo* in Spanish) is a word or expression whose meaning cannot be readily understood by analyzing its component words. It is, however, still considered an acceptable part of the standard vocabulary of the language. We use English idioms all the time without even realizing it. Here are some common examples:

| | |
|---|---|
| I ate like a pig! | We were bored stiff! |
| He slept like a log! | Let's let bygones be bygones! |

Idioms and slang are different. *Slang* refers to colorful, popular, informal words or phrases that are *not* part of the standard vocabulary of a language. Slang is considered unconventional. It has evolved to describe particular items or situations in street language and is composed of coinages, arbitrarily changed words, and extravagant, forced, or facetious figures of speech. Some common examples of slang are:

| | |
|---|---|
| He dissed me. | That's tacky. |
| That's a copout! | He flipped out. |

Idioms are acceptable in oral and written phrases; slang, although freely used in informal conversations, is generally considered substandard in formal writing and speaking. Much slang is, at best, X-rated, and will not appear in this book.

## Idioms with Regular, Reflexive, and Changing Verbs

Some idiomatic expressions are formed with regular verbs, reflexive verbs, or verbs with stem or spelling changes. Table 12.1 lists popular phrases with verbs in these categories, which are highlighted for your reference.

### Table 12.1    Idioms with Regular, Reflexive, and Changing Verbs

| Idiom | Meaning |
| --- | --- |
| aburrir**se** como una ostra | to be bored stiff |
| ac**o**star**se** con las gallinas | to go to bed early |
| aho**gar**se en un vaso de agua | to make a mountain out of a molehill |
| amar**gar** la vida a (alguien) | to make someone's life miserable |
| andar**se** con chiquitas | to beat around the bush |
| arran**car** a perderse | to make a dash for it |
| as**e**ntar la cabeza | to settle down |
| bus**car**le cinco patas al gato | to complicate matters |
| cal**e**ntar el asiento | to stay a long time |
| cal**e**ntarle la cabeza a (alguien) | to pester someone |
| cal**e**ntarse la cabeza por ... | to agonize about something |
| cantar las cuarenta a (alguien) | to give someone a piece of one's mind |
| co**ger** (captar, cal**zar**) al vuelo | to be quick to understand something |
| co**ger** el toro por los cuernos | to take the bull by the horns |
| comer como un cerdo | to eat like a pig |
| consultar ... en la almohada | to sleep on something |
| cre**cer** como la espuma | to mushroom |
| crispar los nervios a (alguien) | to get on someone's nerves |
| dañar la vista | to be an eyesore |
| dejar a (alguien) bizco/a | to leave someone open-mouthed |
| dejar a (alguien) en bragas | to leave someone empty-handed |
| dejar a (alguien) en la estacada | to leave someone in a lurch |
| dejar ... atado y bien atado | to leave no loose ends |
| dejar frío alguien | to leave someone out in the cold |
| distin**guir** lo blanco de lo negro | to distinguish right from wrong |
| d**o**rmir como una marmota (un bendito, un lirón) | to sleep like a log |
| echar la casa por la ventana | to spare no expense |
| echar las campanas a vuelo | to celebrate |
| echar un cable (capote) a (alguien) | to give someone a helping hand |
| emp**ez**ar de cero | to start from scratch |
| enc**o**ntrar(**se**) con la horma de su zapato | to meet one's match |

*continues*

## Table 12.1   Idioms with Regular, Reflexive, and Changing Verbs
### (continued)

| Idiom | Meaning |
|---|---|
| enseñar el cobre | to show one's true colors |
| esperar … como agua de mayo | to await something with eager anticipation |
| estrujarse el cerebro (la mollera) | to rack one's brains |
| examinar … con lupa | to go over something with a fine-tooth comb |
| forzar la máquina | to go full steam ahead |
| guardar … en el buche | to keep something quiet |
| guardarse un as en la manga | to have an ace up one's sleeve |
| jugar una baza | to play one's cards right |
| leer entre líneas | to read between the lines |
| leer la cartilla a (alguien) | to tell someone off |
| llegar a oídos de alguien | to come to someone's attention |
| llevar la batuta | to be the boss |
| llorar a moco tendido | to cry one's eyes out |
| llover a cántaros | to rain cats and dogs |
| matar dos pájaros de un tiro | to kill two birds with one stone |
| meterse en belenes | to get into trouble |
| pagar a (alguien) con la misma moneda | to give someone a taste of his own medicine |
| partir el corazón a (alguien) | to break someone's heart |
| pasar a la historia | to go down in history |
| pasar la noche en blanco | to have a sleepless night |
| perder hasta la camisa | to lose one's shirt |
| perder la brújula | to lose one's bearings |
| perder los estribos | to lose one's temper |
| prestar oídos a … | to pay attention to something |
| quedarse tan ancho | to feel pleased with oneself |
| quemar etapas | to make rapid progress |
| quemar las naves | to burn one's bridges |
| romperse la cabeza | to rack one's brains |
| sacar a (alguien) de quicio | to drive someone up the wall |

| Idiom | Meaning |
|---|---|
| sa**car** a (alguien) de sus casillas | to infuriate someone |
| sa**car** a (alguien) las castañas del fuego | to get someone off the hook |
| sa**car** fuerzas de flaqueza | to make a supreme effort |
| sa**car** los colores a (alguien) | to make someone blush |
| s**o**ltar**se** la melena | to let one's hair down |
| tirar la toalla | to throw in the towel |
| to**car** fondo | to hit rock bottom |
| trabajar como un burro | to work like a dog |
| vender**se** como rosquilla | to sell like hotcakes |
| vivir a todo tren | to live in style |

¡No te ahoges en un vaso de agua!
Don't make a mountain out of a molehill!
(*Literally: Don't drown in a glass of water!*)

Tenemos que examinar con lupa este documento.
We have to go over this document with a fine-tooth comb.

Pasará a la historia como el primer hombre en el espacio.
He will go down in history as the first man in space.

Él me sacó los colores.
He made me blush.

## Práctica 1

Complete each sentence by using a phrase found in the word bank:

aburrirse como una ostra
acostarse con las gallinas
arrancar a perderse
cantar las cuarenta
comer como un cerdo
crispar los nervios
distinguir lo blanco de lo negro
echar la casa por la ventana

estrujarse el cerebro
llorar a moco tendido
llover a cántaros
matar dos pájaros de un tiro
pagar con la misma moneda
sacar fuerzas de flaqueza
tirar la toalla
vender como rosquilla

*continues*

*continued*

1. Si él come mucho, él _____.

2. Ella escucha pero el profesor no dice nada interestante. Entonces ella
   _____.

3. Me acuesto a la ocho porque estoy cansada. Yo _____.

4. Una tempestad estalla sin aviso y el señor González no tiene paraguas. Por
   eso él _____.

5. Ud. se pone furioso contra su amiga y Ud. le _____.

6. Uds. hablan demasiado y hacen demasiado ruido. Uds. me
   _____.

7. Eduardo es un criminal peligroso y nunca va a cambiar. Él no
   _____.

8. Ellas gastan mucho dinero todo el tiempo. Ellas _____.

9. Él estudió anoche y ahora pasa un examen. Desgraciadamente, él no sabe
   las respuestas correctas y él _____.

10. Su novio le dice que no quiere casarse con ella. Al entender eso, ella
    _____.

11. Continúa lloviendo mucho. Se puede decir que _____.

12. Ella trabaja mientras mira la televisión. Ella _____.

13. Él trata de hacerlo pero por fin él no puede hacer el trabajo. Por eso él
    _____.

14. Los postres son deliciosos. No hay sorpresa de que _____.

15. Julio no le prestó un libro a su amigo Carlos. Ahora Julio quiere pedirle
    algo a Carlos. Carlos quiere darle una lección a Julio. Él le
    _____.

16. Ellos trabajan muy duro. Ellos _____.

## Idioms with Irregular Verbs

Many idiomatic expressions are formed with irregular verbs. Table 12.2 lists phrases that begin with the most frequency used irregular Spanish verbs.

### Table 12.2 Idioms with Irregular Verbs

| Idiom | Meaning |
|---|---|
| dar alas a (alguien) | to encourage someone |
| dar la vuelta a la tortilla | to turn the tables |
| dar oídos a … | to listen to something |
| dar un espectáculo | to make a scene |
| darse aires | to put on airs |
| decir … con la boca chica | to say something without really meaning it |
| decir cuatro cosas a (alguien) | to give someone a piece of one's mind |
| estar bobo/a por … (alguien) | to be crazy about something/someone |
| estar cantado | to be totally predictable |
| estar colado/a por (alguien) | to be madly in love with |
| estar como pez en el agua | to feel completely at home |
| estar de buenas | to be in a good mood |
| estar de capa caída | to be crestfallen |
| estar en ayunas | to be completely in the dark |
| estar en el ajo | to be in on the secret |
| estar en la edad del pavo | to be at that awkward age |
| estar en la luna | to have one's head in the clouds |
| estar hasta el gorro | to be fed up |
| estar pez en … | to know nothing about something |
| estar sin blanca | to be broke |
| estar todavía en pañales | to still be wet behind the ears |
| estar verde de envidia | to be green with envy |
| estar vivito y coleando | to be alive and kicking |
| hacer … en las barbas de alguien | to do something right under someone's nose |
| hacer borrón y cuenta nueva | to let bygones be bygones |
| hacer el canelo | to play the fool |

*continues*

## Table 12.2 Idioms with Irregular Verbs (continued)

| Idiom | Meaning |
| --- | --- |
| hacer historia | to make history |
| hacer la vista gorda | to turn a blind eye |
| hacer las cosas a su aire | to do things one's own way |
| hacer maromas | to do a balancing act |
| hacérsele agua la boca a (alguien) | to make someone's mouth water |
| ir a la cargada | to jump on the bandwagon |
| ir al grano | to get to the point |
| nacer de pie | to be born lucky |
| oír campanas y no saber dónde | to not have a clue |
| poner … en bandeja de plata a (alguien) | to hand someone something on a silver platter |
| poner cara de circunstancias | to look serious |
| poner el grito en el cielo | to scream bloody murder |
| poner las cartas sobre la mesa | to put one's cards on the table |
| poner rojo/a a (alguien) | to make someone blush |
| ponerse de mil colores | to become bright red |
| saber … a ciencia cierta | to know something for sure |
| saber la Biblia en verso | to know everything |
| ser canela fina | to be wonderful, exquisite |
| ser como un libro abierto | to be an open book |
| ser el vivo retrato de (alguien) | to be the spitting image of someone |
| ser la niña de los ojos de (alguien) | to be the apple of someone's eye |
| ser más listo que el hambre | to be as sharp as a tack |
| ser todo un poema | to be quite a site |
| ser todo oídos | to be all ears |
| ser una bala perdida | to be a good-for-nothing |
| ser un cerebro | to be brillant |
| ser un lince | to be very shrewd |
| ser una perita en dulce | to be gorgeous |
| tener a (alguien) en el bolsillo | to have someone eating out of |
| tener cara de vinagre | to have a sour look on one's face |
| tener carta blanca | to have a free hand |
| tener manos de trapo | to have butterfingers |

| Idiom | Meaning |
|---|---|
| tener sus más y sus menos | to have its good and bad points |
| tener un hambre de lobo | to be extremely hungry |
| traer a (alguien) por la calle de la amargura | to make someone's life miserable |
| valer su peso en oro | to be worth one's weight in gold |

Él dijó eso con la boca chica.
He said that without really meaning it.

Se me hace la boca agua de pensar en el postre.
It makes my mouth water to think about the dessert.

Ella nació de pie.
She was born lucky.

Su jefe le traía por la calle de la amargura.
His boss was making his life miserable.

## Práctica 2

Match the expressions that convey the same meanings:

1. quererlo mucho
2. decir mentiras
3. estar alegre
4. estar triste
5. escuchar
6. animar a alguien
7. no saber nada
8. saber el secreto
9. no tener dinero
10. perdonar a alguien
11. explicar directamente
12. parecerse a

a. dar oídos
b. ser el vivo retrato de alguien
c. estar en el ajo
d. hacer borrón y cuenta nueva
e. dar alas a alguien
f. decir algo con la boca chica
g. estar boba por él
h. estar de buenas
i. estar de capa caída
j. estar sin blanca
k. estar en ayunas
l. ir al grano

# Common Verbal Expressions

The irregular verbs *dar* (to give), *hacer* (to make, do), and *tener* (to have) are used in many expressions that are frequently used in everyday conversations. For this reason, it is important to make sure that you know these three verbs well in all their tenses.

## Expressions with *dar*

The most commonly used expressions with *dar* are listed in Table 12.3.

### Table 12.3   Common Expressions with *dar*

| Expression | Meaning |
|---|---|
| dar un abrazo | to hug, embrace |
| dar celos a | to make jealous |
| dar cuerda a | to wind |
| dar las gracias (a) | to thank |
| dar gritos | to shout |
| dar la hora | to strike the hour |
| dar un paseo | to take a walk |
| dar recuerdos (a) | to give regards (to) |
| dar una vuelta | to take a stroll |
| darse cuenta de | to realize |
| darse la mano | to shake hands |
| darse prisa | to hurry |

Le dí un abrazo.
I gave him a hug.

Él dio cuerda a su reloj.
He wound his watch.

Dieron gritos de miedo.
They screamed in fear.

Voy a dar un paseo.
I'm going to take a walk.

Le dió celos a su amigo.
He made his friend jealous.

Quiero darte gracias.
I want to thank you.

Ha dado la una en el reloj.
The clock struck one.

Dale mis recuerdos a Ana.
Give my regards to Ana.

Dí una vuelta por el parque.
I took a walk in the park.

¡Date prisa!
Hurry up!

No me dí cuenta de mi error.
I didn't realize my error.

Los niños se dieron la mano.
The children shook hands.

---

### Práctica 3

Complete each sentence with the correct form of the verb *dar:*

| diéramos | daría | des | dí |
|---|---|---|---|
| dé | dará | doy | daban |

1. (present) Siempre _____ abrazos a mis hijos.

2. (pres. subj.) Es necesario que Ud. le _____ recuerdos a Carlota.

3. (imperfect) Ellas _____ un paseo cuando él telefoneó.

4. (future) El reloj _____ las dos en tres minutos.

5. (imperative) ¡No te _____ prisa!

6. (imperfect subj.) Era necesario que nosotros _____ gritos.

7. (conditional) Esto me _____ celos.

8. (preterit) Yo no me _____ cuento de eso.

---

## Expressions with *hacer*

*Hacer* is frequently used in time and weather expressions. Table 12.4 lists the most common expressions with this irregular verb.

### Table 12.4   Expressions with *hacer*

| Expression | Meaning |
|---|---|
| hacer + time + que + preterit | ago |
| preterit + hace + time | ago |
| hacer mucho (poco) | a long (short) while ago |
| hacer buen (mal) tiempo | to be nice (bad) weather |

*continues*

## Table 12.4 Expressions with *hacer* (continued)

| Expression | Meaning |
| --- | --- |
| hacer frío (calor) | to be cold (hot) weather |
| hacer caso | to pay attention |
| hacer como si | to act as if |
| hacer el papel de | to play the role of |
| hacer el tonto | to act foolishly |
| hacer pedazos | to break into pieces |
| hacer una pregunta | to ask a question |
| hacer una visita | to pay a visit |
| hacer un viaje | to take a trip |
| hacer viento | to be windy |
| hacerse tarde | to grow late |
| hacer(se) daño | to hurt (oneself) |
| hacerse una idea de algo | to imagine what something is like |

Hace una semana que él llegó.
(Él llegó hace una semana.)
He arrived a week ago.

Yo vine hace mucho (poco).
I came a long (short) time ago.

¿Qué tiempo hace? Hace calor (frío, viento, buen/mal tiempo.)
What's the weather? It's hot (cold, windy, good/bad weather).

No le hagas caso.
Don't pay attention to him.

Él hace como si no le importa.
He acts as if it doesn't bother him.

Ud. se hizo el tonto.
You acted like a fool.

Ella hace el papel de la princesa.
She is playing the role of the princess.

Él hizo pedazos la carta.
He ripped the letter to pieces.

Quiero hacer una pregunta (una visita a mi tío, un viaje).
I want to ask a question (visit my uncle, take a trip).

Se hace tarde.
It's getting late.

¡No te hagas daño!
Don't hurt yourself.

Me hago una idea de su casa.
I imagine what their house is like.

**¡Mira!** _____

To ask or answer how long something has been going on, use hace + time + que:
¿Cuánto tiempo hace(hacías)que vivías aquí? (How long have [had] you been living here?) Hace (Hacía) dos meses. (For two months.)

---

## Práctica 4

Select the form of the verb that best completes the sentence:

1. (present) Se enoja y él _____ pedazos el papel.

   a. hizo   b. hace   c. hará   d. haga

2. (conditional) Si yo tuviera bastante dinero, yo _____ un viaje a España.

   a. haré   b. hiciera   c. haría   d. hago

3. (future) Ellos _____ el papel de los detectives.

   a. harán   b. harían   c. hacían   d. hagan

4. (imperfect subj.) Era imposible que tú _____ una visita a tu familia.

   a. hicieras   b. hagas   c. harías   d. haces

5. (preterit) Uds. _____ como si tenían miedo.

   a. hicieran   b. hacían   c. harían   d. hicieron

6. (imperfect) Es verdad. Nosotros _____ el tonto.

   a. hacíamos   b. haríamos   c. hiciéramos   d. hagamos

*continues*

*continued*

7. (imperative) ¡No se _____ Uds. daño!

   a. hacen   b. hagan   c. hiciéran   d. hicieron

8. (subjunctive) Quiero que tú te _____ una idea de lo que quieres estudiar.

   a. haces   b. hacías   c. hagas   d. hicieras

# Expressions with *tener*

*Tener* (to have) is frequently used in expressions that show physical conditions and emotions where English uses "to be." Table 12.5 lists the most common expressions with this irregular verb.

## Table 12.5    Expressions with *tener*

| Expression | Meaning |
| --- | --- |
| tener aspecto | to look like |
| tener calor (frío) | to be warm (cold) |
| tener celos de | to be jealous of |
| tener cuidado | to be careful |
| tener dolor de … | to have a … ache |
| tener éxito | to succeed |
| tener ganas de | to feel like |
| tener hambre (sed) | to be hungry (thirsty) |
| tener la culpa (de) | to be to blame (for something) |
| tener lugar | to take place |
| tener miedo de | to be afraid of |
| tener prisa | to be in a hurry |
| tener razón | to be right |
| tener sueño | to be sleepy |
| tener suerte | to be lucky |
| tener vergüenza (de) + inf. | to be ashamed (of) |

¿Qué aspecto tenía ella?
What did she look like?

Yo tengo calor (frío, cuidado, hambre, sed, razón, sueño, suerte).
I'm hot (cold, careful, hungry, thirsty, right, sleepy, lucky).

Tengo celos de mi hermana.
I'm jealous of my sister.

¿Tienes dolor de cabeza?
Do you have a headache?

Él tuvo éxito.
He succeeded.

¿Tienes ganas de ir al cine?
Do you feel like going to the movies?

Ud. tiene la culpa de este problema.
You are to blame for this problem.

¿Cuándo tendrá lugar el partido de tenis?
When will the tennis match take place?

¿De qué tienes miedo?
What are you afraid of?

Tenían prisa.
They were in a hurry.

¿No tienes vergüenza de lo que hiciste?
Aren't you ashamed of what you did?

---

## Práctica 5

Match the verb with the sentence it completes:

1. (preterit) Ayer ella ___ un dolor de cabeza.

2. (future) El niño ___ sueño pronto.

3. (imperfect) María ___ celos de ella.

4. (imperfect subj.) Era probable que él ___ prisa.

5. (present) Jorge no ___ ganas de trabajar.

6. (conditional) ¿En ese caso, no ___ él vergüenza?

7. (subjunctive) Es imposible que Ud. ___ éxito.

8. (imperative) ¡___ cuidado, mi amigo!

a. tenga

b. tiene

c. ten

d. tendría

e. tendrá

f. tuvo

g. tenía

h. tuviera

# Other Verbal Expressions

There are a small number of other verbs that express ideas that may come in handy. Table 12.6 lists some regular, reflexive, spelling and stem changing verbs, and irregular verbs that are found in only a few phrases.

## Table 12.6    Other Common Expressions

| Expression | Meaning |
|---|---|
| dejar caer | to drop |
| echar al correo | to mail |
| echar de menos | to miss |
| echar la culpa (a) | to blame |
| enco**gerse** de hombros | to shrug one's shoulders |
| guardar cama | to stay in bed |
| lle**gar** a ser | to become |
| oír decir que | to hear that |
| oír hablar de | to hear about |
| pe**n**sar + infinitive | to intend |
| pe**r**der de vista | to lose sight of |
| que**r**er decir | to mean |
| sa**car** una fotografía | to take a picture |
| valer la pena | to be worth the effort |
| vol**verse** + adjective | to become |

No dejes caer tu vaso.
Don't drop your glass.

Echaré las cartas al correo.
I'll mail the letters.

Yo echo de menos a mi amigo.
I miss my friend.

Ella le echó la culpa a Lupe.
She blamed Lupe.

Cuando no supo la respuesta, se encogió de hombros.
When he didn't know the answer, he shrugged his shoulders.

Tengo que guardar cama porque estoy muy enfermo.
I have to stay in bed because I'm very sick.

Mi hermana llegó a ser abogada.
My sister became a lawyer.

Oí decir que ellos se casaron.
I heard that they got married.

Oímos hablar del accidente.
We heard about the accident.

Pienso aprender español.
I intend to learn Spanish.

Lo perdieron de vista.
They lost sight of him.

¿Qué quiere decir esta palabra?
What does this word mean?

Saqué una fotografía de mi familia.
I took a picture of my family.

Vale la pena estudiar.
It's worth the effort to study.

Se volvió nervioso.
He became nervous.

---

## Práctica 6

Give the Spanish for the words in parenthesis:

1. (I intended) _____ ir al supermercado.

2. (She heard that) _____ él no llegará a tiempo.

3. ¿Que (means) _____ esta frase?

4. (It will be worth the effort) _____ ver esta exposición.

5. (They would mail) _____ las cartas para Ud.

6. Es imposible que ella (is becoming) _____ médica.

# *Gustar* and Other Verbs Like It

Translated literally, *gustar* means "to be pleasing to." Unfortunately, in Spanish you can't simply say "I like …" You must say "_____ is pleasing to me." The word "to" is of paramount importance because it instructs you to use an indirect object pronoun to get your point across. The verb *gustar* must agree with the noun, because that word is now the subject of the sentence. In general, the verb will be in either the third person singular (*él, ella, Ud.*) or third person plural form (*ellos, ellas, Uds.*).

> Me gusta el chocolate.
> Chocolate is pleasing to me.
> I like chocolate.

In the above example, *gusta* agrees with *chocolate*, which is the subject of the sentence.

> Me gustan las galletitas.
> Cookies are pleasing to me.
> I like cookies.

In the above example, *gustan* agrees with *galletitas*, which is the subject of the sentence.

Don't allow the reverse word order to trick you. Pick the direct object that expresses the person to whom the noun is pleasing, as shown in Table 12.7.

## Table 12.7    Indirect Object Pronouns

| Indirect Object Pronoun | Meaning |
| --- | --- |
| me | (to) me |
| te | (to) you (familiar) |
| le | (to) him, her, you, it |
| nos | (to) us |
| os | (to) you (familiar) |
| les | (to) them |

If you remember that the subject follows the verb *gustar*, you'll have little trouble.

Note that when gustar refers to two activities, the third person singular of the verb is used:

> Me gusta cantar y bailar.
> I like to sing and dance.

## Table 12.8   Other Verbs Like *gustar* (to like)

| Expression | Meaning |
| --- | --- |
| agradar | to like |
| apete**cer** | to like (food) |
| bastar | to be enough |
| d**o**ler | to be painful, to cause sorrow |
| con**venir** | to be suitable, convenient |
| disgustar | to upset, displease |
| encantar | to adore |
| faltar | to be lacking, to need |
| fascinar | to fascinate |
| importar | to be important |
| interesar | to interest |
| molestar | to bother |
| ocurrir | to happen, occur |
| pare**cer** | to seem |
| pasar | to happen |
| pla**cer** | to be pleasing, to be pleased |
| quedar | to remain (to someone), to have left |
| sobrar | to be left over, to have too much |
| to**car** | to be one's turn |

Me duelen los pies.
My feet hurt.

¿Te interesa cantar y bailar?
Do you like to sing and dance?

Le quedan dos minutos.
He only has two minutes left.

Nos faltan diez dólares.
We need ten dollars.

¿Os molesta el ruido?
Does the noise bother you?

Les encanta leer.
They adore reading.

---

### Práctica 7

Complete each sentence with the correct form of the verb:

1. (gustar) Les _____ nadar.

2. (faltar) Me _____ mis libros.

3. (apetecer) Os _____ el café.

4. (tocar) Nos _____ lavar el coche.

5. (sobrar) Le _____ cinco dólares.

6. (agradar) ¿Te _____ esos deportes?

---

# The Passive Voice

In general, we use the active voice when speaking or writing. In this voice, the subject noun or pronoun performs the action. In the passive voice, something or someone else acts upon the subject. It is usually considered preferable to avoid the passive whenever possible.

Active:
La profesora escribió el libro.
The teacher wrote the book.

Passive:
El libro fue escrito por la profesora.
The book was written by the teacher.

The passive construction in Spanish mirrors the English construction:

subject + *ser* + past participle + *por* + agent (doer if mentioned)

El banco fue atracado por ese hombre.
The bank was robbed by that man.

El ladrón ha sido atrapado.
The thief has been caught.

El será detenido.
He will be arrested.

In the passive, because the past participle is used like an adjective, it agrees in number and gender with the subject:

Las mujeres fueron heridas.
The women were injured.

## Substitute Constructions for the Passive

Because the passive is used less frequently in Spanish than in English, the reflexive construction may be substituted for the passive. The subject usually follows the verb:

Aquí se habla español.            Se perdieron los billetes.
Spanish is spoken here.           The tickets were lost.

Sometimes an action is expressed without any indication of who is performing the action that the verb implies. In English, when the speaker does not want to refer to anyone in particular, the subjects "one," "people," "they," and "you" are used. In Spanish, the pronoun *se* may be used as an indefinite subject or as a substitute for the passive with the third person singular form of the verb.

Se dice que el español es fácil.       Se puede decir que Ud. es muy rico.
It is said that Spanish is easy.       It can be said (One can say) that you
                                       are very rich.

Se cree que son inteligentes.          ¿Cuánto tiempo se necesita?
People believe that they are smart.    How much time is needed?

Se sabe que ella es muy famosa.
They say that she is very famous.

### ¡Mira!

The third person plural verb form may replace the se construction for *decir: dicen* (they say); *saber: saben* (they know); and *creer: creen* (they believe):

*Dicen que el español es fácil.*
They say Spanish is easy.

*Creen que son inteligentes.*
They believe they are intelligent.

*Saben que ella es muy famosa.*
They know she is famous.

The indefinite *se* may also be used to express the passive when a person or persons are acted upon and when the person performing the action is not mentioned or implied:

> Se ayudó a la mujer.
> The woman was helped (by someone).

> Se compensará a los muchachos.
> The boys will be rewarded (by someone).

The third person plural active voice is often used to avoid the indefinite *se* construction:

> Ayudaron a la mujer.
> They (someone indefinite) helped the woman.

> Compensarán a los muchachos.
> They (someone indefinite) will reward the boys.

## Práctica 8

Express what each person did to help around the house:

Ejemplo:
Sergio preparó la cena.
La cena fue preparada por Sergio.

1. Isabel lavó los platos. _____

2. Javier pusó la mesa. _____

3. Estela limpió el baño. _____

4. Eduardo pasó la aspiradora. _____

5. Alfredo cortó el césped. _____

6. Clara planchó los vestidos. _____

7. Carolina compró las provisiones. _____

8. Pepe sacó la basura. _____

## Práctica 9

Complete the sentences in two ways by using the appropriate form of the verb:

Ejemplo:
(pasar) por esta calle para ir a la biblioteca
Se pasa (Pasan) por esta calle para ir a la biblioteca.

1. (salir) por esa puerta para ir afuera _____

2. (necesitar) un bolígrafo para escribir _____

3. (pagar) en la caja registradora _____

4. (preparar) la comida en la cocina _____

5. (poner) un abrigo cuando hace frío _____

6. (decir) "disculpe" cuando hay un error _____

# Repaso

1. An idiom is a word or expression whose meaning cannot be readily understood by analyzing its component words.

2. An idiom is considered an acceptable part of the standard vocabulary of the language.

3. Slang refers to colorful, popular, informal words or phrases that are not part of the standard vocabulary of a language.

4. Slang has evolved to describe particular items or situations in street language and is composed of coinages, arbitrarily changed words, and extravagant, forced, or facetious figures of speech.

5. Idioms are acceptable in oral and written phrases, whereas slang is considered substandard in formal writing and speaking.

6. Some idiomatic expressions are formed with regular verbs, reflexive verbs, or verbs with stem or spelling changes.

7. Many idiomatic expressions are formed with irregular verbs.

8. It is important to learn the irregular verbs *dar* (to give), *hacer* (to make, do), and *tener* (to have) because they are used in common expressions.

9. The verb *gustar* (and other similar verbs requiring a direct object) must agree with the noun that follows it, because that word is now the subject of the sentence. In general, the verb will be in either the third person singular (*él, ella, Ud.*) or third person plural form (*ellos, ellas, Uds.*)

10. The active voice is most commonly used in speaking and writing.

11. The passive voice is generally avoided where possible.

12. In the passive, the past participle is used like an adjective and agrees in number and gender with the subject.

13. The reflexive construction may be substituted for the passive, and the subject will usually follow the verb.

14. *Se* + third person singular of verb expresses "one," "they," "people," "you," etc.

15. The third person plural active voice is often used to avoid the indefinite *se* construction.

## The Least You Need to Know

- Every language has its own peculiar idioms that can't be translated word for word because there is no logic or understandable grammar that explains them.

- Many idioms are introduced by irregular verbs, which must be memorized in all forms.

- Many useful Spanish expressions are introduced by *dar* (to give), *hacer* (to make, do), and *tener* (to have).

- *Gustar* and other verbs like it that require an indirect object pronoun agree with the noun subject, which follows the verb.

- In Spanish the passive voice is expressed by: subject + *ser* + past participle (which agrees with the subject) + *por* + agent (doer if mentioned).

- The passive voice may be avoided by using a reflexive or an indefinite construction.

# Answer Key

## Chapter 1

### Práctica 1

| | | |
|---|---|---|
| 1. ayudado | 2. mirado | 3. bebido |
| 4. prometido | 5. decidido | 6. vivido |
| 7. atraído | 8. supuesto | 9. contradicho |
| 10. revuelto | | |

### Práctica 2

1. Yo he bailado.
2. Tú hubiste escrito.
3. Él había comido.
4. Nosotros habremos leído.
5. Vosotros habríais reído.
6. Es imposible que ellos hayan escrito.
7. Era urgente que Uds. hubieran vuelto.

## Práctica 3

1. buscando
2. aprendiendo
3. asistiendo
4. reconstruyendo
5. sonriendo
6. despidiendo
7. desvistiendo
8. previniendo

## Práctica 4

1. Yo estoy estudiando.
2. Tú estuviste aplaudiendo.
3. Él estaba corriendo.
4. Nosotros estaremos leyendo.
5. Vosotros estaríais riendo.
6. Ellos están durmiendo.

# Chapter 2

## Práctica 1

1. to accept
2. to decide
3. to comprehend
4. to persuade
5. to consider
6. to offend
7. to omit
8. to respond
9. to function
10. to admit
11. to sell
12. to participate

## Práctica 2

1. toque
2. llegue
3. pague
4. organice
5. apacigüe
6. obedezca
7. zurza
8. dirija
9. escoja
10. distinga

## Práctica 3

1. despierta
2. remienda
3. acuesta
4. cuenta
5. pierde
6. vuelve
7. prefiere
8. duerme
9. expide
10. distribuye
11. envía
12. continúa

## Práctica 4

1. denieguen
2. jueguen
3. empiecen
4. almuercen
5. descuelguen
6. cuezan
7. corrijan
8. sigan

# Chapter 3

## Práctica 1

1. caminan
2. grito
3. celebramos
4. viaja
5. nadas
6. esperáis
7. descansa
8. miran
9. dibuja
10. enseñan

## Práctica 2

1. bebemos
2. comen
3. lee
4. prometes
5. comprende
6. debéis
7. responden
8. corresponde
9. intercedo
10. tejen

## Práctica 3

1. sufren
2. escribe
3. vivimos
4. recibe
5. parten
6. decides
7. describen
8. insistís
9. permito
10. sube

## Práctica 4

1. venzo
2. apaciguo
3. frunzo
4. escojo
5. explico
6. padezco
7. analizo
8. traduzco
9. exijo
10. investigo

## Práctica 5

| Verb | Yo | Nosotros | Ellos |
|---|---|---|---|
| enc**o**mendar | enc**o**miendo | enc**o**mendamos | enc**o**miendan |
| m**o**strar | m**ue**stro | m**o**stramos | m**ue**stran |
| esqu**i**ar | esqu**í**o | esqu**i**amos | esqu**í**an |
| ade**cuar** | ade**cú**o | ade**cua**mos | ade**cú**an |
| atesti**guar** | atesti**gu**o | atesti**gua**mos | atesti**gua**n |
| eval**uar** | eval**ú**o | eval**ua**mos | eval**ú**an |
| ent**e**nder | ent**ie**ndo | ent**e**ndemos | ent**ie**nden |
| res**o**lver | res**ue**lvo | res**o**lvemos | res**ue**lven |
| excl**uir** | excl**u**yo | excl**u**imos | excl**u**yen |
| extin**guir** | extin**g**o | extin**gu**imos | extin**gu**en |
| inqu**i**rir | inqu**ie**ro | inqu**i**rimos | inqu**ie**ren |
| m**e**dir | m**i**do | m**e**dimos | m**i**den |

## Práctica 6

1. se acuerda
2. se casan
3. me enfado
4. se equivoca
5. se despiden
6. nos preocupamos
7. te despiertas
8. os negáis

## Práctica 7

1. dice
2. vienen
3. somos
4. ríes
5. oís
6. tengo
7. va
8. está

## Práctica 8

1. tienen
2. te acuestas
3. entiende
4. cojo
5. siguen
6. adquirís
7. se habitúa
8. distribuyen
9. sé
10. somos
11. envías
12. nos adecuamos

## Práctica 9

1. hemos consumido
2. habéis estudiado
3. ha bebido
4. he visto
5. has hecho
6. han escrito

## Práctica 10

1. están huyendo
2. estoy cantando
3. está sirviendo
4. estás conduciendo
5. estamos recogiendo
6. estáis durmiendo

# Chapter 4

## Práctica 1

1. invitó
2. prepararon
3. bailamos
4. cantaste
5. pasasteis
6. regresé

## Práctica 2

1. salieron
2. comí
3. asististeis
4. corrió
5. recibiste
6. aprendimos

## Práctica 3

1. almorcé
2. toqué
3. castigué
4. amortigüé
5. abracé
6. encargué
7. pesqué
8. apacigüé

## Práctica 4

1. leyó
2. oyeron
3. concluyeron
4. bulló
5. cayó
6. poseyeron

## Práctica 5

1. sonrieron
2. durmió
3. prefirieron
4. pidió
5. consintieron
6. sirvieron

## Práctica 6

1. me cepillé
2. se vistieron
3. nos despertamos
4. te bañaste
5. os desayunasteis
6. se afeitó

## Práctica 7

1. fui
2. hicimos
3. pusisteis
4. tuvieron
5. pudiste
6. anduvo
7. estuvieron
8. quiso
9. condujo
10. vio

## Práctica 8

1. durmió
2. fue
3. hizo
4. sacó
5. pagó
6. dio
7. almorzó
8. trajo
9. puso
10. sirvió
11. condujo
12. pudo

## Práctica 9

1. hubimos abierto
2. hubo dicho
3. hubiste visto
4. hube escrito
5. hubieron vuelto
6. hubisteis puesto

## Práctica 10

1. estuvisteis trabajando
2. estuvieron escribiendo
3. estuviste vendiendo
4. estuve leyendo
5. estuvimos durmiendo
6. estuvo corrigiendo

# Chapter 5

## Práctica 1

1. se afeitaba
2. bebíamos
3. escribían
4. platicabais
5. pagaba
6. almorzaban

7. esquiaba 8. volvías 9. conducían
10. estaba 11. venía 12. tenían

## Práctica 2

1. era 2. brillaba 3. hacía
4. quería 5. estaba 6. llevaba
7. parecía 8. tenía 9. pesaba
10. leía 11. temía 12. esperaba

## Práctica 3

1. Hacía buen tiempo.
2. Los pájaros cantaban.
3. Todo el mundo felicitaba a Carmen.
4. Sus padres lloraban de alegría.
5. Carmen sonreía.
6. Yo sacaba fotografías.
7. Uds. querían abrazar a Carmen.
8. Tú esperabas bailar con ella.

## Práctica 4

1. trabajábamos 2. comían
3. interrumpías 4. ibais
5. jugaba 6. escogía
7. perdía 8. se vestían
9. se despertaban 10. era

## Práctica 5

Era; hacía; tenía; sonó; contesté; era; preguntó; quería; respondí; fui; fuimos; estaba; estaba; encontramos; fuimos; pasamos; estábamos; fue

## Práctica 6

Era; pasaba; vivía; iba; escogía; prefería; me aburrí; tomé; fui; entré; estaba; pregunté; podía; sugirió; expliqué; quería; propuso; rechacé; mostró; eran; dió; escogí

## Práctica 7

1. Arturo se cayó porque no prestaba atención.
2. Tu llamaste a Miguel porque tú querías ir al parque.
3. Ella compró un billete porque ella tenía ganas de ir al teatro.
4. Saqué mi paraguas porque llovía mucho.
5. Nosotros le escribíamos a nuestro amigo porque era su aniversario.
6. Uds. presentaron sus excusas porque Uds. se arrepentían de sus acciones.

## Práctica 8

1. conducía/detuvo
2. salían/atacó.
3. reñía/abrió
4. subía/llamó
5. comía/vi
6. viajaban/se desencadenó
7. corría/se cayó
8. ibas/perdiste

## Práctica 9

1. ¿Cuánto tiempo hacía que Elena iba a la universidad?

   Hacía un año (que iba a la universidad).

2. ¿Cuánto tiempo hacía que Esteban y Jorge eran amigos?

   Hacía diez años (que eran amigos).

3. ¿Cuánto tiempo hacía que nosotros tocábamos la guitarra?

   Hacía dos meses (que tocábamos la guitarra).

4. ¿Cuánto tiempo hacía que tú tenías tu propio carro?

   Hacía una semana (que yo tenía mi propio carro).

5. ¿Cuánto tiempo hacía que vosotros vivíais en los Estados Unidos?

   Hacía cinco años (que nosotros vivíamos en los Estados Unidos).

6. ¿Cuánto tiempo hacía que Uds. estaban a régimen?

   Hacía seis días (que nosotros estábamos a régimen).

## Práctica 10

1. Ellos habían perdido su perro.
2. Ella había comido demasiado.
3. Yo había recibido malas notas.

4. Nosotros habíamos salido sin nuestros sombreros.

5. Tú habías trabajado duro.

6. Vosotros os habíais caído.

## Práctica 11

1. Yo estaba conduciendo al centro.

2. Nosotros estábamos durmiendo al aire libre.

3. Los niños estaban jugando en el parque.

4. Tú estabas corriendo.

5. Vosotros estabais caminando.

6. Mariana estaba plantando flores.

# Chapter 6

## Práctica 1

1. Yo voy a escuchar música.

2. Nosotros vamos a leer.

3. Uds. van a jugar al fútbol.

4. Tú vas a ir al centro comercial.

5. Vosotros vais a escribir mensajes por correo electrónico.

6. Ella va a llamar a sus amigas.

## Práctica 2

| | | |
|---|---|---|
| 1. celebraré | 2. asistirás | 3. venderán |
| 4. anunciará | 5. correremos | 6. acudiréis |
| 7. se comunicarán | 8. investigará | 9. empezaremos |
| 10. merendaréis | 11. se probarán | 12. rociaréis |
| 13. continuarán | 14. dormiré | 15. mentirá |
| 16. reiremos | 17. creerás | 18. se vestirán |
| 19. cocerán | 20. corregiré | |

## Práctica 3

diré; podré; querrán; cabrá; tendré; haré; saldré; iré; sabrán; valdrá; habrá; me pondré

## Práctica 4

1. curarán
2. descubrirán
3. desaparecerá
4. se enterarán
5. establecerán
6. eliminaremos

## Práctica 5

1. será
2. tendrán
3. lloverá
4. estará
5. recibirán
6. tardará

## Práctica 6

1. habremos comido
2. habrán recibido
3. habré platicado
4. habrá puesto
5. habrás resuelto
6. habréis abierto
7. habrán visto
8. habrá escrito

## Práctica 7

1. estaremos tocando
2. estarás pilotando
3. estará ofreciendo
4. estarán navegando
5. estaré mandando
6. estaréis traduciendo

# Chapter 7

## Práctica 1

1. compraríamos
2. viviría
3. aprenderías
4. publicarían
5. jugaríais
6. comenzaría
7. se despertarían
8. continuaría
9. conduciría
10. sonreiría
11. leeríamos
12. protegerían

## Práctica 2

1. No habría citas este día.
2. Los empleados podrían salir temprano.
3. Los directores tendrían que esperar hasta las cinco.
4. Los clientes no vendrían.
5. El gerente no diría nada.
6. Yo saldría con los otros.
7. Ricardo y yo querríamos completar nuestro trabajo.
8. Valdría la pena no tomar el autobús.
9. Tú harías todo lo necesario para ayudarnos.
10. Todo el mundo no cabría en el café de la oficina.
11. Uds. no sabrían como ir a casa.
12. Vosotros pondríais música en la oficina.

## Práctica 3

1. compraríais
2. ayudaríamos
3. tendría
4. darían
5. harías
6. viviría

## Práctica 4

1. haría
2. Nevaría
3. sería
4. tendría
5. Pasarían
6. Iría

## Práctica 5

1. habría mirado
2. habrían salido
3. habría cocinado
4. habríamos ido
5. habríais jugado
6. habrías escrito

## Práctica 6

1. estaríais cocinando
2. estaría limpiando
3. estarían yendo
4. estarías lavando
5. estaríamos sirviendo
6. estaría llevando

# Chapter 8

## Práctica 1

1. Es necesario que los ciudadanos respeten las leyes.

2. Es necesario que yo vote.

3. Es necesario que vosotros no os quejéis de todo.

4. Es necesario que tú aceptes tus responsabilidades humanitarias.

5. Es necesario que nosotros no abusemos del ambiente.

6. Es necesario que la gente evite cometer infracciones.

## Práctica 2

1. Es importante que vosotros corráis una milla cada día.

2. Es importante que tú asumas la responsabilidad de tu salud.

3. Es importante que yo prometa adelgazar.

4. Es importante que ellos combatan la fatiga.

5. Es importante que ella emprenda el entrenamiento.

6. Es importante que nosotros consumamos menos calorías.

## Práctica 3

1. Es posible que nosotros vengamos mañana.

2. Es posible que él se ponga enfermo.

3. Es posible que tú tengas buena suerte.

4. Es posible que yo traiga los documentos importantes.

5. Es posible que vosotros hagáis el trabajo.

6. Es posible que ellos digan la verdad.

7. Es posible que Ud. salga con su familia.

8. Es posible que ella no oiga bien.

## Práctica 4

1. Es preciso que nosotros paguemos la cuenta.

2. Es preciso que tú goces de buena salud.

3. Es preciso que vosotros memoricéis todo.

4. Es preciso que Uds. verifiquen toda la información.

5. Es preciso que yo castigue a mi niño.

6. Es preciso que ella practique sus verbos.

## Práctica 5

1. Es menester que Ud. complazca a sus clientes.

2. Es menester que yo conduzca con cuidado.

3. Es menester que nosotros zurzamos estos vestidos.

4. Es menester que ellos me convenzan de la verdad.

5. Es menester que vosotros erijáis un monumento en su honor.

6. Es menester que tú acojas a estas muchachas.

7. Es menester que Ud. extinga el fuego.

8. Es menester que ellas no delincan.

## Práctica 6

1. Más vale que Ud. concluya pronto su trabajo.

2. Más vale que ellos se depierten temprano.

3. Más vale que nosotros durmamos en nuestra propia casa.

4. Más vale que ella varíe el enfoque de su discurso.

5. Más vale que yo me acueste a las diez en punto.

6. Más vale que vosotros perdáis cinco kilos.

7. Más vale que Uds. vuelvan a buscar sus libros.

8. Más vale que tú midas tu cuarto.

9. Más vale que él pueda ayudarme.

10. Más vale que ellas encierren sus joyas.

11. Más vale que yo contribuya con cincuenta dólares.

12. Más vale que nosotros continuemos nuestros estudios.

## Práctica 7

1. Es dudoso que Ud. vuelque el vaso.

2. Es dudoso que nosotros colguemos el cuadro hoy.

3. Es dudoso que yo tropiece con el escalón.

4. Es dudoso que vosotros torzáis el dedo jugando al tenis.

5. Es dudoso que ellos jueguen bien al golf.

6. Es dudoso que tú almuerces con Julio.

7. Es dudoso que ella consiga su objetivo.

8. Es dudoso que Uds. corrijan el error.

## Práctica 8

1. Es probable que yo dé un paseo.

2. Es probable que tú sepas cocinar.

3. Es probable que vosotros estéis cansados.

4. Es probable que Uds. vayan al centro.

5. Es probable que él sea profesor.

6. Es probable que nosotros hayamos recibido el anuncio.

## Práctica 9

1. venga
2. compraremos (compramos)
3. se diviertan
4. traigan
5. toque
6. estarás (estás)

## Práctica 10

1. haga
2. sepan
3. vaya
4. dices
5. seamos
6. pague
7. salgáis
8. da

## Práctica 11

1. salgan
2. dé
3. reciba
4. siga
5. te vayas
6. estudiemos

## Práctica 12

1. Papá le da dinero a Carlos para que él compre un carro.

2. Rosa no hace mucho ruido de manera que nosotros podamos dormir.

3. Yo escucharé la radio mientras que mi hermana hace (hará) sus tareas.

4. Tomás fregará los platos a condición de que yo ordene la sala.

5. Yo no te presto mi libro a menos que tú me lo devuelvas.

6. Mamá prepara sándwiches en caso de que mis hermanos tengan hambre.

## Práctica 13

| | | |
|---|---|---|
| 1. vaya | 2. puede (pueda) | 3. sea |
| 4. tengas | 5. sabe | 6. Viva |

## Práctica 14

| | |
|---|---|
| 1. se haya perdido | 2. hayas ganado |
| 3. se hayan olvidado | 4. haya hecho |
| 5. hayáis visto | 6. hayamos venido |

## Práctica 15

1. Le manda trabajar.

2. Me deja escribir en la pizarra.

3. Te hace leer.

4. Nos prohibe fumar.

5. Me permite salir de la clase.

6. Te deja hablar en inglés.

## Práctica 16

| | | |
|---|---|---|
| 1. traduzcamos | 2. llegue | 3. escojan |
| 4. traéis | 5. tenga | 6. pierdas |
| 7. dormimos | 8. estudiar | 9. esté |
| 10. vayan | 11. sea | 12. conozca |
| 13. explica | 14. sepa | 15. vengan |
| 16. hagan | | |

# Chapter 9

## Práctica 1

1. acompañáramos, acompañásemos

2. vendiera, vendiese

3. abrieras, abrieses

4. descansaran, descansasen

5. escribiera, escribiese

6. aprendierais, aprendieseis

## Práctica 2

1. Era importante que nosotros almorzáramos (almorzásemos) temprano.

2. Era importante que ella pareciera (pareciese) contenta.

3. Era importante que vosotros apaciguarais (apaciguaseis) a los niños.

4. Era importante que tú no te equivocaras (equivocases).

5. Era importante que Uds. protegieran (protegiesen) a sus amigos.

6. Era importante que yo investigara (investigase) el problema.

7. Era importante que el conductor dirigiera (dirigiese) la orquesta.

8. Era importante que nosotros nos distinguiéramos (distinguiésemos).

## Práctica 3

1. Era posible que el cerdo gruñera (gruñese).

2. Era posible que el agua bullera (bullese).

3. Era posible que los alumnos no oyeran (oyesen) el timbre.

4. Era posible que el paquete no incluyera (incluyese) las mercancías correctas.

5. Era posible que estos muchachos poseyeran (poseyesen) mucho talento.

6. Era posible que el coche cayera (cayese) por un barranco.

## Práctica 4

1. Era una lástima que vosotros mintierais (mintieseis).

2. Era una lástima que ella muriera (muriese).

3. Era una lástima que nosotros no nos refiriéramos (refiriésemos) al diccionario.

4. Era una lástima que tú no te vistieras (vistieses) a la moda.

5. Era una lástima que yo no sonriera (sonriese).

6. Era una lástima que Uds. repitieran (repitiesen) un curso.

## Práctica 5

1. a. tradujera, tradujese
   b. fuera, fuese
   c. satisficiera, satificiese
   d. dijera, dijese
   e. hiciera, hiciese
   f. pusiera, pusiese

2. a. trajeras, trajeses
   b. vieras, vieses
   c. pudieras, pudieses
   d. quisieras, quiseses
   e. tuvieras, tuvieses
   f. dieras, dieses

3. a. anduvieran, anduviesen
   b. estuvieran, estuviesen
   c. supieran, supiesen
   d. cupieran, cupiesen
   e. vinieran, viniesen
   f. fueran, fuesen

## Práctica 6

1. hubiera (hubiese) tenido

2. hubiéramos (hubiésemos) hecho

3. hubiera (hubiese) dicho

4. se hubieran (hubiesen) puesto

5. hubieras (hubieses) escrito

6. hubierais (hubieseis) vuelto

## Práctica 7

1. Si tú tienes sueño, tú duermes.

2. Si nosotros tenemos hambre, nosotros comemos un sándwich.

3. Si ellos tienen frío, ellos se ponen un suéter.

4. Si yo tengo sed, yo bebo agua.

5. Si Ud. tiene vergüenza, Ud. se ruboriza.

6. Si vosotros tenéis dolor de cabeza, vosotros tomais una aspirina.

## Práctica 8

1. olvidara (olvidase)

2. hubieras (hubieses) estado

3. hubieran (hubiesen) tenido

4. iríamos

5. habría hecho (hubiera hecho)

6. se hubiera (hubiese) caído

# Chapter 10

## Práctica 1

1. Escriban (Uds.) el ejercicio.

2. Aprendan (Uds.) las palabras.

3. Trabajen (Uds.) con un compañero de clase.

4. Lean (Uds.) en voz alta.

5. Miren (Uds.) la pizarra.

6. Asistan (Uds.) a la escuela todos los días.

## Práctica 2

1. No mastique chicle.

2. No pida permiso para hablar.

3. No vaya al baño durante la entrevista.

4. No tenga miedo.

5. No mienta.

6. No ofrezca consejos.

7. No cuente chistes.

8. No haga mucho ruido.

9. No interrogue el jefe.

10. No esté nervioso.

## Práctica 3

1. No hagas tus tareas en la sala. Haz tus tareas en tu cuarto.

2. No almuerces en una confitería. Almuerza en un restaurante elegante.

3. No digas mentiras. Di la verdad.

4. No obedezcas a tus amigos. Obedece a tus profesores.

5. No salgas a la escuela tarde. Sal temprano.

6. No exijas demasiado. Exige poco.

7. No vayas a casa de Felipe. Ve a la escuela.

8. No sigas los consejos de tus amigos. Sigue los consejos de tus profesores.

## Práctica 4

1. Abrid las ventanas. No abráis las ventanas.

2. Cerrad la puerta. No cerréis la puerta.

3. Apagad la televisión. No apaguéis la televisión.

4. Sacad la basura. No saquéis la basura.

5. Comenzad a estudiar. No comencéis a estudiar.

6. Subid. No subáis.

7. Seguid jugando. No sigáis jugando.

8. Encended la luz. No encendáis la luz.

## Práctica 5

1. Juguemos al fútbol. Vamos a jugar al fútbol.

2. Vamos al campo. Vamos a ir al campo.

3. Demos un paseo por el bosque. Vamos a dar un paseo por el bosque.

4. Durmamos al aire libre. Vamos a dormir al aire libre.

5. Encendamos un gran fuego. Vamos a encender un gran fuego.

6. Contemos cuentos espantosos. Vamos a contar cuentos espantosos.

## Práctica 6

1. ¡Qué diga la verdad!

2. ¡Qué vengan a la oficina!

3. ¡Qué tengan cuidado!

4. ¡Qué haga caso de sus consejos!

5. ¡Qué vuelvan temprano!

6. ¡Qué llegue en seguida!

## Práctica 7

1. Ayúdame. No me ayudes.

2. Tráeme el libro. No me traigas el libro.

3. Escríbeme una lista de compras. No me escribas una lista de compras.

4. Escúchame. No me escuches.

5. Dime tus problemas. No me digas tus problemas.

6. Pídeme permiso para salir. No me pidas permiso para salir.

## Práctica 8

1. Poneos contentos. No os pongáis tristes.

2. Despertaos a las nueve. No os despertéis a las ocho.

3. Acostaos temprano. No os acostéis tarde.

4. Divertíos en el parque. No os divirtáis en la escuela.

5. Iros más tarde. No os vayáis en seguida.

6. Negaos a fumar. No os neguéis a comer legumbres.

## Práctica 9

1. Apresurémonos.    2. Desayunémonos.

3. Vámonos.    4. Sentémonos.

5. Peinémonos.    6. Divirtámonos.

# Chapter 11

## Práctica 1

| 1. de | 2. a | 3. que | 4. de | 5. con |
|---|---|---|---|---|
| 6. de | 7. contra | 8. que | 9. en | 10. a |

## Práctica 2

1. sienta, se sienta    2. me duermo, duermo

3. te engañas, engaño    4. se baña, baña

5. levanta, se levanta    6. me voy, voy

7. se pone, pone    8. se para, para

## Práctica 3

1. sabe, conozco    2. son, están

3. sale, deja    4. debes, tienes que

5. toca, juega            6. devuelvo, vuelvas
7. pregunta, pides        8. toma, lleva

# Chapter 12

## Práctica 1

1. come como un cerdo            2. se aburre como una ostra
3. me acuesto con las gallinas   4. arranca a perderse
5. canta las cuarenta            6. crispan los nervios
7. distingue lo blanco de lo negro   8. echan la casa por la ventana
9. se estruja el cerebro         10. llora a moco tendido
11. llueve a cántaros            12. mata dos pájaros de un tiro
13. tira la toalla               14. se venden como rosquilla
15. paga con la misma moneda     16. sacan fuerzas de flaqueza

## Práctica 2

1. g     2. f     3. h     4. i     5. a     6. e
7. k     8. c     9. j     10. d    11. l    12. b

## Práctica 3

1. doy   2. dé    3. daban   4. dará
5. des   6. diéramos   7. daría   8. di

## Práctica 4

1. b     2. c     3. a     4. a
5. d     6. a     7. b     8. c

## Práctica 5

1. f     2. e     3. g     4. h
5. b     6. d     7. a     8. c

## Práctica 6

1. pensaba
2. ella oyó decir que
3. quiere decir
4. valdrá la pena
5. echarían al correo
6. llegue a ser

## Práctica 7

1. gusta
2. faltan
3. apetece
4. toca
5. sobran
6. agradan

## Práctica 8

1. Los platos fueron lavados por Isabel.
2. La mesa fue puesta por Javier.
3. El baño fue limpiado por Estela.
4. La aspiradora fue pasada por Eduardo.
5. El césped fue cortado por Alfredo.
6. Los vestidos fueron planchados por Clara.
7. Las provisiones fueron compradas por Carolina.
8. La basura fue sacada por Pepe.

## Práctica 9

1. Se sale (Salen) por esa puerta para ir afuera.
2. Se necesita (Necesitan) un bolígrafo para escribir.
3. Se paga (Pagan) en la caja registradora.
4. Se prepara (Preparan) la comida en la cocina.
5. Se pone (Ponen) un abrigo cuando hace frío.
6. Se dice (Dicen) "disculpe" cuando hay un error.

# Verb Charts

# Regular Verbs

## -ar Verbs

◆ usar (*to wear*); **Gerund:** usando; **Past participle:** usado

**Commands:** usa (tú) no uses (tú) usad (vosotros) no uséis (vosotros) use (Ud.) usen (Uds.) usemos (nosotros)

### Simple Tenses

| Present | Preterit | Imperfect | Future | Conditional | Subjunctive | Imperfect Subjunctive |
|---------|----------|-----------|--------|-------------|-------------|------------------------|
| uso | usé | usaba | usaré | usaría | use | usara |
| usas | usaste | usabas | usarás | usarías | uses | usaras |
| usa | usó | usaba | usará | usaría | use | usara |
| usamos | usamos | usábamos | usaremos | usaríamos | usemos | usáramos |
| usáis | usasteis | usabais | usaréis | usaríais | uséis | usarais |
| usan | usaron | usaban | usarán | usarían | usen | usaran |

### Compound Tenses

| Present Perfect | Preterit Perfect | Pluperfect | Future Perfect | Conditional Perfect | Perfect Subjunctive | Pluperfect Subjunctive |
|-----------------|------------------|------------|----------------|---------------------|---------------------|------------------------|
| he usado | hube usado | había usado | habré usado | habría usado | haya usado | hubiera usado |
| has usado | hubiste usado | habías usado | habrás usado | habrías usado | hayas usado | hubieras usado |
| ha usado | hubo usado | había usado | habrá usado | habría usado | haya usado | hubiera usado |
| hemos usado | hubimos usado | habíamos usado | habremos usado | habríamos usado | hayamos usado | hubiéramos usado |
| habéis usado | hubisteis usado | habíais usado | habréis usado | habríais usado | hayáis usado | hubierais usado |
| han usado | hubieron usado | habían usado | habrán usado | habrían usado | hayan usado | hubieran usado |

## -er Verbs

◆ comer (*to eat*); **Gerund:** comiendo; **Past participle:** comido

**Commands:** come (tú) no comas (tú) comed (vosotros) no comáis (vosotros) coma (Ud.) coman (Uds.) comamos (nosotros)

### Simple Tenses

| Present | Preterit | Imperfect | Future | Conditional | Subjunctive | Imperfect Subjunctive |
|---|---|---|---|---|---|---|
| como | comí | comía | comeré | comería | coma | comiera |
| comes | comiste | comías | comerás | comerías | comas | comieras |
| come | comió | comía | comerá | comería | coma | comiera |
| comemos | comimos | comíamos | comeremos | comeríamos | comamos | comiéramos |
| coméis | comisteis | comíais | comeréis | comeríais | comáis | comierais |
| comen | comieron | comían | comerán | comerían | coman | comieran |

### Compound Tenses

| Present Perfect | Preterit Perfect | Pluperfect | Future Perfect | Conditional Perfect | Perfect Subjunctive | Pluperfect Subjunctive |
|---|---|---|---|---|---|---|
| he comido | hube comido | había comido | habré comido | habría comido | haya comido | hubiera comido |
| has comido | hubiste comido | habías comido | habrás comido | habrías comido | hayas comido | hubieras comido |
| ha comido | hubo comido | había comido | habrá comido | habría comido | haya comido | hubiera comido |
| hemos comido | hubimos comido | habíamos comido | habremos comido | habríamos comido | hayamos comido | hubiéramos comido |
| habéis comido | hubisteis comido | habíais comido | habréis comido | habríais comido | hayáis comido | hubierais comido |
| han comido | hubieron comido | habían comido | habrán comido | habrían comido | hayan comido | hubieran comido |

## *-ir* Verbs

◆ vivir (*to live*); **Gerund:** viviendo; **Past participle:** vivido

**Commands:** vive (tú) no vivas (tú) vivid (vosotros) no viváis (vosotros) viva (Ud.) vivan (Uds.) vivamos (nosotros)

### Simple Tenses

| Present | Preterit | Imperfect | Future | Conditional | Subjunctive | Imperfect Subjunctive |
|---------|----------|-----------|--------|-------------|-------------|-----------------------|
| vivo | viví | vivía | viviré | viviría | viva | viviera |
| vives | viviste | vivías | vivirás | vivirías | vivas | vivieras |
| vive | vivió | vivía | vivirá | viviría | viva | viviera |
| vivimos | vivimos | vivíamos | viviremos | viviríamos | vivamos | viviéramos |
| vivís | vivisteis | vivíais | viviréis | viviríais | viváis | vivierais |
| viven | vivieron | vivían | vivirán | vivirían | vivan | vivieran |

### Compound Tenses

| Present Perfect | Preterit Perfect | Pluperfect | Future Perfect | Conditional Perfect | Perfect Subjunctive | Pluperfect Subjunctive |
|-----------------|------------------|------------|----------------|---------------------|---------------------|------------------------|
| he vivido | hube vivido | había vivido | habré vivido | habría vivido | haya vivido | hubiera vivido |
| has vivido | hubiste vivido | habías vivido | habrás vivido | habrías vivido | hayas vivido | hubieras vivido |
| ha vivido | hubo vivido | había vivido | habrá vivido | habría vivido | haya vivido | hubiera vivido |
| hemos vivido | hubimos vivido | habíamos vivido | habremos vivido | habríamos vivido | hayamos vivido | hubiéramos vivido |
| habéis vivido | hubisteis vivido | habíais vivido | habréis vivido | habríais vivido | hayáis vivido | hubierais vivido |
| han vivido | hubieron vivido | habían vivido | habrán vivido | habrían vivido | hayan vivido | hubieran vivido |

# Spelling-Change Verbs

## -car Verbs

◆ buscar (*to look for*); **Gerund:** buscando; **Past participle:** buscado

**Commands:** busca (tú) no busques (tú) buscad (vosotros) no busquéis (vosotros) busque (Ud.) busquen (Uds.) busquemos (nosotros)

### Simple Tenses

| Present | Preterit | Imperfect | Future | Conditional | Subjunctive | Imperfect Subjunctive |
|---|---|---|---|---|---|---|
| busco | busqué | buscaba | buscaré | buscaría | busque | buscara |
| buscas | buscaste | buscabas | buscarás | buscarías | busques | buscaras |
| busca | buscó | buscaba | buscará | buscaría | busque | buscara |
| **buscamos** | buscamos | buscábamos | buscaremos | buscaríamos | **busquemos** | buscáramos |
| **buscáis** | buscasteis | buscabais | buscaréis | buscaríais | busquéis | buscarais |
| buscan | buscaron | buscaban | buscarán | buscarían | busquen | buscaran |

### Compound Tenses

| Present Perfect | Preterit Perfect | Pluperfect | Future Perfect | Conditional Perfect | Perfect Subjunctive | Pluperfect Subjunctive |
|---|---|---|---|---|---|---|
| he buscado | hube buscado | había buscado | habré buscado | habría buscado | haya buscado | hubiera buscado |
| has buscado | hubiste buscado | habías buscado | habrás buscado | habrías buscado | hayas buscado | hubieras buscado |
| ha buscado | hubo buscado | había buscado | habrá buscado | habría buscado | haya buscado | hubiera buscado |
| hemos buscado | hubimos buscado | habíamos buscado | habremos buscado | habríamos buscado | hayamos buscado | hubiéramos buscado |
| habéis buscado | hubisteis buscado | habíais buscado | habréis buscado | habríais buscado | hayáis buscado | hubierais buscado |
| han buscado | hubieron buscado | habían buscado | habrán buscado | habrían buscado | hayan buscado | hubieran buscado |

## -gar Verbs

◆ llegar (*to arrive*); **Gerund:** llegando; **Past participle:** llegado

**Commands:** llega (tú) no llegues (tú) llegad (vosotros) no lleguéis (vosotros) llegue (Ud.) lleguen (Uds.) lleguemos (nosotros)

### Simple Tenses

| Present | Preterit | Imperfect | Future | Conditional | Subjunctive | Imperfect Subjunctive |
|---|---|---|---|---|---|---|
| llego | llegué | llegaba | llegaré | llegaría | llegue | llegara |
| llegas | llegaste | llegabas | llegarás | llegarías | llegues | llegaras |
| llega | llegó | llegaba | llegará | llegaría | llegue | llegara |
| llegamos | llegamos | llegábamos | llegaremos | llegaríamos | lleguemos | llegáramos |
| llegáis | llegasteis | llegabais | llegaréis | llegaríais | lleguéis | llegarais |
| llegan | llegaron | llegaban | llegarán | llegarían | lleguen | llegaran |

### Compound Tenses

| Present Perfect | Preterit Perfect | Pluperfect | Future Perfect | Conditional Perfect | Perfect Subjunctive | Pluperfect Subjunctive |
|---|---|---|---|---|---|---|
| he llegado | hube llegado | había llegado | habré llegado | habría llegado | haya llegado | hubiera llegado |
| has llegado | hubiste llegado | habías llegado | habrás llegado | habrías llegado | hayas llegado | hubieras llegado |
| ha llegado | hubo llegado | había llegado | habrá llegado | habría llegado | haya llegado | hubiera llegado |
| hemos llegado | hubimos llegado | habíamos llegado | habremos llegado | habríamos llegado | hayamos llegado | hubiéramos llegado |
| habéis llegado | hubisteis llegado | habíais llegado | habréis llegado | habríais llegado | hayáis llegado | hubierais llegado |
| han llegado | hubieron llegado | habían llegado | habrán llegado | habrían llegado | hayan llegado | hubieran llegado |

## *-guar* Verbs

◆ averiguar (*to find out*); **Gerund:** averiguando; **Past participle:** averiguado

**Commands:** averigua (tú) no averigües (tú) averiguad (vosotros) no averigüéis (vosotros) averigüe (Ud.) averigüen (Uds.) averigüemos (nosotros)

### Simple Tenses

| Present | Preterit | Imperfect | Future | Conditional | Subjunctive | Imperfect Subjunctive |
|---|---|---|---|---|---|---|
| averiguo | averigüé | averiguaba | averiguaré | averiguaría | averigüe | averiguara |
| averiguas | averiguaste | averiguabas | averiguarás | averiguarías | averigües | averiguaras |
| averigua | averiguó | averiguaba | averiguará | averiguaría | averigüe | averiguara |
| averiguamos | averiguamos | averiguábamos | averiguaremos | averiguaríamos | averigüemos | averiguáramos |
| averiguáis | averiguasteis | averiguabais | averiguaréis | averiguaríais | averigüéis | averiguarais |
| averiguan | averiguaron | averiguaban | averiguarán | averiguarían | averigüen | averiguaran |

### Compound Tenses

| Present Perfect | Preterit Perfect | Pluperfect | Future Perfect | Conditional Perfect | Perfect Subjunctive | Pluperfect Subjunctive |
|---|---|---|---|---|---|---|
| he averiguado | hube averiguado | había averiguado | habré averiguado | habría averiguado | haya averiguado | hubiera averiguado |
| has averiguado | hubiste averiguado | habías averiguado | habrás averiguado | habrías averiguado | hayas averiguado | hubieras averiguado |
| ha averiguado | hubo averiguado | había averiguado | habrá averiguado | habría averiguado | haya averiguado | hubiera averiguado |
| hemos averiguado | hubimos averiguado | habíamos averiguado | habremos averiguado | habríamos averiguado | hayamos averiguado | hubiéramos averiguado |
| habéis averiguado | hubisteis averiguado | habíais averiguado | habréis averiguado | habríais averiguado | hayáis averiguado | hubierais averiguado |
| han averiguado | hubieron averiguado | habían averiguado | habrán averiguado | habrían averiguado | hayan averiguado | hubieran averiguado |

## -zar Verbs

◆ cruzar (*to cross*); **Gerund:** cruzando; **Past participle:** cruzado

**Commands:** cruza (tú) no cruces (tú) cruzad (vosotros) no crucéis (vosotros) cruce (Ud.) crucen (Uds.) crucemos (nosotros)

### Simple Tenses

| Present | Preterit | Imperfect | Future | Conditional | Subjunctive | Imperfect Subjunctive |
|---|---|---|---|---|---|---|
| cruzo | crucé | cruzaba | cruzaré | cruzaría | cruce | cruzara |
| cruzas | cruzaste | cruzabas | cruzarás | cruzarías | cruces | cruzaras |
| cruza | cruzó | cruzaba | cruzará | cruzaría | cruce | cruzara |
| cruzamos | cruzamos | cruzábamos | cruzaremos | cruzaríamos | crucemos | cruzáramos |
| cruzáis | cruzasteis | cruzabais | cruzaréis | cruzaríais | crucéis | cruzarais |
| cruzan | cruzaron | cruzaban | cruzarán | cruzarían | crucen | cruzaran |

### Compound Tenses

| Present Perfect | Preterit Perfect | Pluperfect | Future Perfect | Conditional Perfect | Perfect Subjunctive | Pluperfect Subjunctive |
|---|---|---|---|---|---|---|
| he cruzado | hube cruzado | había cruzado | habré cruzado | habría cruzado | haya cruzado | hubiera cruzado |
| has cruzado | hubiste cruzado | habías cruzado | habrás cruzado | habrías cruzado | hayas cruzado | hubieras cruzado |
| ha cruzado | hubo cruzado | había cruzado | habrá cruzado | habría cruzado | haya cruzado | hubiera cruzado |
| hemos cruzado | hubimos cruzado | habíamos cruzado | habremos cruzado | habríamos cruzado | hayamos cruzado | hubiéramos cruzado |
| habéis cruzado | hubisteis cruzado | habíais cruzado | habréis cruzado | habríais cruzado | hayáis cruzado | hubierais cruzado |
| han cruzado | hubieron cruzado | habían cruzado | habrán cruzado | habrían cruzado | hayan cruzado | hubieran cruzado |

## *-iar* Verbs

◆ variar (*to vary*): **Gerund:** variando; **Past participle:** variado

**Commands:** varía (tú) no varíes (tú) variad (vosotros) no variéis (vosotros) varíe (Ud.) varíen (Uds.) variemos (nosotros)

### Simple Tenses

| Present | Preterit | Imperfect | Future | Conditional | Subjunctive | Imperfect Subjunctive |
|---|---|---|---|---|---|---|
| varío | varié | variaba | variaré | variaría | varíe | variara |
| varías | variaste | variabas | variarás | variarías | varíes | variaras |
| varía | varió | variaba | variará | variaría | varíe | variara |
| variamos | variamos | variábamos | variaremos | variaríamos | variemos | variáramos |
| variái | variasteis | variabais | variaréis | variaríais | variéis | variarais |
| varían | variaron | variaban | variarán | variarían | varíen | variaran |

### Compound Tenses

| Present Perfect | Preterit Perfect | Pluperfect | Future Perfect | Conditional Perfect | Perfect Subjunctive | Pluperfect Subjunctive |
|---|---|---|---|---|---|---|
| he variado | hube variado | había variado | habré variado | habría variado | haya variado | hubiera variado |
| has variado | hubiste variado | habías variado | habrás variado | habrías variado | hayas variado | hubieras variado |
| ha variado | hubo variado | había variado | habrá variado | habría variado | haya variado | hubiera variado |
| hemos variado | hubimos variado | habíamos variado | habremos variado | habríamos variado | hayamos variado | hubiéramos variado |
| habéis variado | hubisteis variado | habíais variado | habréis variado | habríais variado | hayáis variado | hubierais variado |
| han variado | hubieron variado | habían variado | habrán variado | habrían variado | hayan variado | hubieran variado |

## *-ar* Verbs

◆ continuar (*to continue*); **Gerund:** continuando; **Past participle:** continuado

**Commands:** continúa (tú) no continúes (tú) continuad (vosotros) no continuéis (vosotros) continúe (Ud.) continúen (Uds.) continuemos (nosotros)

### Simple Tenses

| Present | Preterit | Imperfect | Future | Conditional | Subjunctive | Imperfect Subjunctive |
|---------|----------|-----------|--------|-------------|-------------|-----------------------|
| continúo | continué | continuaba | continuaré | continuaría | continúe | continuara |
| continúas | continuaste | continuabas | continuarás | continuarías | continúes | continuaras |
| continúa | continuó | continuaba | continuará | continuaría | continúe | continuara |
| continuamos | continuamos | continuábamos | continuaremos | continuaríamos | continuemos | continuáramos |
| continuáis | continuasteis | continuabais | continuaréis | continuaríais | continuéis | continuarais |
| continúan | continuaron | continuaban | continuarán | continuarían | continúen | continuaran |

### Compound Tenses

| Present Perfect | Preterit Perfect | Pluperfect | Future Perfect | Conditional Perfect | Perfect Subjunctive | Pluperfect Subjunctive |
|-----------------|------------------|------------|----------------|---------------------|---------------------|------------------------|
| he continuado | hube continuado | había continuado | habré continuado | habría continuado | haya continuado | hubiera continuado |
| has continuado | hubiste continuado | habías continuado | habrás continuado | habrías continuado | hayas continuado | hubieras continuado |
| ha continuado | hubo continuado | había continuado | habrá continuado | habría continuado | haya continuado | hubiera continuado |
| hemos continuado | hubimos continuado | habíamos continuado | habremos continuado | habríamos continuado | hayamos continuado | hubiéramos continuado |
| habéis continuado | hubisteis continuado | habíais continuado | habréis continuado | habríais continuado | hayáis continuado | hubierais continuado |
| han continuado | hubieron continuado | habían continuado | habrán continuado | habrían continuado | hayan continuado | hubieran continuado |

# Vowel + -*cer* Verbs

◆ conocer (*to know*); **Gerund:** conociendo; **Past participle:** conocido

**Commands:** conoce (tú) no conozcas (tú) conoced (vosotros) no conozcáis (vosotros) conozca (Ud.) conozcan (Uds.) conozcamos (nosotros)

## Simple Tenses

| Present | Preterit | Imperfect | Future | Conditional | Subjunctive | Imperfect Subjunctive |
|---------|----------|-----------|--------|-------------|-------------|------------------------|
| conozco | conocí | conocía | conoceré | conocería | conozca | conociera |
| conoces | conociste | conocías | conocerás | conocerías | conozcas | conocieras |
| conoce | conoció | conocía | conocerá | conocería | conozca | conociera |
| conocemos | conocimos | conocíamos | conoceremos | conoceríamos | conozcamos | conociéramos |
| conocéis | conocisteis | conocíais | conoceréis | conoceríais | conozcáis | conocierais |
| conocen | conocieron | conocían | conocerán | conocerían | conozcan | conocieran |

## Compound Tenses

| Present Perfect | Preterit Perfect | Pluperfect | Future Perfect | Conditional Perfect | Perfect Subjunctive | Pluperfect Subjunctive |
|-----------------|------------------|------------|----------------|---------------------|---------------------|------------------------|
| he conocido | hube conocido | había conocido | habré conocido | habría conocido | haya conocido | hubiera conocido |
| has conocido | hubiste conocido | habías conocido | habrás conocido | habrías conocido | hayas conocido | hubieras conocido |
| ha conocido | hubo conocido | había conocido | habrá conocido | habría conocido | haya conocido | hubiera conocido |
| hemos conocido | hubimos conocido | habíamos conocido | habremos conocido | habríamos conocido | hayamos conocido | hubiéramos conocido |
| habéis conocido | hubisteis conocido | habíais conocido | habréis conocido | habríais conocido | hayáis conocido | hubierais conocido |
| han conocido | hubieron conocido | habían conocido | habrán conocido | habrían conocido | hayan conocido | hubieran conocido |

## Consonant + -cer Verbs

◆ vencer (*to conquer*); **Gerund:** venciendo; **Past participle:** vencido

**Commands:** vence (tú) no venzas (tú) venced (vosotros) no venzáis (vosotros) venza (Ud.) venzan (Uds.) venzamos (nosotros)

### Simple Tenses

| Present | Preterit | Imperfect | Future | Conditional | Subjunctive | Imperfect Subjunctive |
|---|---|---|---|---|---|---|
| venzo | vencí | vencía | venceré | vencería | venza | venciera |
| vences | venciste | vencías | vencerás | vencerías | venzas | vencieras |
| vence | venció | vencía | vencerá | vencería | venza | venciera |
| vencemos | vencimos | vencíamos | venceremos | venceríamos | venzamos | venciéramos |
| vencéis | vencisteis | vencíais | venceréis | venceríais | venzáis | vencierais |
| vencen | vencieron | vencían | vencerá | vencerían | venzan | vencieran |

### Compound Tenses

| Present Perfect | Pluperfect | Preterit Perfect | Future Perfect | Conditional Perfect | Perfect Subjunctive | Pluperfect Subjunctive |
|---|---|---|---|---|---|---|
| he vencido | había vencido | hube vencido | habré vencido | habría vencido | haya vencido | hubiera vencido |
| has vencido | habías vencido | hubiste vencido | habrás vencido | habrías vencido | hayas vencido | hubieras vencido |
| ha vencido | había vencido | hubo vencido | habrá vencido | habría vencido | haya vencido | hubiera vencido |
| hemos vencido | habíamos vencido | hubimos vencido | habremos vencido | habríamos vencido | hayamos vencido | hubiéramos vencido |
| habéis vencido | habíais vencido | hubisteis vencido | habréis vencido | habríais vencido | hayáis vencido | hubierais vencido |
| han vencido | habían vencido | hubieron vencido | habrán vencido | habrían vencido | hayan vencido | hubieran vencido |

## -ger Verbs

◆ escoger (*to chose*); **Gerund:** escogiendo; **Past participle:** escogido

**Commands:** escoge (tú) no escojas (tú) escoged (vosotros) no escojáis (vosotros) escoja (Ud.) escojan (Uds.) escojamos (nosotros)

### Simple Tenses

| Present | Preterit | Imperfect | Future | Conditional | Subjunctive | Imperfect Subjunctive |
|---|---|---|---|---|---|---|
| escojo | escogí | escogía | escogeré | escogería | escoja | escogiera |
| escoges | escogiste | escogías | escogerás | escogerías | escojas | escogieras |
| escoge | escogió | escogía | escogerá | escogería | escoja | escogiera |
| escogemos | escogimos | escogíamos | escogeremos | escogeríamos | escojamos | escogiéramos |
| escogéis | escogisteis | escogíais | escogeréis | escogeríais | escojáis | escogierais |
| escogen | escogieron | escogían | escogerán | escogerían | escojan | escogieran |

### Compound Tenses

| Present Perfect | Preterit Perfect | Pluperfect | Future Perfect | Conditional Perfect | Perfect Subjunctive | Pluperfect Subjunctive |
|---|---|---|---|---|---|---|
| he escogido | hube escogido | había escogido | habré escogido | habría escogido | haya escogido | hubiera escogido |
| has escogido | hubiste escogido | habías escogido | habrás escogido | habrías escogido | hayas escogido | hubieras escogido |
| ha escogido | hubo escogido | había escogido | habrá escogido | habría escogido | haya escogido | hubiera escogido |
| hemos escogido | hubimos escogido | habíamos escogido | habremos escogido | habríamos escogido | hayamos escogido | hubiéramos escogido |
| habéis escogido | hubisteis escogido | habíais escogido | habréis escogido | habriais escogido | hayáis escogido | hubierais escogido |
| han escogido | hubieron escogido | habían escogido | habrán escogido | habrían escogido | hayan escogido | hubieran escogido |

# Vowel + -*cir* Verbs

◆ lucir (*to shine*); **Gerund:** luciendo; **Past participle:** lucido

**Commands:** luce (tú) no luzcas (tú) lucid (vosotros) no luzcáis (vosotros) luzca (Ud.) luzcan (Uds.) luzcamos (nosotros)

## Simple Tenses

| Present | Preterit | Imperfect | Future | Conditional | Subjunctive | Imperfect Subjunctive |
|---|---|---|---|---|---|---|
| luzco | lucí | lucía | luciré | luciría | luzca | luciera |
| luces | luciste | lucías | lucirás | lucirías | luzcas | lucieras |
| luce | lució | lucía | lucirá | luciría | luzca | luciera |
| lucimos | lucimos | lucíamos | luciremos | luciríamos | luzcamos | luciéramos |
| lucís | lucisteis | lucíais | luciréis | luciríais | luzcáis | lucierais |
| lucen | lucieron | lucían | lucirán | lucirían | luzcan | lucieran |

## Compound Tenses

| Present Perfect | Preterit Perfect | Pluperfect | Future Perfect | Conditional Perfect | Perfect Subjunctive | Pluperfect Subjunctive |
|---|---|---|---|---|---|---|
| he lucido | hube lucido | había lucido | habré lucido | habría lucido | haya lucido | hubiera lucido |
| has lucido | hubiste lucido | habías lucido | habrás lucido | habrías lucido | hayas lucido | hubieras lucido |
| ha lucido | hubo lucido | había lucido | habrá lucido | habría lucido | haya lucido | hubiera lucido |
| hemos lucido | hubimos lucido | habíamos lucido | habremos lucido | habríamos lucido | hayamos lucido | hubiéramos lucido |
| habéis lucido | hubisteis lucido | habíais lucido | habréis lucido | habríais lucido | hayáis lucido | hubierais lucido |
| han lucido | hubieron lucido | habían lucido | habrán lucido | habrían lucido | hayan lucido | hubieran lucido |

# Consonant + -*cir* Verbs

♦ esparcir (*to spread*); **Gerund:** esparciendo; **Past participle:** esparcido

**Commands:** esparce (tú) no esparzas (tú) esparcid (vosotros) no esparzáis (vosotros) esparza (Ud.) esparzan (Uds.) esparzamos (nosotros)

## Simple Tenses

| Present | Preterit | Imperfect | Future | Conditional | Subjunctive | Imperfect Subjunctive |
|---|---|---|---|---|---|---|
| esparzo | esparcí | esparcía | esparciré | esparciría | esparza | esparciera |
| esparces | esparciste | esparcías | esparcirás | esparcirías | esparzas | esparcieras |
| esparce | esparció | esparcía | esparcirá | esparciría | esparza | esparciera |
| esparcimos | esparcimos | esparcíamos | esparciremos | esparciríamos | esparzamos | esparciéramos |
| esparcís | esparcisteis | esparcíais | esparciréis | esparciríais | esparzáis | esparcierais |
| esparcen | esparcieron | esparcían | esparcirán | esparcirían | esparzan | esparcieran |

## Compound Tenses

| Present Perfect | Pluperfect | Preterit Perfect | Future Perfect | Conditional Perfect | Perfect Subjunctive | Pluperfect Subjunctive |
|---|---|---|---|---|---|---|
| he esparcido | había esparcido | hube esparcido | habré esparcido | habría esparcido | haya esparcido | hubiera esparcido |
| has esparcido | habías esparcido | hubiste esparcido | habrás esparcido | habrías esparcido | hayas esparcido | hubieras esparcido |
| ha esparcido | había esparcido | hubo esparcido | habrá esparcido | habría esparcido | haya esparcido | hubiera esparcido |
| hemos esparcido | habíamos esparcido | hubimos esparcido | habremos esparcido | habríamos esparcido | hayamos esparcido | hubiéramos esparcido |
| habéis esparcido | habíais esparcido | hubisteis esparcido | habréis esparcido | habríais esparcido | hayáis esparcido | hubierais esparcido |
| han esparcido | habían esparcido | hubieron esparcido | habrán esparcido | habrían esparcido | hayan esparcido | hubieran esparcido |

## *-ducir* Verbs

◆ conducir (*to drive*); **Gerund:** conduciendo; **Past participle:** conducido

**Commands:** conduce (tú) no conduzcas (tú) conducid (vosotros) no conduzcáis (vosotros) conduzca (Ud.) conduzcan (Uds.) conduzcamos (nosotros)

### Simple Tenses

| Present | Preterit | Imperfect | Future | Conditional | Subjunctive | Imperfect Subjunctive |
|---|---|---|---|---|---|---|
| conduzco | conduje | conducía | conduciré | conduciría | conduzca | condujera |
| conduces | condujiste | conducías | conducirás | conducirías | conduzcas | condujeras |
| conduce | condujo | conducía | conducirá | conduciría | conduzca | condujera |
| conducimos | condujimos | conducíamos | conduciremos | conduciríamos | conduzcamos | condujéramos |
| conducís | condujisteis | conducíais | conduciréis | conduciríais | conduzcáis | condujerais |
| conducen | condujeron | conducían | conducirán | conducirían | conduzcan | condujeran |

### Compound Tenses

| Present Perfect | Preterit Perfect | Pluperfect | Future Perfect | Conditional Perfect | Perfect Subjunctive | Pluperfect Subjunctive |
|---|---|---|---|---|---|---|
| he conducido | hube conducido | había conducido | habré conducido | habría conducido | haya conducido | hubiera conducido |
| has conducido | hubiste conducido | habías conducido | habrás conducido | habrías conducido | hayas conducido | hubieras conducido |
| ha conducido | hubo conducido | había conducido | habrá conducido | habría conducido | haya conducido | hubiera conducido |
| hemos conducido | hubimos conducido | habíamos conducido | habremos conducido | habríamos conducido | hayamos conducido | hubiéramos conducido |
| habéis conducido | hubisteis conducido | habíais conducido | habréis conducido | habríais conducido | hayáis conducido | hubierais conducido |
| han conducido | hubieron conducido | habían conducido | habrán conducido | habrían conducido | hayan conducido | hubieran conducido |

## *-gir* Verbs

◆ dirigir (*to direct*); **Gerund:** dirigiendo; **Past participle:** dirigido

**Commands:** dirige (tú) no dirijas (tú) dirigid (vosotros) no dirijáis (vosotros) dirija (Ud.) dirijan (Uds.) dirijamos (nosotros)

### Simple Tenses

| Present | Preterit | Imperfect | Future | Conditional | Subjunctive | Imperfect Subjunctive |
|---|---|---|---|---|---|---|
| dirijo | dirigí | dirigía | dirigiré | dirigiría | dirija | dirigiera |
| diriges | dirigiste | dirigías | dirigirás | dirigirías | dirijas | dirigieras |
| dirige | dirigió | dirigía | dirigirá | dirigiría | dirija | dirigiera |
| dirigimos | dirigimos | dirigíamos | dirigiremos | dirigiríamos | dirijamos | dirigiéramos |
| dirigís | dirigisteis | dirigíais | dirigiréis | dirigiríais | dirijáis | dirigierais |
| dirigen | dirigieron | dirigían | dirigirán | dirigirían | dirijan | dirigieran |

### Compound Tenses

| Present Perfect | Preterit Perfect | Pluperfect | Future Perfect | Conditional Perfect | Perfect Subjunctive | Pluperfect Subjunctive |
|---|---|---|---|---|---|---|
| he dirigido | hube dirigido | había dirigido | habré dirigido | habría dirigido | haya dirigido | hubiera dirigido |
| has dirigido | hubiste dirigido | habías dirigido | habrás dirigido | habrías dirigido | hayas dirigido | hubieras dirigido |
| ha dirigido | hubo dirigido | había dirigido | habrá dirigido | habría dirigido | haya dirigido | hubiera dirigido |
| hemos dirigido | hubimos dirigido | habíamos dirigido | habremos dirigido | habríamos dirigido | hayamos dirigido | hubiéramos dirigido |
| habéis dirigido | hubisteis dirigido | habíais dirigido | habréis dirigido | habríais dirigido | hayáis dirigido | hubierais dirigido |
| han dirigido | hubieron dirigido | habían dirigido | habrán dirigido | habrían dirigido | hayan dirigido | hubieran dirigido |

## -uir Verbs (but not -guir Verbs)

◆ concluir (*to conclude*); **Gerund:** concluyendo; **Past participle:** concluído

**Commands:** concluye (tú) no concluyas (tú) concluid (vosotros) no concluyáis (vosotros) concluya (Ud.) concluya (Uds.) concluyamos (nosotros)

### Simple Tenses

| Present | Preterit | Imperfect | Future | Conditional | Subjunctive | Imperfect Subjunctive |
|---------|----------|-----------|--------|-------------|-------------|----------------------|
| concluyo | concluí | concluía | concluiré | concluiría | concluya | concluyera |
| concluyes | concluiste | concluías | concluirás | concluirías | concluyas | concluyeras |
| concluye | concluyó | concluía | concluirá | concluiría | concluya | concluyera |
| concluimos | concluimos | concluíamos | concluiremos | concluiríamos | concluyamos | concluyéramos |
| concluís | concluisteis | concluíais | concluiréis | concluiríais | concluyáis | concluyerais |
| concluyen | concluyeron | concluían | concluirán | concluirían | concluyan | concluyeran |

### Compound Tenses

| Present Perfect | Preterit Perfect | Pluperfect | Future Perfect | Conditional Perfect | Perfect Subjunctive | Pluperfect Subjunctive |
|-----------------|------------------|------------|----------------|---------------------|---------------------|------------------------|
| he concluído | hube concluído | había concluído | habré concluído | habría concluído | haya concluído | hubiera concluído |
| has concluído | hubiste concluído | habías concluído | habrás concluído | habrías concluído | hayas concluído | hubieras concluído |
| ha concluído | hubo concluído | había concluído | habrá concluído | habría concluído | haya concluído | hubiera concluído |
| hemos concluído | hubimos concluído | habíamos concluído | habremos concluído | habríamos concluído | hayamos concluído | hubiéramos concluído |
| habéis concluído | hubisteis concluído | habíais concluído | habréis concluído | habríais concluído | hayáis concluído | hubierais concluído |
| han concluído | hubieron concluído | habían concluído | habrán concluído | habrían concluído | hayan concluído | hubieran concluído |

## *-guir* Verbs

◆ distinguir (*to distinguish*); **Gerund:** distinguiendo; **Past participle:** distinguido

**Commands:** distingue (tú) no distingas (tú) distinguid (vosotros) no distingáis (vosotros) distinga (Ud.) distingan (Uds.) distingamos (nosotros)

### Simple Tenses

| Present | Preterit | Imperfect | Future | Conditional | Subjunctive | Imperfect Subjunctive |
|---|---|---|---|---|---|---|
| distingo | distinguí | distinguía | distinguiré | distinguiría | distinga | distinguiera |
| distingues | distinguiste | distinguías | distinguirás | distinguirías | distingas | distinguieras |
| distingue | distinguió | distinguía | distinguirá | distinguiría | distinga | distinguiera |
| distinguimos | distinguimos | distinguíamos | distinguiremos | distinguiríamos | distingamos | distinguiéramos |
| distinguís | distinguisteis | distinguíais | distinguiréis | distinguiríais | distingáis | distinguierais |
| distinguen | distinguieron | distinguían | distinguirán | distinguirían | distingan | distinguieran |

### Compound Tenses

| Present Perfect | Preterit Perfect | Pluperfect | Future Perfect | Conditional Perfect | Perfect Subjunctive | Pluperfect Subjunctive |
|---|---|---|---|---|---|---|
| he distinguido | hube distinguido | había distinguido | habré distinguido | habría distinguido | haya distinguido | hubiera distinguido |
| has distinguido | hubiste distinguido | habías distinguido | habrás distinguido | habrías distinguido | hayas distinguido | hubieras distinguido |
| ha distinguido | hubo distinguido | había distinguido | habrá distinguido | habría distinguido | haya distinguido | hubiera distinguido |
| hemos distinguido | hubimos distinguido | habíamos distinguido | habremos distinguido | habríamos distinguido | hayamos distinguido | hubiéramos distinguido |
| habéis distinguido | hubisteis distinguido | habíais distinguido | habréis distinguido | habríais distinguido | hayáis distinguido | hubierais distinguido |
| han distinguido | hubieron distinguido | habían distinguido | habrán distinguido | habrían distinguido | hayan distinguido | hubieran distinguido |

# *-quir* Verbs

◆ delinquir (*to offend*); **Gerund:** delinquiendo; **Past participle:** delinquido

**Commands:** delinque (tú) no delincas (tú) delinquid (vosotros) no delincáis (vosotros) delinca (Ud.) delincan (Uds.) delincamos (nosotros)

## Simple Tenses

| Present | Preterit | Imperfect | Future | Conditional | Subjunctive | Imperfect Subjunctive |
|---|---|---|---|---|---|---|
| delinco | delinquí | delinquía | delinquiré | delinquiría | delinca | delinquiera |
| delinques | delinquiste | delinquías | delinquirás | delinquirías | delincas | delinquieras |
| delinque | delinquió | delinquía | delinquirá | delinquiría | delinca | delinquiera |
| delinquimos | delinquimos | delinquíamos | delinquiremos | delinquiríamos | delincamos | delinquiéramos |
| delinquís | delinquisteis | delinquíais | delinquiréis | delinquiríais | delincáis | delinquierais |
| delinquen | delinquieron | delinquían | delinquirán | delinquirían | delincan | delinquieran |

## Compound Tenses

| Present Perfect | Preterit Perfect | Pluperfect | Future Perfect | Conditional Perfect | Perfect Subjunctive | Pluperfect Subjunctive |
|---|---|---|---|---|---|---|
| he delinquido | hube delinquido | había delinquido | habré delinquido | habría delinquido | haya delinquido | hubiera delinquido |
| has delinquido | hubiste delinquido | habías delinquido | habrás delinquido | habrías delinquido | hayas delinquido | hubieras delinquido |
| ha delinquido | hubo delinquido | había delinquido | habrá delinquido | habría delinquido | haya delinquido | hubiera delinquido |
| hemos delinquido | hubimos delinquido | habíamos delinquido | habremos delinquido | habríamos delinquido | hayamos delinquido | hubiéramos delinquido |
| habéis delinquido | hubisteis delinquido | habíais delinquido | habréis delinquido | habríais delinquido | hayáis delinquido | hubierais delinquido |
| han delinquido | hubieron delinquido | habían delinquido | habrán delinquido | habrían delinquido | hayan delinquido | hubieran delinquido |

# Verbs Ending in *ll*

◆ bullir (*to boil*); **Gerund:** bullendo; **Past participle:** bullendo

**Commands:** bulle (tú) no bullas (tú) bullid (vosotros) no bulláis (vosotros) bulla (Ud.) bullan (Uds.) bullamos (nosotros)

## Simple Tenses

| Present | Preterit | Imperfect | Future | Conditional | Subjunctive | Imperfect Subjunctive |
|---|---|---|---|---|---|---|
| bullo | bullí | bullía | bulliré | bulliría | bulla | bullera |
| bulles | bulliste | bullías | bullirás | bullirías | bullas | bulleras |
| bulle | bulló | bullía | bullirá | bulliría | bulla | bullera |
| bullimos | bullimos | bullíamos | bulliremos | bulliríamos | bullamos | bulléramos |
| bullís | bullisteis | bullíais | bulliréis | bulliríais | bulláis | bullerais |
| bullen | bulleron | bullían | bullirán | bullirían | bullan | bulleran |

## Compound Tenses

| Present Perfect | Preterit Perfect | Pluperfect | Future Perfect | Conditional Perfect | Perfect Subjunctive | Pluperfect Subjunctive |
|---|---|---|---|---|---|---|
| he bullido | hube bullido | había bullido | habré bullido | habría bullido | haya bullido | hubiera bullido |
| has bullido | hubiste bullido | habías bullido | habrás bullido | habrías bullido | hayas bullido | hubieras bullido |
| ha bullido | hubo bullido | había bullido | habrá bullido | habría bullido | haya bullido | hubiera bullido |
| hemos bullido | hubimos bullido | habíamos bullido | habremos bullido | habríamos bullido | hayamos bullido | hubiéramos bullido |
| habéis bullido | hubisteis bullido | habíais bullido | habréis bullido | habríais bullido | hayáis bullido | hubierais bullido |
| han bullido | hubieron bullido | habían bullido | habrán bullido | habrían bullido | hayan bullido | hubieran bullido |

# Verbs Ending in ñ

- bruñir (*to polish*); **Gerund:** bruñendo; **Past participle:** bruñido

  **Commands:** bruñe (tú) no bruñas (tú) bruñid (vosotros) no bruñáis (vosotros) bruña (Ud.) bruñan (Uds.) bruñamos (nosotros)

## Simple Tenses

| Present | Preterit | Imperfect | Future | Conditional | Subjunctive | Imperfect Subjunctive |
|---------|----------|-----------|--------|-------------|-------------|----------------------|
| bruño | bruñí | bruñía | bruñiré | bruñiría | bruña | bruñera |
| bruñes | bruñiste | bruñías | bruñirás | bruñirías | bruñas | bruñeras |
| bruñe | bruñó | bruñía | bruñirá | bruñiría | bruña | bruñera |
| bruñimos | bruñimos | bruñíamos | bruñiremos | bruñiríamos | bruñamos | bruñéramos |
| bruñís | bruñisteis | bruñíais | bruñiréis | bruñiríais | bruñáis | bruñerais |
| bruñen | bruñeron | bruñían | bruñirán | bruñirían | bruñan | bruñeran |

## Compound Tenses

| Present Perfect | Preterit Perfect | Pluperfect | Future Perfect | Conditional Perfect | Perfect Subjunctive | Pluperfect Subjunctive |
|-----------------|------------------|------------|----------------|---------------------|---------------------|------------------------|
| he bruñido | hube bruñido | había bruñido | habré bruñido | habría bruñido | haya bruñido | hubiera bruñido |
| has bruñido | hubiste bruñido | habías bruñido | habrás bruñido | habrías bruñido | hayas bruñido | hubieras bruñido |
| ha bruñido | hubo bruñido | había bruñido | habrá bruñido | habría bruñido | haya bruñido | hubiera bruñido |
| hemos bruñido | hubimos bruñido | habíamos bruñido | habremos bruñido | habríamos bruñido | hayamos bruñido | hubiéramos bruñido |
| habéis bruñido | hubisteis bruñido | habíais bruñido | habréis bruñido | habríais bruñido | hayáis bruñido | hubierais bruñido |
| han bruñido | hubieron bruñido | habían bruñido | habrán bruñido | habrían bruñido | hayan bruñido | hubieran bruñido |

◆ tañer (*to strum fingers*); **Gerund:** tañendo; **Past participle:** tañido

**Commands:** tañe (tú) no tañas (tú) tañid (vosotros) no tañáis (vosotros) taña (Ud.) tañan (Uds.) tañamos (nosotros)

## Simple Tenses

| Present | Preterit | Imperfect | Future | Conditional | Subjunctive | Imperfect Subjunctive |
|---------|----------|-----------|--------|-------------|-------------|----------------------|
| taño | tañí | tañía | tañeré | tañería | taña | tañera |
| tañes | tañiste | tañías | tañerás | tañerías | tañas | tañeras |
| tañe | tañó | tañía | tañerá | tañería | taña | tañera |
| tañemos | tañimos | tañíamos | tañeremos | tañeríamos | tañamos | tañéramos |
| tañéis | tañisteis | tañíais | tañeréis | tañeríais | tañáis | tañerais |
| tañen | tañeron | tañían | tañerán | tañerían | tañan | tañeran |

## Compound Tenses

| Present Perfect | Preterit Perfect | Pluperfect | Future Perfect | Conditional Perfect | Perfect Subjunctive | Pluperfect Subjunctive |
|-----------------|------------------|------------|----------------|--------------------|--------------------|-----------------------|
| he tañido | hube tañido | había tañido | habré tañido | habría tañido | haya tañido | hubiera tañido |
| has tañido | hubiste tañido | habías tañido | habrás tañido | habrías tañido | hayas tañido | hubieras tañido |
| ha tañido | hubo tañido | había tañido | habrá tañido | habría tañido | haya tañido | hubiera tañido |
| hemos tañido | hubimos tañido | habíamos tañido | habremos tañido | habríamos tañido | hayamos tañido | hubiéramos tañido |
| habéis tañido | hubisteis tañido | habíais tañido | habréis tañido | habríais tañido | hayáis tañido | hubierais tañido |
| han tañido | hubieron tañido | habían tañido | habrán tañido | habrían tañido | hayan tañido | hubieran tañido |

## -eer Verbs

♦ creer (*to believe*); **Gerund:** creyendo; **Past participle:** creído

**Commands:** cree (tú) no creas (tú) creed (vosotros) no creáis (vosotros) crea (Ud.) crean (Uds.) creamos (nosotros)

### Simple Tenses

| Present | Preterit | Imperfect | Future | Conditional | Subjunctive | Imperfect Subjunctive |
|---|---|---|---|---|---|---|
| creo | creí | creía | creeré | creería | crea | creyera |
| crees | creíste | creías | creerás | creerías | creas | creyeras |
| cree | creyó | creía | creerá | creería | crea | creyera |
| creemos | creímos | creíamos | creeremos | creeríamos | creamos | creyéramos |
| creéis | creísteis | creíais | creeréis | creeríais | creáis | creyerais |
| creen | creyeron | creían | creerán | creerían | crean | creyeran |

### Compound Tenses

| Present Perfect | Preterit Perfect | Pluperfect | Future Perfect | Conditional Perfect | Perfect Subjunctive | Pluperfect Subjunctive |
|---|---|---|---|---|---|---|
| he creído | hube creído | había creído | habré creído | habría creído | haya creído | hubiera creído |
| has creído | hubiste creído | habías creído | habrás creído | habrías creído | hayas creído | hubieras creído |
| ha creído | hubo creído | había creído | habrá creído | habría creído | haya creído | hubiera creído |
| hemos creído | hubimos creído | habíamos creído | habremos creído | habríamos creído | hayamos creído | hubiéramos creído |
| habéis creído | hubisteis creído | habíais creído | habréis creído | habríais creído | hayáis creído | hubierais creído |
| han creído | hubieron creído | habían creído | habrán creído | habrían creído | hayan creído | hubieran creído |

# Stem-Changing Verbs

## -ar Verbs e to ie

◆ cerrar (*to close*); **Gerund:** cerrando; **Past participle:** cerrado

**Commands:** cierra (tú) no cierres (tú) cerrad (vosotros) no cerréis (vosotros) cierre (Ud.) cierren (Uds.) cerremos (nosotros)

### Simple Tenses

| Present | Preterit | Imperfect | Future | Conditional | Subjunctive | Imperfect Subjunctive |
|---|---|---|---|---|---|---|
| cierro | cerré | cerraba | cerraré | cerraría | cierre | cerrara |
| cierras | cerraste | cerrabas | cerrarás | cerrarías | cierres | cerraras |
| cierra | cerró | cerraba | cerrará | cerraría | cierre | cerrara |
| cerramos | cerramos | cerrábamos | cerraremos | cerraríamos | cerremos | cerráramos |
| cerráis | cerrasteis | cerrabais | cerraréis | cerraríais | cerréis | cerrarais |
| cierran | cerraron | cerraban | cerrarán | cerrarían | cierren | cerraran |

### Compound Tenses

| Present Perfect | Preterit Perfect | Pluperfect | Future Perfect | Conditional Perfect | Perfect Subjunctive | Pluperfect Subjunctive |
|---|---|---|---|---|---|---|
| he cerrado | hube cerrado | había cerrado | habré cerrado | habría cerrado | haya cerrado | hubiera cerrado |
| has cerrado | hubiste cerrado | habías cerrado | habrás cerrado | habrías cerrado | hayas cerrado | hubieras cerrado |
| ha cerrado | hubo cerrado | había cerrado | habrá cerrado | habría cerrado | haya cerrado | hubiera cerrado |
| hemos cerrado | hubimos cerrado | habíamos cerrado | habremos cerrado | habríamos cerrado | hayamos cerrado | hubiéramos cerrado |
| habéis cerrado | hubisteis cerrado | habíais cerrado | habréis cerrado | habríais cerrado | hayáis cerrado | hubierais cerrado |
| han cerrado | hubieron cerrado | habían cerrado | habrán cerrado | habrían cerrado | hayan cerrado | hubieran cerrado |

## *-ar* Verbs *o* to *ue*

- mostrar (*to show*); **Gerund:** mostrando; **Past participle:** mostrado

  **Commands:** muestra (tú) no muestres (tú) mostrad (vosotros) no mostréis (vosotros) muestre (Ud.) muestren (Uds.) mostremos (nosotros)

### Simple Tenses

| Present | Preterit | Imperfect | Future | Conditional | Subjunctive | Imperfect Subjunctive |
|---|---|---|---|---|---|---|
| muestro | mostré | mostraba | mostraré | mostraría | muestre | mostrara |
| muestras | mostraste | mostrabas | mostrarás | mostrarías | muestres | mostraras |
| muestra | mostró | mostraba | mostrará | mostraría | muestre | mostrara |
| mostramos | mostramos | mostrábamos | mostraremos | mostraríamos | mostremos | mostráramos |
| mostráis | mostrasteis | mostrabais | mostraréis | mostraríais | mostréis | mostrarais |
| muestran | mostraron | mostraban | mostrarán | mostrarían | muestren | mostraran |

### Compound Tenses

| Present Perfect | Preterit Perfect | Pluperfect | Future Perfect | Conditional Perfect | Perfect Subjunctive | Pluperfect Subjunctive |
|---|---|---|---|---|---|---|
| he mostrado | hube mostrado | había mostrado | habré mostrado | habría mostrado | haya mostrado | hubiera mostrado |
| has mostrado | hubiste mostrado | habías mostrado | habrás mostrado | habrías mostrado | hayas mostrado | hubieras mostrado |
| ha mostrado | hubo mostrado | había mostrado | habrá mostrado | habría mostrado | haya mostrado | hubiera mostrado |
| hemos mostrado | hubimos mostrado | habíamos mostrado | habremos mostrado | habríamos mostrado | hayamos mostrado | hubiéramos mostrado |
| habéis mostrado | hubisteis mostrado | habíais mostrado | habréis mostrado | habríais mostrado | hayáis mostrado | hubierais mostrado |
| han mostrado | hubieron mostrado | habían mostrado | habrán mostrado | habrían mostrado | hayan mostrado | hubieran mostrado |

## *-er* Verbs *e* to *ie*

◆ perder (*to lose*); **Gerund:** perdiendo; **Past participle:** perdido

**Commands:** pierde (tú) no pierdas (tú) perded (vosotros) no perdáis (vosotros) pierda (Ud.) pierdan (Uds.) perdamos (nosotros)

### Simple Tenses

| Present | Preterit | Imperfect | Future | Conditional | Subjunctive | Imperfect Subjunctive |
|---|---|---|---|---|---|---|
| pierdo | perdí | perdía | perderé | perdería | pierda | perdiera |
| pierdes | perdiste | perdías | perderás | perderías | pierdas | perdieras |
| pierde | perdió | perdía | perderá | perdería | pierda | perdiera |
| perdemos | perdimos | perdíamos | perderemos | perderíamos | perdamos | perdiéramos |
| perdéis | perdisteis | perdíais | perderéis | perderíais | perdáis | perdierais |
| pierden | perdieron | perdían | perderán | perderían | pierdan | perdieran |

### Compound Tenses

| Present Perfect | Preterit Perfect | Pluperfect | Future Perfect | Conditional Perfect | Perfect Subjunctive | Pluperfect Subjunctive |
|---|---|---|---|---|---|---|
| he perdido | hube perdido | había perdido | habré perdido | habría perdido | haya perdido | hubiera perdido |
| has perdido | hubiste perdido | habías perdido | habrás perdido | habrías perdido | hayas perdido | hubieras perdido |
| ha perdido | hubo perdido | había perdido | habrá perdido | habría perdido | haya perdido | hubiera perdido |
| hemos perdido | hubimos perdido | habíamos perdido | habremos perdido | habríamos perdido | hayamos perdido | hubiéramos perdido |
| habéis perdido | hubisteis perdido | habíais perdido | habréis perdido | habríais perdido | hayáis perdido | hubierais perdido |
| han perdido | hubieron perdido | habían perdido | habrán perdido | habrían perdido | hayan perdido | hubieran perdido |

## -er Verbs o to ue

◆ morder (*to bite*); **Gerund:** mordiendo; **Past participle:** mordido

**Commands:** muerde (tú) no muerdas (tú) morded (vosotros) no mordáis (vosotros) muerda (Ud.) muerdan (Uds.) mordamos (nosotros)

### Simple Tenses

| Present | Preterit | Imperfect | Future | Conditional | Subjunctive | Imperfect Subjunctive |
|---|---|---|---|---|---|---|
| muerdo | mordí | mordía | morderé | mordería | muerda | mordiera |
| muerdes | mordiste | mordías | morderás | morderías | muerdas | mordieras |
| muerde | mordió | mordía | morderá | mordería | muerda | mordiera |
| mordemos | mordimos | mordíamos | morderemos | morderíamos | mordamos | mordiéramos |
| mordéis | mordisteis | mordíais | morderéis | morderíais | mordáis | mordierais |
| muerden | mordieron | mordían | morderán | morderían | muerdan | mordieran |

### Compound Tenses

| Present Perfect | Preterit Perfect | Pluperfect | Future Perfect | Conditional Perfect | Perfect Subjunctive | Pluperfect Subjunctive |
|---|---|---|---|---|---|---|
| he mordido | hube mordido | había mordido | habré mordido | habría mordido | haya mordido | hubiera mordido |
| has mordido | hubiste mordido | habías mordido | habrás mordido | habrías mordido | hayas mordido | hubieras mordido |
| ha mordido | hubo mordido | había mordido | habrá mordido | habría mordido | haya mordido | hubiera mordido |
| hemos mordido | hubimos mordido | habíamos mordido | habremos mordido | habríamos mordido | hayamos mordido | hubiéramos mordido |
| habéis mordido | hubisteis mordido | habíais mordido | habréis mordido | habríais mordido | hayáis mordido | hubierais mordido |
| han mordido | hubieron mordido | habían mordido | habrán mordido | habrían mordido | hayan mordido | hubieran mordido |

## -ir Verbs e to ie

◆ mentir (*to lie*); **Gerund:** mintiendo; **Past participle:** mentido

**Commands:** miente (tú) no mientas (tú) mentid (vosotros) no mintáis (vosotros) mienta (Ud.) mientan (Uds.) mintamos (nosotros)

### Simple Tenses

| Present | Preterit | Imperfect | Future | Conditional | Subjunctive | Imperfect Subjunctive |
|---|---|---|---|---|---|---|
| miento | mentí | mentía | mentiré | mentiría | mienta | mintiera |
| mientes | mentiste | mentías | mentirás | mentirías | mientas | mintieras |
| miente | mintió | mentía | mentirá | mentiría | mienta | mintiera |
| mentimos | mentimos | mentíamos | mentiremos | mentiríamos | mintamos | mintiéramos |
| mentís | mentisteis | mentíais | mentiréis | mentiríais | mintáis | mintierais |
| mienten | mintieron | mentían | mentirán | mentirían | mientan | mintieran |

### Compound Tenses

| Present Perfect | Preterit Perfect | Pluperfect | Future Perfect | Conditional Perfect | Perfect Subjunctive | Pluperfect Subjunctive |
|---|---|---|---|---|---|---|
| he mentido | hube mentido | había mentido | habré mentido | habría mentido | haya mentido | hubiera mentido |
| has mentido | hubiste mentido | habías mentido | habrás mentido | habrías mentido | hayas mentido | hubieras mentido |
| ha mentido | hubo mentido | había mentido | habrá mentido | habría mentido | haya mentido | hubiera mentido |
| hemos mentido | hubimos mentido | habíamos mentido | habremos mentido | habríamos mentido | hayamos mentido | hubiéramos mentido |
| habéis mentido | hubisteis mentido | habíais mentido | habréis mentido | habríais mentido | hayáis mentido | hubierais mentido |
| han mentido | hubieron mentido | habían mentido | habrán mentido | habrían mentido | hayan mentido | hubieran mentido |

## -ir Verbs *i* to *ie*

- adquirir (*to acquire*) is conjugated in the same manner as inquirir, simply substitute *ad* for *in* as the prefix.
- inquirir (*to inquire*); **Gerund:** inquiriendo; **Past participle:** inquirido

**Commands:** inquiere (tú) no inquieras (tú) inquirid (vosotros) no inquiráis (vosotros) inquiera (Ud.) inquieran (Uds.) inquiramos (nosotros)

### Simple Tenses

| Present | Preterit | Imperfect | Future | Conditional | Subjunctive | Imperfect Subjunctive |
|---|---|---|---|---|---|---|
| inquiero | inquirí | inquiría | inquiriré | inquiriría | inquiera | inquiriera |
| inquieres | inquiriste | inquirías | inquirirás | inquirirías | inquieras | inquirieras |
| inquiere | inquirió | inquiría | inquirirá | inquiriría | inquiera | inquiriera |
| inquirimos | inquirimos | inquiríamos | inquiriremos | inquiriríamos | inquiramos | inquiriéramos |
| inquirís | inquiristeis | inquiríais | inquiriréis | inquiriríais | inquiráis | inquirierais |
| inquieren | inquirieron | inquirían | inquirirán | inquirirían | inquieran | inquirieran |

### Compound Tenses

| Present Perfect | Preterit Perfect | Pluperfect | Future Perfect | Conditional Perfect | Perfect Subjunctive | Pluperfect Subjunctive |
|---|---|---|---|---|---|---|
| he inquirido | hube inquirido | había inquirido | habré inquirido | habría inquirido | haya inquirido | hubiera inquirido |
| has inquirido | hubiste inquirido | habías inquirido | habrás inquirido | habrías inquirido | hayas inquirido | hubieras inquirido |
| ha inquirido | hubo inquirido | había inquirido | habrá inquirido | habría inquirido | haya inquirido | hubiera inquirido |
| hemos inquirido | hubimos inquirido | habíamos inquirido | habremos inquirido | habríamos inquirido | hayamos inquirido | hubiéramos inquirido |
| habéis inquirido | hubisteis inquirido | habíais inquirido | habréis inquirido | habríais inquirido | hayáis inquirido | hubierais inquirido |
| han inquirido | hubieron inquirido | habían inquirido | habrán inquirido | habrían inquirido | hayan inquirido | hubieran inquirido |

## -ir Verbs o to ue

◆ dormir (*to sleep*); **Gerund:** durmiendo; **Past participle:** dormido

**Commands:** duerme (tú) no duermas (tú) dormid (vosotros) no durmáis (vosotros) duerma (Ud.) duerman (Uds.) durmamos (nosotros)

### Simple Tenses

| Present | Preterit | Imperfect | Future | Conditional | Subjunctive | Imperfect Subjunctive |
|---------|----------|-----------|--------|-------------|-------------|------------------------|
| duermo | dormí | dormía | dormiré | dormiría | duerma | durmiera |
| duermes | dormiste | dormías | dormirás | dormirías | duermas | durmieras |
| duerme | durmió | dormía | dormirá | dormiría | duerma | durmiera |
| dormimos | dormimos | dormíamos | dormiremos | dormiríamos | durmamos | durmiéramos |
| dormís | dormisteis | dormíais | dormiréis | dormiríais | durmáis | durmierais |
| duermen | durmieron | dormían | dormirán | dormirían | duerman | durmieran |

### Compound Tenses

| Present Perfect | Preterit Perfect | Pluperfect | Future Perfect | Conditional Perfect | Perfect Subjunctive | Pluperfect Subjunctive |
|-----------------|------------------|------------|----------------|---------------------|---------------------|------------------------|
| he dormido | hube dormido | había dormido | habré dormido | habría dormido | haya dormido | hubiera dormido |
| has dormido | hubiste dormido | habías dormido | habrás dormido | habrías dormido | hayas dormido | hubieras dormido |
| ha dormido | hubo dormido | había dormido | habrá dormido | habría dormido | haya dormido | hubiera dormido |
| hemos dormido | hubimos dormido | habíamos dormido | habremos dormido | habríamos dormido | hayamos dormido | hubiéramos dormido |
| habéis dormido | hubisteis dormido | habíais dormido | habréis dormido | habríais dormido | hayáis dormido | hubierais dormido |
| han dormido | hubieron dormido | habían dormido | habrán dormido | habrían dormido | hayan dormido | hubieran dormido |

## *-ir* Verbs *e* to *i*

◆ pedir (*to ask*); **Gerund:** pidiendo; **Past participle:** pedido

**Commands:** pide (tú) no pidas (tú) pedid (vosotros) no pidáis (vosotros) pida (Ud.) pidan (Uds.) pidamos (nosotros)

### Simple Tenses

| Present | Preterit | Imperfect | Future | Conditional | Subjunctive | Imperfect Subjunctive |
|---|---|---|---|---|---|---|
| pido | pedí | pedía | pediré | pediría | pida | pidiera |
| pides | pediste | pedías | pedirás | pedirías | pidas | pidieras |
| pide | pidió | pedía | pedirá | pediría | pida | pidiera |
| pedimos | pedimos | pedíamos | pediremos | pediríamos | pidamos | pidiéramos |
| pedís | pedisteis | pedíais | pediréis | pediríais | pidáis | pidierais |
| piden | pidieron | pedían | pedirán | pedirían | pidan | pidieran |

### Compound Tenses

| Present Perfect | Preterit Perfect | Pluperfect | Future Perfect | Conditional Perfect | Perfect Subjunctive | Pluperfect Subjunctive |
|---|---|---|---|---|---|---|
| he pedido | hube pedido | había pedido | habré pedido | habría pedido | haya pedido | hubiera pedido |
| has pedido | hubiste pedido | habías pedido | habrás pedido | habrías pedido | hayas pedido | hubieras pedido |
| ha pedido | hubo pedido | había pedido | habrá pedido | habría pedido | haya pedido | hubiera pedido |
| hemos pedido | hubimos pedido | habíamos pedido | habremos pedido | habríamos pedido | hayamos pedido | hubiéramos pedido |
| habéis pedido | hubisteis pedido | habíais pedido | habréis pedido | habríais pedido | hayáis pedido | hubierais pedido |
| han pedido | hubieron pedido | habían pedido | habrán pedido | habrían pedido | hayan pedido | hubieran pedido |

# Verbs with *ai to aí, au to aú,* or *eu to eú*

◆ reunir (to join); **Gerund:** reuniendo; **Past participle:** reunido

**Commands:** reúne (tú) no reúnas (tú) reunid (vosotros) no reunáis (vosotros) reúna (Ud.) reúnan (Uds.) reunamos (nosotros)

## Simple Tenses

| Present | Preterit | Imperfect | Future | Conditional | Subjunctive | Imperfect Subjunctive |
|---|---|---|---|---|---|---|
| reúno | reuní | reunía | reuniré | reuniría | reúna | reuniera |
| reúnes | reuniste | reunías | reunirás | reunirías | reúnas | reunieras |
| reúne | reunió | reunía | reunirá | reuniría | reúna | reuniera |
| reunimos | reunimos | reuníamos | reuniremos | reuniríamos | reunamos | reuniéramos |
| reunís | reunisteis | reuníais | reuniréis | reuniríais | reunáis | reunierais |
| reúnen | reunieron | reunían | reunirán | reunirían | reúnan | reunieran |

## Compound Tenses

| Present Perfect | Preterit Perfect | Pluperfect | Future Perfect | Conditional Perfect | Perfect Subjunctive | Pluperfect Subjunctive |
|---|---|---|---|---|---|---|
| he reunido | hube reunido | había reunido | habré reunido | habría reunido | haya reunido | hubiera reunido |
| has reunido | hubiste reunido | habías reunido | habrás reunido | habrías reunido | hayas reunido | hubieras reunido |
| ha reunido | hubo reunido | había reunido | habrá reunido | habría reunido | haya reunido | hubiera reunido |
| hemos reunido | hubimos reunido | habíamos reunido | habremos reunido | habríamos reunido | hayamos reunido | hubiéramos reunido |
| habéis reunido | hubisteis reunido | habíais reunido | habréis reunido | habríais reunido | hayáis reunido | hubierais reunido |
| han reunido | hubieron reunido | habían reunido | habrán reunido | habrían reunido | hayan reunido | hubieran reunido |

Note *ai* to *aí*, and *au* to *aú* place accents in the persons and tenses shown above.

## -*car* Verbs with *o* to *ue* Spelling Change

◆ volcar (*to overturn*); Gerund: volcando; Past participle: volcado

**Commands:** vuelca (tú) no vuelques (tú) volcad (vosotros) no volquéis (vosotros) vuelque (Ud.) vuelquen (Uds.) volquemos (nosotros)

### Simple Tenses

| Present | Preterit | Imperfect | Future | Conditional | Subjunctive | Imperfect Subjunctive |
|---|---|---|---|---|---|---|
| vuelco | volqué | volcaba | volcaré | volcaría | vuelque | volcara |
| vuelcas | volcaste | volcabas | volcarás | volcarías | vuelques | volcaras |
| vuelca | volcó | volcaba | volcará | volcaría | vuelque | volcara |
| volcamos | volcamos | volcábamos | volcaremos | volcaríamos | volquemos | volcáramos |
| volcáis | volcasteis | volcabais | volcaréis | volcaríais | volquéis | volcarais |
| vuelcan | volcaron | volcaban | volcarán | volcarían | vuelquen | volcaran |

### Compound Tenses

| Present Perfect | Preterit Perfect | Pluperfect | Future Perfect | Conditional Perfect | Perfect Subjunctive | Pluperfect Subjunctive |
|---|---|---|---|---|---|---|
| he volcado | hube volcado | había volcado | habré volcado | habría volcado | haya volcado | hubiera volcado |
| has volcado | hubiste volcado | habías volcado | habrás volcado | habrías volcado | hayas volcado | hubieras volcado |
| ha volcado | hubo volcado | había volcado | habrá volcado | habría volcado | haya volcado | hubiera volcado |
| hemos volcado | hubimos volcado | habíamos volcado | habremos volcado | habríamos volcado | hayamos volcado | hubiéramos volcado |
| habéis volcado | hubisteis volcado | habíais volcado | habréis volcado | habríais volcado | hayáis volcado | hubierais volcado |
| han volcado | hubieron volcado | habían volcado | habrán volcado | habrían volcado | hayan volcado | hubieran volcado |

## -*gar* Verbs with *i* to *ie* Spelling Change

◆ negar (*to deny*); **Gerund:** negando; **Past participle:** negado

**Commands:** niega (tú) no niegues (tú) negad (vosotros) no neguéis (vosotros) niegue (Ud.) nieguen (Uds.) neguemos (nosotros)

### Simple Tenses

| Present | Preterit | Imperfect | Future | Conditional | Subjunctive | Imperfect Subjunctive |
|---------|----------|-----------|--------|-------------|-------------|-----------------------|
| niego | negué | negaba | negaré | negaría | niegue | negara |
| niegas | negaste | negabas | negarás | negarías | niegues | negaras |
| niega | negó | negaba | negará | negaría | niegue | negara |
| negamos | negamos | negábamos | negaremos | negaríamos | neguemos | negáramos |
| negáis | negasteis | negabais | negaréis | negaríais | neguéis | negarais |
| niegan | negaron | negaban | negarán | negarían | nieguen | negaran |

### Compound Tenses

| Present Perfect | Preterit Perfect | Pluperfect | Future Perfect | Conditional Perfect | Perfect Subjunctive | Pluperfect Subjunctive |
|-----------------|------------------|------------|----------------|---------------------|---------------------|------------------------|
| he negado | hube negado | había negado | habré negado | habría negado | haya negado | hubiera negado |
| has negado | hubiste negado | habías negado | habrás negado | habrías negado | hayas negado | hubieras negado |
| ha negado | hubo negado | había negado | habrá negado | habría negado | haya negado | hubiera negado |
| hemos negado | hubimos negado | habíamos negado | habremos negado | habríamos negado | hayamos negado | hubiéramos negado |
| habéis negado | hubisteis negado | habíais negado | habréis negado | habríais negado | hayáis negado | hubierais negado |
| han negado | hubieron negado | habían negado | habrán negado | habrían negado | hayan negado | hubieran negado |

## -gar Verbs with o to ue Spelling Change

◆ rogar (*to beg*); **Gerund:** rogando; **Past participle:** rogado

**Commands:** ruega (tú) no ruegues (tú) rogad (vosotros) no roguéis (vosotros) ruegue (Ud.) rueguen (Uds.) roguemos (nosotros)

### Simple Tenses

| Present | Preterit | Imperfect | Future | Conditional | Subjunctive | Imperfect Subjunctive |
|---|---|---|---|---|---|---|
| ruego | rogué | rogaba | rogaré | rogaría | ruegue | rogara |
| ruegas | rogaste | rogabas | rogarás | rogarías | ruegues | rogaras |
| ruega | rogó | rogaba | rogará | rogaría | ruegue | rogara |
| rogamos | rogamos | rogábamos | rogaremos | rogaríamos | roguemos | rogáramos |
| rogáis | rogasteis | rogabais | rogaréis | rogaríais | roguéis | rogarais |
| ruegan | rogaron | rogaban | rogarán | rogarían | rueguen | rogaran |

### Compound Tenses

| Present Perfect | Preterit Perfect | Pluperfect | Future Perfect | Conditional Perfect | Perfect Subjunctive | Pluperfect Subjunctive |
|---|---|---|---|---|---|---|
| he rogado | hube rogado | había rogado | habré rogado | habría rogado | haya rogado | hubiera rogado |
| has rogado | hubiste rogado | habías rogado | habrás rogado | habrías rogado | hayas rogado | hubieras rogado |
| ha rogado | hubo rogado | había rogado | habrá rogado | habría rogado | haya rogado | hubiera rogado |
| hemos rogado | hubimos rogado | habíamos rogado | habremos rogado | habríamos rogado | hayamos rogado | hubiéramos rogado |
| habéis rogado | hubisteis rogado | habíais rogado | habréis rogado | habríais rogado | hayáis rogado | hubierais rogado |
| han rogado | hubieron rogado | habían rogado | habrán rogado | habrían rogado | hayan rogado | hubieran rogado |

◆ jugar (*to play*); **Gerund:** jugando; **Past participle:** jugado

   **Commands:** juega (tú) no juegues (tú) jugad (vosotros) no juguéis (vosotros) juegue (Ud.) jueguen (Uds.) jueguemos (nosotros)

## Simple Tenses

| Present | Preterit | Imperfect | Future | Conditional | Subjunctive | Imperfect Subjunctive |
|---------|----------|-----------|--------|-------------|-------------|------------------------|
| juego | jugué | jugaba | jugaré | jugaría | juegue | jugara |
| juegas | jugaste | jugabas | jugarás | jugarías | juegues | jugaras |
| juega | jugó | jugaba | jugará | jugaría | juegue | jugara |
| jugamos | jugamos | jugábamos | jugaremos | jugaríamos | juguemos | jugáramos |
| jugáis | jugasteis | jugabais | jugaréis | jugaríais | juguéis | jugarais |
| juegan | jugaron | jugaban | jugarán | jugarían | jueguen | jugaran |

## Compound Tenses

| Present Perfect | Preterit Perfect | Pluperfect | Future Perfect | Conditional Perfect | Perfect Subjunctive | Pluperfect Subjunctive |
|-----------------|------------------|------------|----------------|---------------------|---------------------|------------------------|
| he jugado | hube jugado | había jugado | habré jugado | habría jugado | haya jugado | hubiera jugado |
| has jugado | hubiste jugado | habías jugado | habrás jugado | habrías jugado | hayas jugado | hubieras jugado |
| ha jugado | hubo jugado | había jugado | habrá jugado | habría jugado | haya jugado | hubiera jugado |
| hemos jugado | hubimos jugado | habíamos jugado | habremos jugado | habríamos jugado | hayamos jugado | hubiéramos jugado |
| habéis jugado | hubisteis jugado | habíais jugado | habréis jugado | habríais jugado | hayáis jugado | hubierais jugado |
| han jugado | hubieron jugado | habían jugado | habrán jugado | habrían jugado | hayan jugado | hubieran jugado |

## *-zar* Verbs with *i* to *ie* Spelling Change

◆ comenzar (*to begin*); **Gerund:** comenzando; **Past participle:** comenzado

**Commands:** comienza (tú) no comiences (tú) comenzad (vosotros) no comencéis (vosotros) comience (Ud.) comiencen (Uds.) comencemos (nosotros)

### Simple Tenses

| Present | Preterit | Imperfect | Future | Conditional | Subjunctive | Imperfect Subjunctive |
|---|---|---|---|---|---|---|
| comienzo | comencé | comenzaba | comenzaré | comenzaría | comience | comenzara |
| comienzas | comenzaste | comenzabas | comenzarás | comenzarías | comiences | comenzaras |
| comienza | comenzó | comenzaba | comenzará | comenzaría | comience | comenzara |
| comenzamos | comenzamos | comenzábamos | comenzaremos | comenzaríamos | comencemos | comenzáramos |
| comenzáis | comenzasteis | comenzabais | comenzaréis | comenzaríais | comencéis | comenzarais |
| comienzan | comenzaron | comenzaban | comenzarán | comenzarían | comiencen | comenzaran |

### Compound Tenses

| Present Perfect | Preterit Perfect | Pluperfect | Future Perfect | Conditional Perfect | Perfect Subjunctive | Pluperfect Subjunctive |
|---|---|---|---|---|---|---|
| he comenzado | hube comenzado | había comenzado | habré comenzado | habría comenzado | haya comenzado | hubiera comenzado |
| has comenzado | hubiste comenzado | habías comenzado | habrás comenzado | habrías comenzado | hayas comenzado | hubieras comenzado |
| ha comenzado | hubo comenzado | había comenzado | habrá comenzado | habría comenzado | haya comenzado | hubiera comenzado |
| hemos comenzado | hubimos comenzado | habíamos comenzado | habremos comenzado | habríamos comenzado | hayamos comenzado | hubiéramos comenzado |
| habéis comenzado | hubisteis comenzado | habíais comenzado | habréis comenzado | habríais comenzado | hayáis comenzado | hubierais comenzado |
| han comenzado | hubieron comenzado | habían comenzado | habrán comenzado | habrían comenzado | hayan comenzado | hubieran comenzado |

## *-zar* Verbs with *o* to *ue* Spelling Change

◆ almorzar (*to eat lunch*); **Gerund:** almorzando; **Past participle:** almorzado

**Commands:** almuerza (tú) no almuerces (tú) almorzad (vosotros) no almorcéis (vosotros) almuerce (Ud.) almuercen (Uds.) almorcemos (nosotros)

### Simple Tenses

| Present | Preterit | Imperfect | Future | Conditional | Subjunctive | Imperfect Subjunctive |
|---|---|---|---|---|---|---|
| almuerzo | almorcé | almorzaba | almorzaré | almorzaría | almuerce | almorzara |
| almuerzas | almorzaste | almorzabas | almorzarás | almorzarías | almuerces | almorzaras |
| almuerza | almorzó | almorzaba | almorzará | almorzaría | almuerce | almorzara |
| almorzamos | almorzamos | almorzábamos | almonzaremos | almorzaríamos | almorcemos | almorzáramos |
| almorzáis | almorzasteis | almorzabais | almonzaréis | almorzaríais | almorcéis | almorzarais |
| almuerzan | almorzaron | almorzaban | almorzarán | almorzarían | almuercen | almorzaran |

### Compound Tenses

| Present Perfect | Preterit Perfect | Pluperfect | Future Perfect | Conditional Perfect | Perfect Subjunctive | Pluperfect Subjunctive |
|---|---|---|---|---|---|---|
| he almorzado | hube almorzado | había almorzado | habré almorzado | habría almorzado | haya almorzado | hubiera almorzado |
| has almorzado | hubiste almorzado | habías almorzado | habrás almorzado | habrías almorzado | hayas almorzado | hubieras almorzado |
| ha almorzado | hubo almorzado | había almorzado | habrá almorzado | habría almorzado | haya almorzado | hubiera almorzado |
| hemos almorzado | hubimos almorzado | habíamos almorzado | habremos almorzado | habríamos almorzado | hayamos almorzado | hubiéramos almorzado |
| habéis almorzado | hubisteis almorzado | habíais almorzado | habréis almorzado | habríais almorzado | hayáis almorzado | hubierais almorzado |
| han almorzado | hubieron almorzado | habían almorzado | habrán almorzado | habrían almorzado | hayan almorzado | hubieran almorzado |

## -zar Verbs with o to üe Spelling Change

◆ avergonzar (*shame*); **Gerund:** avergonzando; **Past participle:** avergonzado

**Commands:** avergüenza (tú) no avergüences (tú) avergonzad (vosotros) no avergoncéis (vosotros) avergüence (Ud.) avergüencen (Uds.) avergoncemos (nosotros)

### Simple Tenses

| Present | Preterit | Imperfect | Future | Conditional | Subjunctive | Imperfect Subjunctive |
|---|---|---|---|---|---|---|
| avergüenzo | avergoncé | avergonzaba | avergonzaré | avergonzaría | avergüence | avergonzara |
| avergüenzas | avergonzaste | avergonzabas | avergonzarás | avergonzarías | avergüences | avergonzaras |
| avergüenza | avergonzó | avergonzaba | avergonzará | avergonzaría | avergüence | avergonzara |
| avergonzamos | avergonzamos | avergonzábamos | avergonzaremos | avergonzaríamos | avergoncemos | avergonzáramos |
| avergonzáis | avergonzasteis | avergonzabais | avergonzaréis | avergonzaríais | avergoncéis | avergonzarais |
| avergüenzan | avergonzaron | avergonzaban | avergonzarán | avergonzarían | avergüencen | avergonzaran |

### Compound Tenses

| Present Perfect | Preterit Perfect | Pluperfect | Future Perfect | Conditional Perfect | Perfect Subjunctive | Pluperfect Subjunctive |
|---|---|---|---|---|---|---|
| he avergonzado | hube avergonzado | había avergonzado | habré avergonzado | habría avergonzado | haya avergonzado | hubiera avergonzado |
| has avergonzado | hubiste avergonzado | habías avergonzado | habrás avergonzado | habrías avergonzado | hayas avergonzado | hubieras avergonzado |
| ha avergonzado | hubo avergonzado | había avergonzado | habrá avergonzado | habría avergonzado | haya avergonzado | hubiera avergonzado |
| hemos avergonzado | hubimos avergonzado | habíamos avergonzado | habremos avergonzado | habríamos avergonzado | hayamos avergonzado | hubiéramos avergonzado |
| habéis avergonzado | hubisteis avergonzado | habíais avergonzado | habréis avergonzado | habríais avergonzado | hayáis avergonzado | hubierais avergonzado |
| han avergonzado | hubieron avergonzado | habían avergonzado | habrán avergonzado | habrían avergonzado | hayan avergonzado | hubieran avergonzado |

## *-cer* Verbs with *o* to *ue* Spelling Change

◆ cocer (*to cook*); **Gerund:** cociendo; **Past participle:** cocido

**Commands:** cuece (tú) no cuezas (tú) coced (vosotros) no cozáis (vosotros) cueza (Ud.) cuezan (Uds.) cozamos (nosotros)

### Simple Tenses

| Present | Preterit | Imperfect | Future | Conditional | Subjunctive | Imperfect Subjunctive |
|---|---|---|---|---|---|---|
| **cuezo** | cocí | cocía | coceré | cocería | **cueza** | cociera |
| **cueces** | cociste | cocías | cocerás | cocerías | **cuezas** | cocieras |
| **cuece** | coció | cocía | cocerá | cocería | **cueza** | cociera |
| **cocemos** | cocimos | cocíamos | coceremos | coceríamos | **cozamos** | cociéramos |
| **cocéis** | cocisteis | cocíais | coceréis | coceríais | **cozáis** | cocierais |
| **cuecen** | cocieron | cocían | cocerán | cocerían | **cuezan** | cocieran |

### Compound Tenses

| Present Perfect | Preterit Perfect | Pluperfect | Future Perfect | Conditional Perfect | Perfect Subjunctive | Pluperfect Subjunctive |
|---|---|---|---|---|---|---|
| he cocido | hube cocido | había cocido | habré cocido | habría cocido | haya cocido | hubiera cocido |
| has cocido | hubiste cocido | habías cocido | habrás cocido | habrías cocido | hayas cocido | hubieras cocido |
| ha cocido | hubo cocido | había cocido | habrá cocido | habría cocido | haya cocido | hubiera cocido |
| hemos cocido | hubimos cocido | habíamos cocido | habremos cocido | habríamos cocido | hayamos cocido | hubiéramos cocido |
| habéis cocido | hubisteis cocido | habíais cocido | habréis cocido | habríais cocido | hayáis cocido | hubierais cocido |
| han cocido | hubieron cocido | habían cocido | habrán cocido | habrían cocido | hayan cocido | hubieran cocido |

The verb *torcer* (*to twist*) undergoes the same changes in the same persons and tenses shown in the preceding table.

## -gir Verbs with e to i Spelling Change

- colegir (to collect); **Gerund:** coligiendo; **Past participle:** colegido

**Commands:** colige (tú) no colijas (tú) colegid (vosotros) no colijáis (vosotros) colija (Ud.) colijan (Uds.) colijamos (nosotros)

### Simple Tenses

| Present | Preterit | Imperfect | Future | Conditional | Subjunctive | Imperfect Subjunctive |
|---|---|---|---|---|---|---|
| colijo | colegí | colegía | colegiré | colegiría | colija | coligiera |
| coliges | colegiste | colegías | colegirás | colegirías | colijas | coligieras |
| colige | coligió | colegía | colegirá | colegiría | colija | coligiera |
| colegimos | colegimos | colegíamos | colegiremos | colegiríamos | colijamos | coligiéramos |
| colegís | colegisteis | colegíais | colegiréis | colegiríais | colijáis | coligierais |
| coligen | coligieron | colegían | colegirán | colegirían | colijan | coligieran |

### Compound Tenses

| Present Perfect | Preterit Perfect | Pluperfect | Future Perfect | Conditional Perfect | Perfect Subjunctive | Pluperfect Subjunctive |
|---|---|---|---|---|---|---|
| he colegido | hube colegido | había colegido | habré colegido | habría colegido | haya colegido | hubiera colegido |
| has colegido | hubiste colegido | habías colegido | habrás colegido | habrías colegido | hayas colegido | hubieras colegido |
| ha colegido | hubo colegido | había colegido | habrá colegido | habría colegido | haya colegido | hubiera colegido |
| hemos colegido | hubimos colegido | habíamos colegido | habremos colegido | habríamos colegido | hayamos colegido | hubiéramos colegido |
| habéis colegido | hubisteis colegido | habíais colegido | habréis colegido | habríais colegido | hayáis colegido | hubierais colegido |
| han colegido | hubieron colegido | habían colegido | habrán colegido | habrían colegido | hayan colegido | hubieran colegido |

# *-guir* Verbs with *i* to *ie* Spelling Change

◆ seguir (*to follow*); **Gerund:** siguiendo; **Past participle:** seguido

**Commands:** sigue (tú) no sigas (tú) seguid (vosotros) no sigáis (vosotros) siga (Ud.) sigan (Uds.) sigamos (nosotros)

## Simple Tenses

| Present | Preterit | Imperfect | Future | Conditional | Subjunctive | Imperfect Subjunctive |
|---|---|---|---|---|---|---|
| sigo | seguí | seguía | seguiré | seguiría | siga | siguiera |
| sigues | seguiste | seguías | seguirás | seguirías | sigas | siguieras |
| sigue | siguió | seguía | seguirá | seguiría | siga | siguiera |
| seguimos | seguimos | seguíamos | seguiremos | seguiríamos | sigamos | siguiéramos |
| seguís | seguisteis | seguíais | seguiréis | seguiríais | sigáis | siguierais |
| siguen | siguieron | seguían | seguirán | seguirían | sigan | siguieran |

## Compound Tenses

| Present Perfect | Preterit Perfect | Pluperfect | Future Perfect | Conditional Perfect | Perfect Subjunctive | Pluperfect Subjunctive |
|---|---|---|---|---|---|---|
| he seguido | hube seguido | había seguido | habré seguido | habría seguido | haya seguido | hubiera seguido |
| has seguido | hubiste seguido | habías seguido | habrás seguido | habrías seguido | hayas seguido | hubieras seguido |
| ha seguido | hubo seguido | había seguido | habrá seguido | habría seguido | haya seguido | hubiera seguido |
| hemos seguido | hubimos seguido | habíamos seguido | habremos seguido | habríamos seguido | hayamos seguido | hubiéramos seguido |
| habéis seguido | hubisteis seguido | habíais seguido | habréis seguido | habríais seguido | hayáis seguido | hubierais seguido |
| han seguido | hubieron seguido | habían seguido | habrán seguido | habrían seguido | hayan seguido | hubieran seguido |

# Irregular Verbs

- andar (*to walk*); **Gerund:** andando; **Past participle:** andado

    **Commands:** anda (tú) no andes (tú) andad (vosotros) no andéis (vosotros) ande (Ud.) anden (Uds.) andemos (nosotros)

## Simple Tenses

| Present | Preterit | Imperfect | Future | Conditional | Subjunctive | Imperfect Subjunctive |
|---|---|---|---|---|---|---|
| ando | anduve | andaba | andaré | andaría | ande | anduviera |
| andas | anduviste | andabas | andarás | andarías | andes | anduvieras |
| anda | anduvo | andaba | andará | andaría | ande | anduviera |
| andamos | anduvimos | andábamos | andaremos | andaríamos | andemos | anduviéramos |
| andáis | anduvisteis | andabais | andaréis | andaríais | andéis | anduvierais |
| andan | anduvieron | andaban | andarán | andarían | anden | anduvieran |

## Compound Tenses

| Present Perfect | Preterit Perfect | Pluperfect | Future Perfect | Conditional Perfect | Perfect Subjunctive | Pluperfect Subjunctive |
|---|---|---|---|---|---|---|
| he andado | hube andado | había andado | habré andado | habría andado | haya andado | hubiera andado |
| has andado | hubiste andado | habías andado | habrás andado | habrías andado | hayas andado | hubieras andado |
| ha andado | hubo andado | había andado | habrá andado | habría andado | haya andado | hubiera andado |
| hemos andado | hubimos andado | habíamos andado | habremos andado | habríamos andado | hayamos andado | hubiéramos andado |
| habéis andado | hubisteis andado | habíais andado | habréis andado | habríais andado | hayáis andado | hubierais andado |
| han andado | hubieron andado | habían andado | habrán andado | habrían andado | hayan andado | hubieran andado |

◆ argüir (*to argue*); **Gerund:** arguyendo; **Past participle:** argüido

**Commands: arguye** (tú) no **arguyas** (tú) argüid (vosotros) no **arguyáis** (vosotros) **arguya** (Ud.) **arguyan** (Uds.) **arguyamos** (nosotros)

## Simple Tenses

| Present | Preterit | Imperfect | Future | Conditional | Subjunctive | Imperfect Subjunctive |
|---|---|---|---|---|---|---|
| **arguyo** | argüí | argüía | argüiré | argüiría | **arguya** | **arguyera** |
| **arguyes** | argüiste | argüías | argüirás | argüirías | **arguyas** | **arguyeras** |
| **arguye** | **arguyó** | argüía | argüirá | argüiría | **arguya** | **arguyera** |
| **argüimos** | argüimos | argüíamos | argüiremos | argüiríamos | **arguyamos** | **arguyéramos** |
| **argüís** | argüisteis | argüíais | argüiréis | argüiríais | **arguyáis** | **arguyerais** |
| **arguyen** | **arguyeron** | argüían | argüirán | argüirían | **arguyan** | **arguyeran** |

## Compound Tenses

| Present Perfect | Preterit Perfect | Pluperfect | Future Perfect | Conditional Perfect | Perfect Subjunctive | Pluperfect Subjunctive |
|---|---|---|---|---|---|---|
| he argüido | hube argüido | había argüido | habré argüido | habría argüido | haya argüido | hubiera argüido |
| has argüido | hubiste argüido | habías argüido | habrás argüido | habrías argüido | hayas argüido | hubieras argüido |
| ha argüido | hubo argüido | había argüido | habrá argüido | habría argüido | haya argüido | hubiera argüido |
| hemos argüido | hubimos argüido | habíamos argüido | habremos argüido | habríamos argüido | hayamos argüido | hubiéramos argüido |
| habéis argüido | hubisteis argüido | habíais argüido | habréis argüido | habríais argüido | hayáis argüido | hubierais argüido |
| han argüido | hubieron argüido | habían argüido | habrán argüido | habrían argüido | hayan argüido | hubieran argüido |

◆ bendecir (*to bless*); **Gerund:** bendiciendo; **Past participle:** bendecido/bendito

**Commands: bendice** (tú) no **bendigas** (tú) bendecid (vosotros) no **bendigáis** (vosotros) **bendiga** (Ud.) **bendigan** (Uds.) **bendigamos** (nosotros)

## Simple Tenses

| Present | Preterit | Imperfect | Future | Conditional | Subjunctive | Imperfect Subjunctive |
|---|---|---|---|---|---|---|
| **bendigo** | **bendije** | bendecía | **bendeciré** | **bendeciría** | **bendiga** | **bendijera** |
| **bendices** | **bendijiste** | bendecías | **bendecirás** | **bendecirías** | **bendigas** | **bendijeras** |
| **bendice** | **bendijo** | bendecía | **bendecirá** | **bendeciría** | **bendiga** | **bendijera** |
| bendecimos | **bendijimos** | bendecíamos | **bendeciremos** | **bendeciríamos** | **bendigamos** | **bendijéramos** |
| bendecís | **bendijisteis** | bendecíais | **bendeciréis** | **bendeciríais** | **bendigáis** | **bendijerais** |
| bendicen | **bendijeron** | bendecían | **bendecirán** | **bendecirían** | **bendigan** | **bendijeran** |

## Compound Tenses

| Present Perfect | Preterit Perfect | Pluperfect | Future Perfect | Conditional Perfect | Perfect Subjunctive | Pluperfect Subjunctive |
|---|---|---|---|---|---|---|
| he bendecido | hube bendecido | había bendecido | habré bendecido | habría bendecido | haya bendecido | hubiera bendecido |
| has bendecido | hubiste bendecido | habías bendecido | habrás bendecido | habrías bendecido | hayas bendecido | hubieras bendecido |
| ha bendecido | hubo bendecido | había bendecido | habrá bendecido | habría bendecido | haya bendecido | hubiera bendecido |
| hemos bendecido | hubimos bendecido | habíamos bendecido | habremos bendecido | habríamos bendecido | hayamos bendecido | hubiéramos bendecido |
| habéis bendecido | hubisteis bendecido | habíais bendecido | habréis bendecido | habríais bendecido | hayáis bendecido | hubierais bendecido |
| han bendecido | hubieron bendecido | habían bendecido | habrán bendecido | habrían bendecido | hayan bendecido | hubieran bendecido |

♦ caber (*to fit*); **Gerund:** cabiendo; **Past participle:** cabido

**Commands:** cabe (tú) no quepas (tú) cabed (vosotros) no quepáis (vosotros) quepa (Ud.) quepan (Uds.) quepamos (nosotros)

## Simple Tenses

| Present | Imperfect | Preterit | Future | Conditional | Subjunctive | Imperfect Subjunctive |
|---|---|---|---|---|---|---|
| **quepo** | cabía | **cupe** | **cabré** | **cabría** | **quepa** | **cupiera** |
| cabes | cabías | **cupiste** | **cabrás** | **cabrías** | **quepas** | **cupieras** |
| cabe | cabía | **cupo** | **cabrá** | **cabría** | **quepa** | **cupiera** |
| cabemos | cabíamos | **cupimos** | **cabremos** | **cabríamos** | **quepamos** | **cupiéramos** |
| cabéis | cabíais | **cupisteis** | **cabréis** | **cabríais** | **quepáis** | **cupierais** |
| caben | cabían | **cupieron** | **cabrán** | **cabrían** | **quepan** | **cupieran** |

## Compound Tenses

| Present Perfect | Pluperfect | Preterit Perfect | Future Perfect | Conditional Perfect | Perfect Subjunctive | Pluperfect Subjunctive |
|---|---|---|---|---|---|---|
| he cabido | había cabido | hube cabido | habré cabido | habría cabido | haya cabido | hubiera cabido |
| has cabido | habías cabido | hubiste cabido | habrás cabido | habrías cabido | hayas cabido | hubieras cabido |
| ha cabido | había cabido | hubo cabido | habrá cabido | habría cabido | haya cabido | hubiera cabido |
| hemos cabido | habíamos cabido | hubimos cabido | habremos cabido | habríamos cabido | hayamos cabido | hubiéramos cabido |
| habéis cabido | habíais cabido | hubisteis cabido | habréis cabido | habríais cabido | hayáis cabido | hubierais cabido |
| han cabido | habían cabido | hubieron cabido | habrán cabido | habrían cabido | hayan cabido | hubieran cabido |

◆ caer (*to fall*); **Gerund:** cayendo; **Past participle:** caído

**Commands:** cae (tú) no caigas (tú) caed (vosotros) no caigáis (vosotros) caiga (Ud.) caigan (Uds.) caigamos (nosotros)

## Simple Tenses

| Present | Preterit | Imperfect | Future | Conditional | Subjunctive | Imperfect Subjunctive |
|---------|----------|-----------|--------|-------------|-------------|----------------------|
| **caigo** | caí | caía | caeré | caería | **caiga** | **cayera** |
| caes | caiste | caías | caerás | caerías | **caigas** | **cayeras** |
| cae | **cayó** | caía | caerá | caería | **caiga** | **cayera** |
| caemos | caímos | caíamos | caeremos | caeríamos | **caigamos** | **cayéramos** |
| caéis | caisteis | caíais | caeréis | caeríais | **caigáis** | **cayerais** |
| caen | **cayeron** | caían | caerán | caerían | **caigan** | **cayeran** |

## Compound Tenses

| Present Perfect | Preterit Perfect | Pluperfect | Future Perfect | Conditional Perfect | Perfect Subjunctive | Pluperfect Subjunctive |
|-----------------|------------------|------------|----------------|---------------------|---------------------|------------------------|
| he caído | hube caído | había caído | habré caído | habría caído | haya caído | hubiera caído |
| has caído | hubiste caído | habías caído | habrás caído | habrías caído | hayas caído | hubieras caído |
| ha caído | hubo caído | había caído | habrá caído | habría caído | haya caído | hubiera caído |
| hemos caído | hubimos caído | habíamos caído | habremos caído | habríamos caído | hayamos caído | hubiéramos caído |
| habéis caído | hubisteis caído | habíais caído | habréis caído | habríais caído | hayáis caído | hubierais caído |
| han caído | hubieron caído | habían caído | habrán caído | habrían caído | hayan caído | hubieran caído |

◆ dar (*to give*); **Gerund:** dando; **Past participle:** dado

**Commands:** da (tú) no des (tú) dad (vosotros) no deis (vosotros) **dé** (Ud.) den (Uds.) demos (nosotros)

## Simple Tenses

| Present | Preterit | Imperfect | Future | Conditional | Subjunctive | Imperfect Subjunctive |
|---|---|---|---|---|---|---|
| **doy** | **di** | daba | daré | daría | **dé** | **diera** |
| das | **diste** | dabas | darás | darías | des | **dieras** |
| da | **dió** | daba | dará | daría | **dé** | **diera** |
| damos | **dimos** | dábamos | daremos | daríamos | demos | **diéramos** |
| dáis | **disteis** | dabais | daréis | daríais | deis | **dierais** |
| dan | **dieron** | daban | darán | darían | den | **dieran** |

## Compound Tenses

| Present Perfect | Preterit Perfect | Pluperfect | Future Perfect | Conditional Perfect | Perfect Subjunctive | Pluperfect Subjunctive |
|---|---|---|---|---|---|---|
| he dado | hube dado | había dado | habré dado | habría dado | haya dado | hubiera dado |
| has dado | hubiste dado | habías dado | habrás dado | habrías dado | hayas dado | hubieras dado |
| ha dado | hubo dado | había dado | habrá dado | habría dado | haya dado | hubiera dado |
| hemos dado | hubimos dado | habíamos dado | habremos dado | habríamos dado | hayamos dado | hubiéramos dado |
| habéis dado | hubisteis dado | habíais dado | habréis dado | habríais dado | hayáis dado | hubierais dado |
| han dado | hubieron dado | habían dado | habrán dado | habrían dado | hayan dado | hubieran dado |

◆ decir (*to say, tell*); **Gerund:** diciendo; **Past participle:** dicho

**Commands: di** (tú) no digas (tú) decid (vosotros) no **digáis** (vosotros) **diga** (Ud.) **digan** (Uds.) **digamos** (nosotros)

## Simple Tenses

| Present | Preterit | Imperfect | Future | Conditional | Subjunctive | Imperfect Subjunctive |
|---|---|---|---|---|---|---|
| digo | dije | decía | diré | diría | diga | dijera |
| dices | dijiste | decías | dirás | dirías | digas | dijeras |
| dice | dijo | decía | dirá | diría | diga | dijera |
| decimos | dijimos | decíamos | diremos | diríamos | digamos | dijéramos |
| decís | dijisteis | decíais | diréis | diríais | digáis | dijerais |
| dicen | dijeron | decían | dirán | dirían | digan | dijeran |

## Compound Tenses

| Present Perfect | Preterit Perfect | Pluperfect | Future Perfect | Conditional Perfect | Perfect Subjunctive | Pluperfect Subjunctive |
|---|---|---|---|---|---|---|
| he dicho | hube dicho | había dicho | habré dicho | habría dicho | haya dicho | hubiera dicho |
| has dicho | hubiste dicho | habías dicho | habrás dicho | habrías dicho | hayas dicho | hubieras dicho |
| ha dicho | hubo dicho | había dicho | habrá dicho | habría dicho | haya dicho | hubiera dicho |
| hemos dicho | hubimos dicho | habíamos dicho | habremos dicho | habríamos dicho | hayamos dicho | hubiéramos dicho |
| habéis dicho | hubisteis dicho | habíais dicho | habréis dicho | habríais dicho | hayáis dicho | hubierais dicho |
| han dicho | hubieron dicho | habían dicho | habrán dicho | habrían dicho | hayan dicho | hubieran dicho |

◆ erguir (*to raise*); **Gerund: irguiendo; Past participle:** erguido

**Commands: yergue** (irgue) (tú) no **yergas** (irgas) (tú) erguid (vosotros) no **irgáis** (vosotros) **yerga** (irga) (Ud.) **yergan** (irgan) (Uds.) **yergamos** (nosotros)

## Simple Tenses

| Present | Preterit | Imperfect | Future | Conditional | Subjunctive | Imperfect Subjunctive |
|---|---|---|---|---|---|---|
| **yergo (irgo)** | erguí | erguía | erguiré | erguiría | **yerga (irga)** | irguiera |
| **yergues (irgues)** | erguiste | erguías | erguirás | erguirías | **yergas (irgas)** | irguieras |
| **yergue (irgue)** | **irguió** | erguía | erguirá | erguiría | **yerga (irga)** | irguiera |
| erguimos | erguimos | erguíamos | erguiremos | erguiríamos | **yergamos** | irguiéramos |
| erguís | erguisteis | erguíais | erguiréis | erguiríais | **yergáis** | irguierais |
| **yerguen (irguen)** | **irguieron** | erguían | erguirán | erguirían | **yergan (irgan)** | irguieran |

## Compound Tenses

| Present Perfect | Preterit Perfect | Pluperfect | Future Perfect | Conditional Perfect | Perfect Subjunctive | Pluperfect Subjunctive |
|---|---|---|---|---|---|---|
| he erguido | hube erguido | había erguido | habré erguido | habría erguido | haya erguido | hubiera erguido |
| has erguido | hubiste erguido | habías erguido | habrás erguido | habrías erguido | hayas erguido | hubieras erguido |
| ha erguido | hubo erguido | había erguido | habrá erguido | habría erguido | haya erguido | hubiera erguido |
| hemos erguido | hubimos erguido | habíamos erguido | habremos erguido | habríamos erguido | hayamos erguido | hubiéramos erguido |
| habéis erguido | hubisteis erguido | habíais erguido | habréis erguido | habríais erguido | hayáis erguido | hubierais erguido |
| han erguido | hubieron erguido | habían erguido | habrán erguido | habrían erguido | hayan erguido | hubieran erguido |

◆ errar (*to wander, err*); **Gerund:** errando; **Past participle:** errado

**Commands: yerra** (tú) no **yerres** (tú) errad (vosotros) no erréis (vosotros) **yerre** (Ud.) **yerren** (Uds.) erremos (nosotros)

## Simple Tenses

| Present | Preterit | Imperfect | Future | Conditional | Subjunctive | Imperfect Subjunctive |
|---------|----------|-----------|--------|-------------|-------------|-----------------------|
| yerro | erré | erraba | erraré | erraría | yerre | errara |
| yerras | erraste | errabas | errarás | errarías | yerres | erraras |
| yerra | erró | erraba | errará | erraría | yerre | errara |
| erramos | erramos | errábamos | erraremos | erraríamos | erremos | erráramos |
| erráis | errasteis | errabais | erraréis | erraríais | erréis | errarais |
| yerran | erraron | erraban | errarán | errarían | yerren | erraran |

## Compound Tenses

| Present Perfect | Preterit Perfect | Pluperfect | Future Perfect | Conditional Perfect | Perfect Subjunctive | Pluperfect Subjunctive |
|-----------------|------------------|------------|----------------|---------------------|---------------------|------------------------|
| he errado | hube errado | había errado | habré errado | habría errado | haya errado | hubiera errado |
| has errado | hubiste errado | habías errado | habrás errado | habrías errado | hayas errado | hubieras errado |
| ha errado | hubo errado | había errado | habrá errado | habría errado | haya errado | hubiera errado |
| hemos errado | hubimos errado | habíamos errado | habremos errado | habríamos errado | hayamos errado | hubiéramos errado |
| habéis errado | hubisteis errado | habíais errado | habréis errado | habríais errado | hayáis errado | hubierais errado |
| han errado | hubieron errado | habían errado | habrán errado | habrían errado | hayan errado | hubieran errado |

◆ estar (*to be*); **Gerund:** estando; **Past participle:** estado

**Commands:** está (tú) no **estés** (tú) estad (vosotros) no **estéis** (vosotros) **esté** (Ud.) **estén** (Uds.) **estemos** (nosotros)

## Simple Tenses

| Present | Preterit | Imperfect | Future | Conditional | Subjunctive | Imperfect Subjunctive |
|---|---|---|---|---|---|---|
| estoy | estuve | estaba | estaré | estaría | esté | estuviera |
| estás | estuviste | estabas | estarás | estarías | estés | estuvieras |
| está | estuvo | estaba | estará | estaría | esté | estuviera |
| estamos | estuvimos | estábamos | estaremos | estaríamos | estemos | estuviéramos |
| estáis | estuvisteis | estabais | estaréis | estaríais | estéis | estuvierais |
| están | estuvieron | estaban | estarán | estarían | estén | estuvieran |

## Compound Tenses

| Present Perfect | Pluperfect | Preterit Perfect | Future Perfect | Conditional Perfect | Perfect Subjunctive | Pluperfect Subjunctive |
|---|---|---|---|---|---|---|
| he estado | había estado | hube estado | habré estado | habría estado | haya estado | hubiera estado |
| has estado | habías estado | hubiste estado | habrás estado | habrías estado | hayas estado | hubieras estado |
| ha estado | había estado | hubo estado | habrá estado | habría estado | haya estado | hubiera estado |
| hemos estado | habíamos estado | hubimos estado | habremos estado | habríamos estado | hayamos estado | hubiéramos estado |
| habéis estado | habíais estado | hubisteis estado | habréis estado | habríais estado | hayáis estado | hubierais estado |
| han estado | habían estado | hubieron estado | habrán estado | habrían estado | hayan estado | hubieran estado |

◆ haber (*to have*); **Gerund:** habiendo; **Past participle:** habido

**Commands** (infrequently used): **hé** (tú) no hayas (tú) habed (vosotros) no hayáis (vosotros) haya (Ud.) hayan (Uds.) hayamos (nosotros)

## Simple Tenses

| Present | Preterit | Imperfect | Future | Conditional | Subjunctive | Imperfect Subjunctive |
|---|---|---|---|---|---|---|
| he | hube | había | habré | habría | haya | hubiera |
| has | hubiste | habías | habrás | habrías | hayas | hubieras |
| ha | hubo | había | habrá | habría | haya | hubiera |
| hemos | hubimos | habíamos | habremos | habríamos | hayamos | hubiéramos |
| habéis | hubisteis | habíais | habréis | habríais | hayáis | hubierais |
| han | hubieron | habían | habrán | habrían | hayan | hubieran |

## Compound Tenses

| Present Perfect | Preterit Perfect | Pluperfect | Future Perfect | Conditional Perfect | Perfect Subjunctive | Pluperfect Subjunctive |
|---|---|---|---|---|---|---|
| he habido | hube habido | había habido | habré habido | habría habido | haya habido | hubiera habido |
| has habido | hubiste habido | habías habido | habrás habido | habrías habido | hayas habido | hubieras habido |
| ha habido | hubo habido | había habido | habrá habido | habría habido | haya habido | hubiera habido |
| hemos habido | hubimos habido | habíamos habido | habremos habido | habríamos habido | hayamos habido | hubiéramos habido |
| habéis habido | hubisteis habido | habíais habido | habréis habido | habríais habido | hayáis habido | hubierais habido |
| han habido | hubieron habido | habían habido | habrán habido | habrían habido | hayan habido | hubieran habido |

◆ hacer (*to make, do*); **Gerund:** haciendo; **Past participle: hecho**

**Commands: haz** (tú) no **hagas** (tú) haced (vosotros) no **hagáis** (vosotros) **haga** (Ud.) **hagan** (Uds.) **hagamos** (nosotros)

## Simple Tenses

| Present | Preterit | Imperfect | Future | Conditional | Subjunctive | Imperfect Subjunctive |
|---|---|---|---|---|---|---|
| **hago** | **hice** | **hacía** | **haré** | **haría** | **haga** | **hiciera** |
| haces | hiciste | hacías | harás | harías | hagas | hicieras |
| hace | hizo | hacía | hará | haría | haga | hiciera |
| hacemos | hicimos | hacíamos | haremos | haríamos | hagamos | hiciéramos |
| hacéis | hicisteis | hacíais | haréis | haríais | hagáis | hicierais |
| hacen | hicieron | hacían | harán | harían | hagan | hicieran |

## Compound Tenses

| Present Perfect | Preterit Perfect | Pluperfect | Future Perfect | Conditional Perfect | Perfect Subjunctive | Pluperfect Subjunctive |
|---|---|---|---|---|---|---|
| he hecho | hube hecho | había hecho | habré hecho | habría hecho | haya hecho | hubiera hecho |
| has hecho | hubiste hecho | habías hecho | habrás hecho | habrías hecho | hayas hecho | hubieras hecho |
| ha hecho | hubo hecho | había hecho | habrá hecho | habría hecho | haya hecho | hubiera hecho |
| hemos hecho | hubimos hecho | habíamos hecho | habremos hecho | habríamos hecho | hayamos hecho | hubiéramos hecho |
| habéis hecho | hubisteis hecho | habíais hecho | habréis hecho | habríais hecho | hayáis hecho | hubierais hecho |
| han hecho | hubieron hecho | habían hecho | habrán hecho | habrían hecho | hayan hecho | hubieran hecho |

- The verb *satisfacer* (to satisfy) is conjugated like the verb *hacer*.

- ir (*to go*); Gerund: **yendo**; Past participle: ido

  Commands: **ve** (tú) no **vayas** (tú) **id** (vosotros) no **vayáis** (vosotros) **vaya** (Ud.) **vayan** (Uds.) **vayamos** (nosotros)

## Simple Tenses

| Present | Preterit | Imperfect | Future | Conditional | Subjunctive | Imperfect Subjunctive |
|---|---|---|---|---|---|---|
| voy | fuí | iba | iré | iría | vaya | fuera |
| vas | fuiste | ibas | irás | irías | vayas | fueras |
| va | fué | iba | irá | iría | vaya | fuera |
| vamos | fuimos | íbamos | iremos | iríamos | vayamos | fuéramos |
| vais | fuisteis | ibais | iréis | iríais | vayáis | fuerais |
| van | fueron | iban | irán | irían | vayan | fueran |

## Compound Tenses

| Present Perfect | Preterit Perfect | Pluperfect | Future Perfect | Conditional Perfect | Perfect Subjunctive | Pluperfect Subjunctive |
|---|---|---|---|---|---|---|
| he ido | hube ido | había ido | habré ido | habría ido | haya ido | hubiera ido |
| has ido | hubiste ido | habías ido | habrás ido | habrías ido | hayas ido | hubieras ido |
| ha ido | hubo ido | había ido | habrá ido | habría ido | haya ido | hubiera ido |
| hemos ido | hubimos ido | habíamos ido | habremos ido | habríamos ido | hayamos ido | hubiéramos ido |
| habéis ido | hubisteis ido | habíais ido | habréis ido | habríais ido | hayáis ido | hubierais ido |
| han ido | hubieron ido | habían ido | habrán ido | habrían ido | hayan ido | hubieran ido |

◆ oír (*to hear*); **Gerund: oyendo; Past participle: oído**

**Commands:** **oye** (tú) no **oigas** (tú) **oíd** (vosotros) no **oyáis** (vosotros) **oiga** (Ud.) **oigan** (Uds.) **oigamos** (nosotros)

## Simple Tenses

| Present | Preterit | Imperfect | Future | Conditional | Subjunctive | Imperfect Subjunctive |
|---|---|---|---|---|---|---|
| oigo | oí | oía | oiré | oiría | oiga | oyera |
| oyes | oíste | oías | oirás | oirías | oigas | oyeras |
| oye | oyó | oía | oirá | oiría | oiga | oyera |
| oímos | oímos | oíamos | oiremos | oiríamos | oigamos | oyéramos |
| oís | oísteis | oíais | oiréis | oiríais | oigáis | oyerais |
| oyen | oyeron | oían | oirán | oirían | oigan | oyeran |

## Compound Tenses

| Present Perfect | Preterit Perfect | Pluperfect | Future Perfect | Conditional Perfect | Perfect Subjunctive | Pluperfect Subjunctive |
|---|---|---|---|---|---|---|
| he oído | hube oído | había oído | habré oído | habría oído | haya oído | hubiera oído |
| has oído | hubiste oído | habías oído | habrás oído | habrías oído | hayas oído | hubieras oído |
| ha oído | hubo oído | había oído | habrá oído | habría oído | haya oído | hubiera oído |
| hemos oído | hubimos oído | habíamos oído | habremos oído | habríamos oído | hayamos oído | hubiéramos oído |
| habéis oído | hubisteis oído | habíais oído | habréis oído | habríais oído | hayáis oído | hubierais oído |
| han oído | hubieron oído | habían oído | habrán oído | habrían oído | hayan oído | hubieran oído |

◆ oler (*to smell*); **Gerund:** oliendo; **Past participle:** olido

**Commands: huele** (tú) no **huelas** (tú) oled (vosotros) no oláis (vosotros) **huela** (Ud.) **huelan** (Uds.) olamos (nosotros)

## Simple Tenses

| Present | Preterit | Imperfect | Future | Conditional | Subjunctive | Imperfect Subjunctive |
|---|---|---|---|---|---|---|
| **huelo** | olí | olía | oleré | olería | **huela** | oliera |
| **hueles** | oliste | olías | olerás | olerías | **huelas** | olieras |
| **huele** | olió | olía | olerá | olería | **huela** | oliera |
| olemos | olimos | olíamos | oleremos | oleríamos | olamos | oliéramos |
| oléis | olisteis | olíais | oleréis | oleríais | oláis | olierais |
| **huelen** | olieron | olían | olerán | olerían | **huelan** | olieran |

## Compound Tenses

| Present Perfect | Preterit Perfect | Pluperfect | Future Perfect | Conditional Perfect | Perfect Subjunctive | Pluperfect Subjunctive |
|---|---|---|---|---|---|---|
| he olido | hube olido | había olido | habré olido | habría olido | haya olido | hubiera olido |
| has olido | hubiste olido | habías olido | habrás olido | habrías olido | hayas olido | hubieras olido |
| ha olido | hubo olido | había olido | habrá olido | habría olido | haya olido | hubiera olido |
| hemos olido | hubimos olido | habíamos olido | habremos olido | habríamos olido | hayamos olido | hubiéramos olido |
| habéis olido | hubisteis olido | habíais olido | habréis olido | habríais olido | hayáis olido | hubierais olido |
| han olido | hubieron olido | habían olido | habrán olido | habrían olido | hayan olido | hubieran olido |

◆ placer (*to please*); **Gerund:** placiendo; **Past participle:** placido

**Commands:** place (tú) no **plazcas** (tú) placed (vosotros) no **plazcáis** (vosotros) **plazca** (Ud.) **plazcan** (Uds.) **plazcamos** (nosotros)

## Simple Tenses

| Present | Preterit | Imperfect | Future | Conditional | Subjunctive | Imperfect Subjunctive |
|---|---|---|---|---|---|---|
| **plazco (plazgo)** | plací | placía | placeré | placería | **plazca (plazga)** | placiera |
| places | placiste | placías | placerás | placerías | **plazcas** | placieras |
| place | plació **(plugo)** | placía | placerá | placería | **plazca** | placiera **(pluguiera)** |
| placemos | placimos | placíamos | placeremos | placeríamos | **plazcamos** | placiéramos |
| placéis | placisteis | placíais | placeréis | placeríais | **plazcáis** | placierais |
| placen | placieron | placían | placerán | placerían | **plazcan** | placieran |

## Compound Tenses

| Present Perfect | Preterit Perfect | Pluperfect | Future Perfect | Conditional Perfect | Perfect Subjunctive | Pluperfect Subjunctive |
|---|---|---|---|---|---|---|
| he placido | hube placido | había placido | habré placido | habría placido | haya placido | hubiera placido |
| has placido | hubiste placido | habías placido | habrás placido | habrías placido | hayas placido | hubieras placido |
| ha placido | hubo placido | había placido | habrá placido | habría placido | haya placido | hubiera placido |
| hemos placido | hubimos placido | habíamos placido | habremos placido | habríamos placido | hayamos placido | hubiéramos placido |
| habéis placido | hubisteis placido | habíais placido | habréis placido | habríais placido | hayáis placido | hubierais placido |
| han placido | hubieron placido | habían placido | habrán placido | habrían placido | hayan placido | hubieran placido |

◆ poder (*to be able*); **Gerund: pudiendo; Past participle:** podido

Note that there are no commands with *poder*.

## Simple Tenses

| Present | Preterit | Imperfect | Future | Conditional | Subjunctive | Imperfect Subjunctive |
|---|---|---|---|---|---|---|
| **puedo** | **pude** | podía | **podré** | **podría** | **pueda** | **pudiera** |
| **puedes** | **pudiste** | podías | **podrás** | **podrías** | **puedas** | **pudieras** |
| **puede** | **pudo** | podía | **podrá** | **podría** | **pueda** | **pudiera** |
| podemos | **pudimos** | podíamos | **podremos** | **podríamos** | podamos | **pudiéramos** |
| podéis | **pudisteis** | podíais | **podréis** | **podríais** | podáis | **pudierais** |
| **pueden** | **pudieron** | podían | **podrán** | **podrían** | **puedan** | **pudieran** |

## Compound Tenses

| Present Perfect | Preterit Perfect | Pluperfect | Future Perfect | Conditional Perfect | Perfect Subjunctive | Pluperfect Subjunctive |
|---|---|---|---|---|---|---|
| he podido | hube podido | había podido | habré podido | habría podido | haya podido | hubiera podido |
| has podido | hubiste podido | habías podido | habrás podido | habrías podido | hayas podido | hubieras podido |
| ha podido | hubo podido | había podido | habrá podido | habría podido | haya podido | hubiera podido |
| hemos podido | hubimos podido | habíamos podido | habremos podido | habríamos podido | hayamos podido | hubiéramos podido |
| habéis podido | hubisteis podido | habíais podido | habréis podido | habríais podido | hayáis podido | hubierais podido |
| han podido | hubieron podido | habían podido | habrán podido | habrían podido | hayan podido | hubieran podido |

◆ poner (*to put*); **Gerund:** poniendo; **Past participle: puesto**

**Commands:** pon (tú) no **pongas** (tú) poned (vosotros) no **pongáis** (vosotros) **ponga** (Ud.) **pongan** (Uds.) **pongamos** (nosotros)

## Simple Tenses

| Present | Preterit | Imperfect | Future | Conditional | Subjunctive | Imperfect Subjunctive |
|---|---|---|---|---|---|---|
| **pongo** | **puse** | ponía | **pondré** | **pondría** | **ponga** | **pusiera** |
| pones | pusiste | ponías | **pondrás** | **pondrías** | **pongas** | **pusieras** |
| pone | **puso** | ponía | **pondrá** | **pondría** | **ponga** | **pusiera** |
| ponemos | **pusimos** | poníamos | **pondremos** | **pondríamos** | **pongamos** | **pusiéramos** |
| ponéis | **pusisteis** | poníais | **pondréis** | **pondríais** | **pongáis** | **pusierais** |
| ponen | **pusieron** | ponían | **pondrán** | **pondrían** | **pongan** | **pusieran** |

## Compound Tenses

| Present Perfect | Preterit Perfect | Pluperfect | Future Perfect | Conditional Perfect | Perfect Subjunctive | Pluperfect Subjunctive |
|---|---|---|---|---|---|---|
| he puesto | hube puesto | había puesto | habré puesto | habría puesto | haya puesto | hubiera puesto |
| has puesto | hubiste puesto | habías puesto | habrás puesto | habrías puesto | hayas puesto | hubieras puesto |
| ha puesto | hubo puesto | había puesto | habrá puesto | habría puesto | haya puesto | hubiera puesto |
| hemos puesto | hubimos puesto | habíamos puesto | habremos puesto | habríamos puesto | hayamos puesto | hubiéramos puesto |
| habéis puesto | hubisteis puesto | habíais puesto | habréis puesto | habríais puesto | hayáis puesto | hubierais puesto |
| han puesto | hubieron puesto | habían puesto | habrán puesto | habrían puesto | hayan puesto | hubieran puesto |

◆ querer (*to wish, want*); **Gerund:** queriendo; **Past participle:** querido

**Commands: quiere** (tú) no **quieras** (tú) quered (vosotros) no queráis (vosotros) **quiera** (Ud.) **quieran** (Uds.)
queramos (nosotros)

## Simple Tenses

| Present | Preterit | Imperfect | Future | Conditional | Subjunctive | Imperfect Subjunctive |
|---|---|---|---|---|---|---|
| quiero | quise | quería | querré | querría | quiera | quisiera |
| quieres | quisiste | querías | querrás | querrías | quieras | quisieras |
| quiere | quiso | quería | querrá | querría | quiera | quisiera |
| queremos | quisimos | queríamos | querremos | querríamos | queramos | quisiéramos |
| queréis | quisisteis | queríais | querréis | querríais | queráis | quisierais |
| quieren | quisieron | querían | querrán | querrían | quieran | quisieran |

## Compound Tenses

| Present Perfect | Preterit Perfect | Pluperfect | Future Perfect | Conditional Perfect | Perfect Subjunctive | Pluperfect Subjunctive |
|---|---|---|---|---|---|---|
| he querido | hube querido | había querido | habré querido | habría querido | haya querido | hubiera querido |
| has querido | hubiste querido | habías querido | habrás querido | habrías querido | hayas querido | hubieras querido |
| ha querido | hubo querido | había querido | habrá querido | habría querido | haya querido | hubiera querido |
| hemos querido | hubimos querido | habíamos querido | habremos querido | habríamos querido | hayamos querido | hubiéramos querido |
| habéis querido | hubisteis querido | habíais querido | habréis querido | habríais querido | hayáis querido | hubierais querido |
| han querido | hubieron querido | habían querido | habrán querido | habrían querido | hayan querido | hubieran querido |

◆ raer (*to scrape, smooth*); **Gerund:** rayendo; **Past participle: raído**

**Commands:** rae (tú) no **raigas** (tú) raed (vosotros) no **raigáis** (vosotros) **raiga** (Ud.) **raigan** (Uds.) **raigamos** (nosotros)

## Simple Tenses

| Present | Preterit | Imperfect | Future | Conditional | Subjunctive | Imperfect Subjunctive |
|---------|----------|-----------|--------|-------------|-------------|----------------------|
| **raigo (rayo)** | **raí** | raía | raeré | raería | **raiga (raya)** | rayera |
| raes | **raíste** | raías | raerás | raerías | **raigas** | rayeras |
| rae | **rayó** | raía | raerá | raería | **raiga** | rayera |
| raímos | **raímos** | raíamos | raeremos | raeríamos | **raigamos** | rayéramos |
| raéis | **raísteis** | raíais | raeréis | raeríais | **raigáis** | rayerais |
| raen | **rayeron** | raían | raerán | raerían | **raigan** | rayeran |

## Compound Tenses

| Present Perfect | Preterit Perfect | Pluperfect | Future Perfect | Conditional Perfect | Perfect Subjunctive | Pluperfect Subjunctive |
|-----------------|------------------|------------|----------------|---------------------|---------------------|------------------------|
| he raído | hube raído | había raído | habré raído | habría raído | haya raído | hubiera raído |
| has raído | hubiste raído | habías raído | habrás raído | habrías raído | hayas raído | hubieras raído |
| ha raído | hubo raído | había raído | habrá raído | habría raído | haya raído | hubiera raído |
| hemos raído | hubimos raído | habíamos raído | habremos raído | habríamos raído | hayamos raído | hubiéramos raído |
| habéis raído | hubisteis raído | habíais raído | habréis raído | habríais raído | hayáis raído | hubierais raído |
| han raído | hubieron raído | habían raído | habrán raído | habrían raído | hayan raído | hubieran raído |

◆ reír (*to laugh*); **Gerund:** riendo; **Past participle:** reído

**Commands:** ríe (tú) no rías (tú) reíd (vosotros) no riáis (vosotros) ría (Ud.) rían (Uds.) riamos (nosotros)

## Simple Tenses

| Present | Preterit | Imperfect | Future | Conditional | Subjunctive | Imperfect Subjunctive |
|---|---|---|---|---|---|---|
| río | reí | reía | reiré | reiría | ría | riera |
| ríes | reíste | reías | reirás | reirías | rías | rieras |
| ríe | rió | reía | reirá | reiría | ría | riera |
| reímos | reímos | reíamos | reiremos | reiríamos | riamos | riéramos |
| reís | reísteis | reíais | reiréis | reiríais | riáis | rierais |
| ríen | rieron | reían | reirán | reirían | rían | rieran |

## Compound Tenses

| Present Perfect | Preterit Perfect | Pluperfect | Future Perfect | Conditional Perfect | Perfect Subjunctive | Pluperfect Subjunctive |
|---|---|---|---|---|---|---|
| he reído | hube reído | había reído | habré reído | habría reído | haya reído | hubiera reído |
| has reído | hubiste reído | habías reído | habrás reído | habrías reído | hayas reído | hubieras reído |
| ha reído | hubo reído | había reído | habrá reído | habría reído | haya reído | hubiera reído |
| hemos reído | hubimos reído | habíamos reído | habremos reído | habríamos reído | hayamos reído | hubiéramos reído |
| habéis reído | hubisteis reído | habíais reído | habréis reído | habríais reído | hayáis reído | hubierais reído |
| han reído | hubieron reído | habían reído | habrán reído | habrían reído | hayan reído | hubieran reído |

◆ saber (*to know*); **Gerund:** sabiendo; **Past participle:** sabido

**Commands:** sabe (tú) no **sepas** (tú) sabed (vosotros) **sepáis** (vosotros) **sepa** (Ud.) **sepan** (Uds.) **sepamos** (nosotros)

## Simple Tenses

| Present | Preterit | Imperfect | Future | Conditional | Subjunctive | Imperfect Subjunctive |
|---------|----------|-----------|--------|-------------|-------------|-----------------------|
| **sé** | **supe** | sabía | **sabré** | **sabría** | **sepa** | **supiera** |
| sabes | **supiste** | sabías | **sabrás** | **sabrías** | **sepas** | **supieras** |
| sabe | **supo** | sabía | **sabrá** | **sabría** | **sepa** | **supiera** |
| sabemos | **supimos** | sabíamos | **sabremos** | **sabríamos** | **sepamos** | **supiéramos** |
| sabéis | **supisteis** | sabíais | **sabréis** | **sabríais** | **sepáis** | **supierais** |
| saben | **supieron** | sabían | **sabrán** | **sabrían** | **sepan** | **supieran** |

## Compound Tenses

| Present Perfect | Preterit Perfect | Pluperfect | Future Perfect | Conditional Perfect | Perfect Subjunctive | Pluperfect Subjunctive |
|-----------------|------------------|------------|----------------|---------------------|---------------------|------------------------|
| he sabido | hube sabido | había sabido | habré sabido | habría sabido | haya sabido | hubiera sabido |
| has sabido | hubiste sabido | habías sabido | habrás sabido | habrías sabido | hayas sabido | hubieras sabido |
| ha sabido | hubo sabido | había sabido | habrá sabido | habría sabido | haya sabido | hubiera sabido |
| hemos sabido | hubimos sabido | habíamos sabido | habremos sabido | habríamos sabido | hayamos sabido | hubiéramos sabido |
| habéis sabido | hubisteis sabido | habíais sabido | habréis sabido | habriais sabido | hayáis sabido | hubierais sabido |
| han sabido | hubieron sabido | habían sabido | habrán sabido | habrían sabido | hayan sabido | hubieran sabido |

◆ salir (*to go out*); **Gerund:** saliendo; **Past participle:** salido

**Commands: sal** (tú) no **salgas** (tú) salid (vosotros) no **salgáis** (vosotros) **salga** (Ud.) **salgan** (Uds.) **salgamos** (nosotros)

## Simple Tenses

| Present | Preterit | Imperfect | Future | Conditional | Subjunctive | Imperfect Subjunctive |
|---------|----------|-----------|--------|-------------|-------------|------------------------|
| **salgo** | salí | salía | **saldré** | **saldría** | **salga** | saliera |
| sales | saliste | salías | **saldrás** | **saldrías** | **salgas** | salieras |
| sale | salió | salía | **saldrá** | **saldría** | **salga** | saliera |
| salimos | salimos | salíamos | **saldremos** | **saldríamos** | **salgamos** | saliéramos |
| salís | salisteis | salíais | **saldréis** | **saldríais** | **salgáis** | salierais |
| salen | salieron | salían | **saldrán** | **saldrían** | **salgan** | salieran |

## Compound Tenses

| Present Perfect | Preterit Perfect | Pluperfect | Future Perfect | Conditional Perfect | Perfect Subjunctive | Pluperfect Subjunctive |
|-----------------|------------------|------------|----------------|---------------------|---------------------|------------------------|
| he salido | hube salido | había salido | habré salido | habría salido | haya salido | hubiera salido |
| has salido | hubiste salido | habías salido | habrás salido | habrías salido | hayas salido | hubieras salido |
| ha salido | hubo salido | había salido | habrá salido | habría salido | haya salido | hubiera salido |
| hemos salido | hubimos salido | habíamos salido | habremos salido | habríamos salido | hayamos salido | hubiéramos salido |
| habéis salido | hubisteis salido | habíais salido | habréis salido | habríais salido | hayáis salido | hubierais salido |
| han salido | hubieron salido | habían salido | habrán salido | habrían salido | hayan salido | hubieran salido |

◆ ser (*to be*); Gerund: **siendo**; Past participle: **sido**

**Commands: sé** (tú) no **seas** (tú) **sed** (vosotros) no **seáis** (vosotros) **sea** (Ud.) **sean** (Uds.) **seamos** (nosotros)

## Simple Tenses

| Present | Preterit | Imperfect | Future | Conditional | Subjunctive | Imperfect Subjunctive |
|---|---|---|---|---|---|---|
| soy | fuí | era | seré | sería | sea | fuera |
| eres | fuiste | eras | serás | serías | seas | fueras |
| es | fué | era | será | sería | sea | fuera |
| somos | fuimos | éramos | seremos | seríamos | seamos | fuéramos |
| sois | fuisteis | erais | seréis | seríais | seáis | fuerais |
| son | fueron | eran | serán | serían | sean | fueran |

## Compound Tenses

| Present Perfect | Preterit Perfect | Pluperfect | Future Perfect | Conditional Perfect | Perfect Subjunctive | Pluperfect Subjunctive |
|---|---|---|---|---|---|---|
| he sido | hube sido | había sido | habré sido | habría sido | haya sido | hubiera sido |
| has sido | hubiste sido | habías sido | habrás sido | habrías sido | hayas sido | hubieras sido |
| ha sido | hubo sido | había sido | habrá sido | habría sido | haya sido | hubiera sido |
| hemos sido | hubimos sido | habíamos sido | habremos sido | habríamos sido | hayamos sido | hubiéramos sido |
| habéis sido | hubisteis sido | habíais sido | habréis sido | habríais sido | hayáis sido | hubierais sido |
| han sido | hubieron sido | habían sido | habrán sido | habrían sido | hayan sido | hubieran sido |

◆ tener (*to have*); **Gerund:** teniendo; **Past participle:** tenido

**Commands:** ten (tú) no **tengas** (tú) tened (vosotros) no **tengáis** (vosotros) **tenga** (Ud.) **tengan** (Uds.) **tengamos** (nosotros)

## Simple Tenses

| Present | Preterit | Imperfect | Future | Conditional | Subjunctive | Imperfect Subjunctive |
|---|---|---|---|---|---|---|
| **tengo** | **tuve** | tenía | **tendré** | **tendría** | **tenga** | **tuviera** |
| **tienes** | **tuviste** | tenías | **tendrás** | **tendrías** | **tengas** | **tuvieras** |
| **tiene** | **tuvo** | tenía | **tendrá** | **tendría** | **tenga** | **tuviera** |
| tenemos | **tuvimos** | teníamos | **tendremos** | **tendríamos** | **tengamos** | **tuviéramos** |
| tenéis | **tuvisteis** | teníais | **tendréis** | **tendríais** | **tengáis** | **tuvierais** |
| **tienen** | **tuvieron** | tenían | **tendrán** | **tendrían** | **tengan** | **tuvieran** |

## Compound Tenses

| Present Perfect | Preterit Perfect | Pluperfect | Future Perfect | Conditional Perfect | Perfect Subjunctive | Pluperfect Subjunctive |
|---|---|---|---|---|---|---|
| he tenido | hube tenido | había tenido | habré tenido | habría tenido | haya tenido | hubiera tenido |
| has tenido | hubiste tenido | habías tenido | habrás tenido | habrías tenido | hayas tenido | hubieras tenido |
| ha tenido | hubo tenido | había tenido | habrá tenido | habría tenido | haya tenido | hubiera tenido |
| hemos tenido | hubimos tenido | habíamos tenido | habremos tenido | habríamos tenido | hayamos tenido | hubiéramos tenido |
| habéis tenido | hubisteis tenido | habíais tenido | habréis tenido | habríais tenido | hayáis tenido | hubierais tenido |
| han tenido | hubieron tenido | habían tenido | habrán tenido | habrían tenido | hayan tenido | hubieran tenido |

◆ traer (*to bring*); Gerund: trayendo; Past participle: traído

**Commands:** trae (tú) no **traigas** (tú) traed (vosotros) no **traigáis** (vosotros) **traiga** (Ud.) traigan (Uds.) **traigamos** (nosotros)

## Simple Tenses

| Present | Preterit | Imperfect | Future | Conditional | Subjunctive | Imperfect Subjunctive |
|---|---|---|---|---|---|---|
| **traigo** | **traje** | traía | traeré | traería | **traiga** | **trajera** |
| traes | **trajiste** | traías | traerás | traerías | **traigas** | **trajeras** |
| trae | **trajo** | traía | traerá | traería | **traiga** | **trajera** |
| traemos | **trajimos** | traíamos | traeremos | traeríamos | **traigamos** | **trajéramos** |
| traéis | **trajisteis** | traíais | traeréis | traeríais | **traigáis** | **trajerais** |
| traen | **trajeron** | traían | traerán | traerían | **traigan** | **trajeran** |

## Compound Tenses

| Present Perfect | Preterit Perfect | Pluperfect | Future Perfect | Conditional Perfect | Perfect Subjunctive | Pluperfect Subjunctive |
|---|---|---|---|---|---|---|
| he traído | hube traído | había traído | habré traído | habría traído | haya traído | hubiera traído |
| has traído | hubiste traído | habías traído | habrás traído | habrías traído | hayas traído | hubieras traído |
| ha traído | hubo traído | había traído | habrá traído | habría traído | haya traído | hubiera traído |
| hemos traído | hubimos traído | habíamos traído | habremos traído | habríamos traído | hayamos traído | hubiéramos traído |
| habéis traído | hubisteis traído | habíais traído | habréis traído | habríais traído | hayáis traído | hubietrais traído |
| han traído | hubieron traído | habían traído | habrán traído | habrían traído | hayan traído | hubieran traído |

◆ valer (*to be worth*); **Gerund:** valiendo; **Past participle:** valido

**Commands: val (vale)** (tú) no **valgas** (tú) valed (vosotros) no **valgáis** (vosotros) **valga** (Ud.) **valgan** (Uds.) **valgamos** (nosotros)

## Simple Tenses

| Present | Preterit | Imperfect | Future | Conditional | Subjunctive | Imperfect Subjunctive |
|---|---|---|---|---|---|---|
| **valgo** | valí | valía | **valdré** | **valdría** | **valga** | valiera |
| vales | valiste | valías | **valdrás** | **valdrías** | **valgas** | valieras |
| vale | valió | valía | **valdrá** | **valdría** | **valga** | valiera |
| valemos | valimos | valíamos | **valdremos** | **valdríamos** | **valgamos** | valiéramos |
| valéis | valisteis | valíais | **valdréis** | **valdríais** | **valgáis** | valierais |
| valen | valieron | valían | **valdrán** | **valdrían** | **valgan** | valieran |

## Compound Tenses

| Present Perfect | Preterit Perfect | Pluperfect | Future Perfect | Conditional Perfect | Perfect Subjunctive | Pluperfect Subjunctive |
|---|---|---|---|---|---|---|
| he valido | hube valido | había valido | habré valido | habría valido | haya valido | hubiera valido |
| has valido | hubiste valido | habías valido | habrás valido | habrías valido | hayas valido | hubieras valido |
| ha valido | hubo valido | había valido | habrá valido | habría valido | haya valido | hubiera valido |
| hemos valido | hubimos valido | habíamos valido | habremos valido | habríamos valido | hayamos valido | hubiéramos valido |
| habéis valido | hubisteis valido | habíais valido | habréis valido | habríais valido | hayáis valido | hubierais valido |
| han valido | hubieron valido | habían valido | habrán valido | habrían valido | hayan valido | hubieran valido |

◆ venir (*to come*); **Gerund: viniendo; Past participle:** venido

**Commands: ven** (tú) no **vengas** (tú) venid (vosotros) no **vengáis** (vosotros) **venga** (Ud.) **vengan** (Uds.) **vengamos** (nosotros)

## Simple Tenses

| Present | Preterit | Imperfect | Future | Conditional | Subjunctive | Imperfect Subjunctive |
|---------|----------|-----------|--------|-------------|-------------|----------------------|
| **vengo** | **vine** | venía | **vendré** | **vendría** | **venga** | **viniera** |
| **vienes** | **viniste** | venías | **vendrás** | **vendrías** | **vengas** | **vinieras** |
| **viene** | **vino** | venía | **vendrá** | **vendría** | **venga** | **viniera** |
| **venimos** | **vinimos** | veníamos | **vendremos** | **vendríamos** | **vengamos** | **viniéramos** |
| **venís** | **vinisteis** | veníais | **vendréis** | **vendríais** | **vengáis** | **vinierais** |
| **vienen** | **vinieron** | venían | **vendrán** | **vendrían** | **vengan** | **vinieran** |

## Compound Tenses

| Present Perfect | Preterit Perfect | Pluperfect | Future Perfect | Conditional Perfect | Perfect Subjunctive | Pluperfect Subjunctive |
|-----------------|------------------|------------|----------------|---------------------|---------------------|------------------------|
| he venido | hube venido | había venido | habré venido | habría venido | haya venido | hubiera venido |
| has venido | hubiste venido | habías venido | habrás venido | habrías venido | hayas venido | hubieras venido |
| ha venido | hubo venido | había venido | habrá venido | habría venido | haya venido | hubiera venido |
| hemos venido | hubimos venido | habíamos venido | habremos venido | habríamos venido | hayamos venido | hubiéramos venido |
| habéis venido | hubisteis venido | habíais venido | habréis venido | habríais venido | hayáis venido | hubierais venido |
| han venido | hubieron venido | habían venido | habrán venido | habrían venido | hayan venido | hubieran venido |

◆ ver (*to see*); **Gerund:** viendo; **Past participle: visto**

**Commands:** ve (tú) no **veas** (tú) ved (vosotros) no **veáis** (vosotros) **vea** (Ud.) **vean** (Uds.) **veamos** (nosotros)

## Simple Tenses

| Present | Preterit | Imperfect | Future | Conditional | Subjunctive | Imperfect Subjunctive |
|---|---|---|---|---|---|---|
| **veo** | ví | **veía** | veré | vería | **vea** | viera |
| ves | viste | **veías** | verás | verías | **veas** | vieras |
| ve | vió | **veía** | verá | vería | **vea** | viera |
| vemos | vimos | **veíamos** | veremos | veríamos | **veamos** | viéramos |
| veis | visteis | **veíais** | veréis | veríais | **veáis** | vierais |
| ven | vieron | **veían** | verán | verían | **vean** | vieran |

## Compound Tenses

| Present Perfect | Preterit Perfect | Pluperfect | Future Perfect | Conditional Perfect | Perfect Subjunctive | Pluperfect Subjunctive |
|---|---|---|---|---|---|---|
| he visto | hube visto | había visto | habré visto | habría visto | haya visto | hubiera visto |
| has visto | hubiste visto | habías visto | habrás visto | habrías visto | hayas visto | hubieras visto |
| ha visto | hubo visto | había visto | habrá visto | habría visto | haya visto | hubiera visto |
| hemos visto | hubimos visto | habíamos visto | habremos visto | habríamos visto | hayamos visto | hubiéramos visto |
| habéis visto | hubisteis visto | habíais visto | habréis visto | habríais visto | hayáis visto | hubierais visto |
| han visto | hubieron visto | habían visto | habrán visto | habrían visto | hayan visto | hubieran visto |

◆ yacer (*to lie*; resting); **Gerund:** yaciendo; **Past participle:** yacido

**Commands: yaz** (yace) (tú) no **yazcas** (tú) yaced (vosotros) no **yazcáis** (vosotros) **yazca** (Ud.) **yazcan** (Uds.) **yazcamos** (nosotros)

## Simple Tenses

| Present | Preterit | Imperfect | Future | Conditional | Subjunctive | Imperfect Subjunctive |
|---|---|---|---|---|---|---|
| **yazco** (yazgo) (yago) | yací | yacía | yaceré | yacería | **yazca** (yazga) (yaga) | yaciera |
| yaces | yaciste | yacías | yacerás | yacerías | **yazcas** | yacieras |
| yace | yació | yacía | yacerá | yacería | **yazca** | yaciera |
| yacemos | yacimos | yacíamos | yaceremos | yaceríamos | **yazcamos** | yaciéramos |
| yacéis | yacisteis | yacíais | yaceréis | yaceríais | **yazcáis** | yacierais |
| yacen | yacieron | yacían | yacerán | yacerían | **yazcan** | yacieran |

## Compound Tenses

| Present Perfect | Preterit Perfect | Pluperfect | Future Perfect | Conditional Perfect | Perfect Subjunctive | Pluperfect Subjunctive |
|---|---|---|---|---|---|---|
| he yacido | hube yacido | había yacido | habré yacido | habría yacido | haya yacido | hubiera yacido |
| has yacido | hubiste yacido | habías yacido | habrás yacido | habrías yacido | hayas yacido | hubieras yacido |
| ha yacido | hubo yacido | había yacido | habrá yacido | habría yacido | haya yacido | hubiera yacido |
| hemos yacido | hubimos yacido | habíamos yacido | habremos yacido | habríamos yacido | hayamos yacido | hubiéramos yacido |
| habéis yacido | hubisteis yacido | habíais yacido | habréis yacido | habríais yacido | hayáis yacido | hubierais yacido |
| han yacido | hubieron yacido | habían yacido | habrán yacido | habrían yacido | hayan yacido | hubieran yacido |

# Compound Verbs

abrir   to open

    entreabrir   to half open

absolver   to absolve

    disolver   to dissolve

    resolver   to resolve

caer   to fall

    decaer   to decay

cubrir   to cover

    descubrir   to discover

decir   to say, tell

    contradecir   to contradict

    desdecir   to denegrate

    interdecir   to interdict

    predecir   to predict

escribir   to write

    adscribir   to ascribe

    circunscribir   to circumscribe

    describir   to describe

    inscribir   to inscribe

    prescribir   to prescribe

    proscribir   to proscribe

    sobrescribir   to superscribe

    suscribir (subscribir)   to subscribe

gustar   to please

    disgustar   to displease

hacer   to make, do

    contrahacer   to copy, imitate

    deshacer   to undo

    rehacer   to redo

nacer   to be born

    renacer   to be reborn

poner   to put

    anteponer   to put before

    contraponer   to set in front; to compose

    deponer   to set aside

    disponer   to dispose

    exponer   to expose

    imponer   to impose

    indisponer   to indispose

    interponer   to interpose

    oponer   to oppose

    posponer   to postpone

    predisponer   to predispose

    preponer   to put before, prefer

    presuponer   to presuppose

    proponer   to propose

    reponer   to replace

    superponer   to superimpose

    suponer   to suppose

    transponer   to transpose

    yuxtaponer   to juxtapose

réir   to laugh

    sonréir   to smile

salir   to go out

    sobresalir   to project, stand out

tener   to have

    contener   to contain

    detener   to detain

    entretener   to amuse, entertain

    mantener   to maintain

    obtener   to obtain

    retener   to retain

    sostener   to sustain

traer   to bring

    abstraer   to abstract

    atraer   to attract

    contraer   to contract

    extraer   to extract

    retraer   to retract

    retrotraer   to date back

    substraer   to subtract

ver   to see

    entrever   to glimpse

    prever   to foresee

    rever   to see again

venir   to come

    advenir   to come, happen

    avenir   to reconcile

    convenir   to be suitable

    prevenir   to prepare; warn

    provenir   to originate

    sobrevenir   to happen

    subvenir   to provide

    supervenir   to provide

volver   to return

    devolver   to return, give back

    envolver   to wrap up

    revolver   to revolve, turn around

# -ar Verbs

## Regular Verbs

abajar    to go down

abalar    to move, shake

abanderar    to champion

abandonar    to abandon

abaratar    to reduce prices

abarrotar    to pack

aberrar    to be mistaken

abismar    to amaze

abjurar    to renounce

ablandar    to soften

abofetear    to slap

abollar    to dent

abominar    to hate

abonar    to subscribe

abordar    to board

abotonar    to button up

abrasar    to burn

abreviar    to abbreviate

abrillantar    to polish

abrochar    to fasten

abrumar    to crush, oppress

abundar    to be plentiful

abusar    to abuse

acabar    to finish

acallar    to silence

acaparar    to hoard

accionar    to activate

aceitar    to oil

acelerar    to accelerate

acentuar    to accent

aceptar   to accept

aclamar   to acclaim

aclarar   to clarify

aclimatar   to acclimatize

acomodar   to accommodate

acompañar   to accompany

acondicionar   to arrange

aconsejar   to advise

acostumbrar   to be accustomed

acreditar   to credit

activar   to activate

acumular   to accumulate

acusar   to accuse

adaptar   to adapt

adelantar   to advance

adeudar   to owe

adiestrar   to train

adivinar   to guess

administrar   to administer

admirar   to admire

adoptar   to adopt

adorar   to adore

adornar   to adorn

adosar   to lean against

adular   to flatter

afectar   to affect

afeitar   to shave

aficionar   to induce a liking for

afilar   to sharpen

afirmar   to affirm

afrentar   to insult

afrontar   to confront

agachar   to bend

agarrar   to grasp

agarrotar   to stiffen

agitar   to agitate, shake

agotar   to wear out

agradar   to please

agrandar   to increase

agravar   to aggravate

agraviar   to wrong, offend

agrupar   to group

aguardar   to expect

ahorrar   to save

aislar   to isolate

ajustar   to adjust

alardear   to boast

alarmar   to alarm

alegrar   to cheer up

alejar   to move away

alertar   to alert

aligerar   to lighten

alimentar   to feed

alisar   to smooth

aliviar   to ease

alojar   to lodge

alquilar   to rent

alterar   to alter

alternar   to alternate

alumbrar   to illuminate

amar   to love

amarrar   to fasten

ambicionar   to aspire

amueblar   to furnish

andar   to walk

anhelar   to yearn for

animar   to animate

anotar   to note down

anticipar   to anticipate

anudar   to tie

anular   to cancel

anunciar   to announce

apenar   to sadden

aplastar   to crush

apoderar   to authorize

apoyar   to rest

apreciar   to appreciate

aprestar   to prepare

apresurar   to hurry

aprovechar   to make use of

aproximar   to approximate

apurar   to drink up

arrastrar   to drag

arreglar   to fix, adjust

arrestar   to arrest

arrojar   to fling

arrollar   to roll up

arrostrar   to face up to

articular   to articulate

asegurar   to assure

asignar   to assign

asomar   to lift

asombrar   to amaze

aspirar   to inhale

asustar   to frighten

atar   to tie

atestar   to attest

atrapar   to trap

atrasar   to delay

atravesar   to cross

atropellar   to knock down

aumentar   to augment, increase

aventajar   to surpass

avisar   to notify, warn

ayudar   to help

ayunar   to fast

azotar   to thrash

bailar   to dance

bajar   to go down

balancear   to rock, swing

balbucear   to stammer

bambolear   to shake

bañar   to bathe

barbotar   to mutter

basar   to base

bastar   to be enough

batallar   to fight

besar   to kiss

blasfemar   to curse

bloquear   to block

bordear   to border

borrar   to erase

botar   to fling

brillar   to shine

brindar   to offer, invite

bromear   to joke

broncear   to tan

bucear   to dive

calar   to soak

calcular   to calculate

callar   to keep quiet

calmar   to calm

cambiar   to change

caminar   to walk

cancelar   to cancel

cansar   to tire

cantar   to sing

capitular   to capitulate

captar   to capture

capturar   to capture

catar   to taste

causar   to cause

cautivar   to capture

celebrar   to celebrate

cenar   to eat dinner

censurar   to censure

centrar   to center

cepillar   to brush

cerrar   to close

cesar   to cease

chafar   to flatten

charlar   to chat

chequear   to examine

chiflar   to whistle

chillar   to scream

chinchar   to annoy

chismorrear   to spread rumors

chupar   to suck

circular   to circulate

citar   to cite, make an appointment

clamar   to exclaim

cobrar   to charge, cash

cocinar   to cook

cohabitar   to coinhabit

colaborar   to collaborate

colapsar   to collapse

coleccionar   to collect

colorear   to color

comandar   to command (military)

combar   to bend

combinar   to combine

comentar   to comment

comparar   to compare

compensar   to compensate

compilar   to compile

completar   to complete

comportar   to involve

comprar   to buy

concentrar   to concentrate

concertar   to agree upon

concienciar   to make aware

conciliar   to reconcile

concursar   to compete

condenar   to condemn

condensar   to condense

confeccionar   to have clothing made

confesar   to confess

configurar   to shape

confinar   to confine

confirmar   to confirm

conformar   to conform

confortar   to comfort

confrontar   to confront

congelar   to freeze

congratular   to congratulate

conjurar   to conjure

conmemorar   to commemorate

conservar   to conserve

considerar   to consider

consolar   to console

consolidar   to consolidate

conspirar   to conspire

constatar   to prove, verify

consternar   to dismay

consultar   to consult

consumar   to complete

contaminar   to contaminate

contemplar   to contemplate

contentar   to please, gratify

contestar   to answer

contrapesar   to counterbalance

contrastar   to contrast

contratar   to contract

controlar   to control

conversar   to converse

convidar   to invite

cooperar   to cooperate

coordinar   to coordinate

copiar   to copy

cortar   to cut

cosechar   to grow, harvest

crear   to create

cuestionar   to question

cuidar   to look after

culminar   to culminate

culpar   to blame

cultivar   to cultivate

curar   to cure

curiosear   to browse

dañar   to harm

datar   to date (a letter)

declamar   to recite

declarar   to declare

declinar   to decline

decorar   to decorate

deformar   to deform

defraudar   to disappoint, defraud

degradar   to degrade

dejar   to let, allow

deletrear   to spell out

deliberar   to deliberate

delimitar   to delimit

demorar   to delay

denotar   to denote

denunciar   to denounce

depositar   to deposit

depreciar   to depreciate

derramar   to spill

derribar   to knock down

desalojar   to move out

desarrollar   to develop

desbaratar   to ruin

descansar   to rest

desear   to desire

desechar   to discard

desempeñar   to carry out

designar   to designate

desnudar   to undress

despachar   to dispatch

destinar   to destine

determinar   to determine

devorar   to devour

dibujar   to draw

dictar   to dictate

disculpar   to excuse

diseminar   to spread

disfrutar   to enjoy

disgustar   to upset, displease

disimular   to hide

disipar   to dispel

dispensar   to excuse

dispersar   to scatter

disputar   to dispute

doblar   to fold, double

documentar   to document

dominar   to dominate

dotar   to endow

dudar   to doubt

durar   to last

echar   to throw

editar   to publish

ejecutar   to execute

ejercitar   to exercise

elaborar   to manufacture

elevar   to raise

eliminar   to eliminate

elogiar   to praise

embalar   to pack

empaquetar   to pack(age)

emplear   to use

empujar   to push

enamorar   to fall in love

encaminar   to direct

encantar   to love

encarar   to confront

enchufar   to connect

endosar   to endorse

enervar   to weaken

enfadar   to anger

enfrontar   to confront

engañar   to deceive

enojar   to annoy

ensayar   to try, rehearse

enseñar   to teach, show

ensuciar   to dirty

enterar   to inform

entrar   to enter

entremezclar   to intermix

entrevistar   to interview

entusiasmar   to enthuse

enumerar   to enumerate

enunciar   to enunciate

envidiar   to envy

equilibrar   to balance

equipar   to equip

escalar   to climb

escapar   to escape

escuchar   to listen (to)

espantar   to frighten

esperar   to hope, wait

estacionar   to park

estimar   to estimate

estimular   to encourage, stimulate

estorbar   to hinder

estrechar   to narrow

estudiar   to study

evacuar   to evacuate

evaporar   to evaporate

evitar   to avoid

exagerar   to exaggerate

examinar   to examine

exasperar   to exasperate

excitar   to excite

exclamar   to exclaim

exculpar   to acquit

excusar   to excuse

experimentar   to experience

explorar   to explore

explotar   to suffer

exportar   to export

expresar   to express

expulsar   to throw out

facilitar   to facilitate

facturar   to bill

falsear   to falsify

faltar   to need, lack

fantasear   to fantasize

fascinar   to fascinate

felicitar   to congratulate

festejar   to celebrate

figurar   to depict

fijar   to fix, fasten

financiar   to finance

firmar   to sign

flotar   to float

formar   to form

formular   to formulate

fotocopiar   to photocopy

fracasar   to fail

fragmentar   to divide

frecuentar   to frequent

frenar   to brake

frotar   to rub

frustrar   to frustrate

fumar   to smoke

funcionar   to function, work

fundar   to found

fusilar   to shoot

fusionar   to merge

galopar   to gallop

ganar   to win; earn

gastar   to spend (money), waste

generar   to generate

gestionar   to negotiate

girar   to turn around

gobernar   to govern

golpear   to hit

grabar   to engrave

gritar   to shout

guardar   to guard, keep

guisar   to cook

gustar   to be pleasing to

habitar   to inhabit

hablar   to speak, talk

hallar   to find

helar   to freeze

heredar   to inherit

hojear   to leaf through

honrar   to honor

hornear   to bake

hospedar   to give lodging to

humillar   to humiliate

hurtar   to steal

idear   to think up

ignorar   to be ignorant of

igualar   to equal

iluminar   to illuminate

ilusionar   to excite

ilustrar   to illustrate, enlighten

imaginar   to imagine

imitar   to imitate

impactar   to impact

implorar   to plead

importar   to matter, be of importance

importunar   to bother

| | |
|---|---|
| impresionar   to impress | jurar   to swear |
| improvisar   to improvise | lamentar   to lament |
| incapacitar   to incapacitate | lavar   to wash |
| incendiar   to set on fire | legitimar   to legitimize |
| incitar   to incite | levantar   to raise, lift |
| inclinar   to bend | limitar   to limit |
| incorporar   to incorporate | limpiar   to clean |
| incriminar   to incriminate | liquidar   to liquidate |
| inflamar   to inflame | llamar   to call, name |
| influenciar   to influence | llenar   to fill |
| informar   to inform | llevar   to wear, carry |
| ingresar   to deposit | llorar   to cry |
| iniciar   to initiate | lograr   to achieve |
| injuriar   to insult | luchar   to fight |
| innovar   to innovate | lustrar   to polish |
| inpulsar   to propel | madrugar   to get up early |
| inquietar   to worry | madurar   to mature |
| insertar   to insert | malgastar   to squander |
| inspirar   to inspire | maltratar   to mistreat |
| insultar   to insult | manchar   to stain |
| integrar   to integrate | mandar   to order |
| intentar   to try | manejar   to handle, drive, operate |
| interceptar   to intercept | manifestar   to show |
| interesar   to interest | manipular   to handle |
| interpretar   to interpret | maquillar   to apply make-up |
| inventar   to invent | marchar   to walk, march |
| invitar   to invite | matar   to kill |
| irritar   to irritate | matricular   to register |
| juntar   to join | meditar   to meditate |

mejorar to improve

mencionar to mention

mezclar to mix

mirar to look at, watch

moderar to moderate

modular to modulate

mojar to wet

molestar to bother

monear to fool around

montar to go up

motivar to motivate

mudar to move

multar to fine

murmurar to murmur

mutilar to mutilate

nadar to swim

narrar to narrate

necesitar to need

negociar to negotiate

nivelar to level

nombrar to name

notar to note

numerar to count

objetar to object

observar to observe

ocultar to hide

ocupar to occupy

odiar to hate

oficiar to officiate

olvidar to forget

ondular to ripple

operar to operate

opinar to believe, think

optar to opt

ordenar to order

orientar to direct

ornar to arrange

osar to dare

oscilar to oscillate

pactar to agree on

paladear to savor, taste

palmear to clap hands

palpar to feel, touch

palpitar to palpitate

parar to stop

participar to participate

pasar to pass, happen, spend (time)

pasear to go for a walk

patinar to skate

pedalear to pedal

pelar to peel

pelear to fight

penetrar to penetrate

pensar to think

perdonar to excuse

perdurar to endure

perfeccionar to perfect

perfilar to outline

perpetrar   to perpetrate

perseverar   to persevere

pesar   to weigh

pilotar   to pilot

pinchar   to prick, puncture

pintar   to paint

planchar   to iron

planear   to plan

plantar   to plant

poblar   to settle

portar   to carry

posar   to put down

precipitar   to precipitate

precisar   to fix, set

predeterminar   to predetermine

predominar   to predominate

preguntar   to ask

premeditar   to premeditate

preocupar   to worry

preparar   to prepare

presentar   to present, introduce

preservar   to protect

presionar   to press

prestar   to lend

privar   to deprive

privilegiar   to favor

procesar   to process

proclamar   to proclaim

procrear   to procreate

procurar   to try to

programar   to program

progresar   to progress

proliferar   to proliferate

pronunciar   to pronounce

prosperar   to prosper

protestar   to protest

pugnar   to fight

pulsar   to press

quebrar   to break

quedar   to remain

quemar   to burn

quitar   to remove

radiar   to radiate

rapar   to shave off

raspar   to scrape

razonar   to reason

rebotar   to rebound

recelar   to suspect

recitar   to recite

reclamar   to reclaim

reclinar   to recline

recobrar   to regain, recover

recompensar   to reward

reconciliar   to reconcile

reconfortar   to comfort

recrear   to amuse

recriminar   to reproach

recular   to recoil

recuperar   to recuperate

reembolsar   to reimburse

refinar   to refine

reflejar   to reflect

reflexionar   to think

reformar   to reform

regalar   to give as a gift

regañar   to tell off

registrar   to register, search

reglamentar   to regulate

regresar   to return

rehusar   to refuse

reiterar   to reiterate

relajar   to relax

relatar   to relate

relevar   to relieve

remedar   to imitate

remediar   to remedy

rememorar   to remember

remojar   to soak

remunerar   to reward

renunciar   to renounce

reparar   to repair

repasar   to review

repostar   to fill up

represar   to repress

representar   to represent

reprochar   to reproach

repudiar   to repudiate

resaltar   to stand out

rescatar   to rescue

reservar   to reserve

respetar   to respect

respirar   to breathe

restaurar   to restore

resucitar   to resuscitate

resultar   to result

retardar   to slow down

retirar   to remove

retrasar   to delay, postpone

retratar   to photograph

revelar   to reveal

revisar   to go over again

revolucionar   to revolutionize

robar   to rob

rodear   to surround

rotar   to rotate

rular   to roll

saborear   to savor

saldar   to settle a debt

saltar   to jump

saludar   to greet

salvar   to save

sanar   to cure, heal

sancionar   to sanction

sangrar   to bleed

saturar   to saturate

seleccionar   to select

sellar   to seal, stamp

semejar   to resemble

senalar   to mark, indicate

separar   to separate

silbar   to whistle

sobrar   to remain

solicitar   to solicit

solucionar   to solve

sombrar   to shade

soplar   to blow (out)

soportar   to support, tolerate

sospechar   to suspect

subordinar   to subordinate

subrayar   to underline

sudar   to sweat

sujetar   to secure

sumar   to add (up)

superar   to surpass

suscitar   to provoke

suspirar   to sigh

sustentar   to support, defend

susurrar   to whisper

tachar   to cross out

tajar   to slice, cut up

tallar   to carve

tardar   to take a long time

tasar   to value

teclear   to key in

telefonear   to phone

televisar   to televise

terminar   to finish

timar   to cheat, swindle

timbrar   to stamp

tirar   to throw, pull

tolerar   to tolerate

tomar   to take

topar   to run into

tornar   to turn something into something

tornear   to turn around

torturar   to torture

trabajar   to work

trabar   to fasten

traicionar   to betray

trajinar   to rush about

transformar   to transform

transitar   to go along

transpirar   to perspire

transplantar   to transplant

transportar   to transport

trasladar   to transfer, move

traspasar   to pierce, go through

tratar   to try

trepar   to climb, mount

tributar   to pay tribute to

triturar   to crush, grind

triunfar   to triumph

tronchar   to snap

trotar   to trot

tumbar   to knock over

turbar   to disturb

tutear   to address as tú

ultimar   to conclude, complete

ultrajar   to insult

ulular   to howl

uniformar   to standardize

untar   to spread with, smear

usar   to use, wear

usurpar   to usurp

vaciar   to empty

vacilar   to hesitate

vagabundear   to roam

validar   to validate

vallar   to fence in

valorar   to value

vaticinar   to predict

vedar   to forbid

velar   to guard, watch over

vendar   to bandage

venerar   to venerate

ventilar   to air

vetar   to vote

viajar   to travel

vibrar   to vibrate

viciar   to corrupt

vigilar   to watch over

vinicular   to relate

violar   to violate, rape

violentar   to embarrass, break into

virar   to turn (round)

visitar   to visit

vocear   to shout

vociferar   to shout

voltear   to turn over, toss

votar   to vote

vulnerar   to harm

yapar   to add a tip

zampar   to gobble

zanjar   to put an end to

zapatear   to stamp one's feet

zarandear   to shake, jostle

zumbar   to buzz, whirr

zurrar   to beat

# -car Verbs

abanicar   to fan

abdicar   to abdicate

acercar   to bring near

achicar   to make smaller

adjudicar   to award

ahorcar   to hang

aplacar   to placate

amplificar   to amplify

aplicar   to apply

apocar   to reduce

arrancar   to pull out

atacar   to attack

autentificar   to authenticate

bonificar   to increase production

brincar   to bounce

buscar   to look for

caducar   to expire

calcar   to trace, copy

calificar   to assess

cascar   to break

certificar   to certify

chascar   to crunch

chocar   to collide

clarificar   to clarify

clasificar   to classify

claudicar   to give in

codificar   to codify

colocar   to put, place

complicar   to complicate

comunicar   to communicate

confiscar   to confiscate

convocar   to convoke

criticar   to criticize

dedicar   to dedicate

diagnosticar   to diagnose

diversificar   to diversify

duplicar   to duplicate

edificar   to build

educar   to educate

ejemplificar   to exemplify

embarcar   to embark, board

enfocar   to focus

enfrascar   to get embroiled in

equivocar   to be wrong

especificar   to specify

evocar   to evoke

explicar   to explain

fabricar   to manufacture

falsificar   to falsify

glorificar   to glorify

gratificar   to gratify

identificar   to identify

implicar   to implicate

indicar   to indicate

intensificar   to intensify

intoxicar   to poison

invocar   to invoke

justificar   to justify

lubricar   to lubricate

marcar   to note

mascar   to chew

masticar   to chew

medicar   to medicate

modificar   to modify

mortificar   to mortify

multiplicar   to multiply

notificar   to notify

ofuscar   to dazzle

pacificar   to pacify

pecar   to sin

perjudicar   to damage

pescar   to fish

picar   to prick, pierce

planificar   to plan

platicar   to chat

practicar   to practice

provocar   to provoke

publicar   to publish

purificar   to purify

rascar   to scratch, itch

recalar   to stress

rectificar   to rectify

replicar   to reply

revocar   to revoke

roncar   to snore

rubricar   to confirm

sacar   to take out, withdraw

sacrificar   to sacrifice

salpicar   to splash

secar   to dry

significar   to mean

simplificar   to simplify

sofocar   to suffocate

solidificar   to solidify

suplicar   to implore

testificar   to testify

tipificar   to classify, typify

tocar   to touch

trabucar   to mix up

traficar   to traffic

trancar   to block

trastocar   to change round

triplicar   to triple

truncar   to cut short, spoil

ubicar   to position, locate

unificar   to unify

verificar   to verify

# -car Verbs with o to ue Stem Changes

trocar   to exchange

revolcar   to knock down

volcar   to overturn, empty

# -gar Verbs

abrigar   to shelter

abrogar   to abrogate

agregar   to add

ahogar   to drown

alargar   to lengthen

albergar   to provide lodging

alegar   to allege

anegar   to flood

apagar   to extinguish

arengar   to harangue

arriesgar   to risk

arrugar   to wrinkle, crumple

bogar   to row

bregar   to fight

cargar   to load

castigar   to punish

catalogar   to catalogue

congregar   to congregate

delegar   to delegate

derogar   to repeal, abolish

descargar   to unload

despegar   to detach, take off (plane)

divulgar   to divulge

embargar   to impede

encargar   to order

entregar   to deliver

fatigar   to tire

fustigar   to whip

galopar   to gallop

halagar   to flatter

instigar   to instigate

interrogar   to interrogate

intrigar   to intrigue

investigar   to investigate

juzgar   to judge

ligar   to bind

llagar   to injure, hurt

llegar   to arrive

mendigar   to beg

mitigar   to mitigate

navegar   to navigate

obligar   to obligate

otorgar   to grant, concede

pagar   to pay

pegar   to stick

prodigar   to lavish

prolongar   to prolong

propagar   to propagate

rasgar   to tear, rip open

relegar   to relegate

segregar   to segregate

tragar   to swallow

vagar   to roam

vengar   to avenge

# -gar Verbs with i to ie Stem Changes

abnegar   to forego

cegar   to blind

denegar   to reject

desplegar   to unfold

fregar   to rub

negar   to deny

plegar   to fold

regar   to water

renegar   to renege

sosegar   to calm

transfregar   to rub together

# -gar Verbs with o to ue Stem Changes

colgar   to hang up

descolgar   to unhook

holgar   to rest

rogar   to beg

# -gar Verbs with u to ue Stem Changes

enjugar   to dry

jugar   to play

# -guar Verbs with u to üe Stem Changes

aguar   to dilute

amortiguar   to deaden

apaciguar   to pacify

atestiguar   to attest

averiguar   to establish

# -uar Verbs with u to ú Stem Changes

actuar   to act

acentuar   to accentuate

continuar   to continue

efectuar   to carry out

evaluar   to evaluate

exceptuar   to exclude

fluctuar   to fluctuate

graduar   to gauge, confer a degree upon

habituar   to accustom someone to

insinuar   to insinuate

perpetuar   to perpetuate

puntuar   to punctuate

situar   to situate

valuar   to value

# -iar Verbs with i to í Stem Changes

| | |
|---|---|
| ampliar   to extend | fotografiar   to photograph |
| confiar   to trust | liar   to tie up |
| criar   to rear | guiar   to guide |
| desafiar   to challenge | obsequiar   to present someone with something |
| desviar   to divert | obviar   to avoid |
| enfriar   to cool | |
| enviar   to send | rociar   to spray, sprinkle |
| espiar   to spy | vaciar   to empty |
| esquiar   to ski | variar   to vary |
| fiar   to trust | |

# -zar Verbs

| | |
|---|---|
| abalanzar   to balance | atenazar   to grip |
| abrazar   to embrace | aterrizar   to land |
| actualizar   to update | autorizar   to authorize |
| acuatizar   to land on water | avanzar   to advance |
| adelgazar   to lose weight | bautizar   to baptize |
| afianzar   to fasten | bostezar   to yawn |
| agilizar   to speed up | calzar   to wear shoes |
| agudizar   to intensify | caracterizar   to characterize |
| aguzar   to sharpen | cazar   to hunt |
| alcanzar   to reach, overtake | civilizar   to civilize |
| alzar   to lift, raise | climatizar   to air condition |
| amenazar   to threaten | colonizar   to colonize |
| analizar   to analyze | cotizar   to quote |
| aplazar   to postpone | cristalizar   to crystallize |
| aromatizar   to scent | cruzar   to cross |
| atemorizar   to frighten | danzar   to dance |

desorganizar   to disorganize

dramatizar   to dramatize

embarazar   to restrict

encolerizar   to infuriate

enderezar   to straighten

enlazar   to tie something up

ensalzar   to praise

entrelazar   to interlace

escandalizar   to scandalize

escolarizar   to provide with schooling

especializar   to specialize

esperanzar   to give hope to

estabilizar   to stabilize

familiarizar   to familiarize

fertilizar   to fertilize

finalizar   to finalize

garantizar   to guarantee

generalizar   to generalize

horrorizar   to horrify

hospitalizar   to hospitalize

humanizar   to humanize

indemnizar   to compensate

individualizar   to single people out

inicializar   to initialize

inmortalizar   to immortalize

inmovilizar   to immobilize

interiorizar   to internalize

intranquilizar   to worry

gozar   to enjoy

lanzar   to throw

localizar   to localize

magnetizar   to magnetize

materializar   to realize, produce

mediatizar   to determine

memorizar   to memorize

modernizar   to modernize

moralizar   to moralize

movilizar   to mobilize

nacionalizar   to nationalize

narcotizar   to drug

naturalizar   to naturalize

neutralizar   to neutralize

normalizar   to normalize

obstaculizar   to hinder

organizar   to organize

particularizar   to go into details

personalizar   to get personal

politizar   to politicize

populizar   to popularize

preconizar   to recommend

profundizar   to study in depth

punzar   to prick

racionalizar   to rationalize

realizar   to realize, fulfill

rechazar   to reject

regularizar   to regulate

relanzar   to throw back

responsabilizar   to hold someone responsible

rezar    to pray

ridiculizar    to ridicule

rivalizar    to compete

rizar    to curl

rozar    to rub

ruborizar    to embarrass

satirizar    to satirize

simbolizar    to symbolize

simpatizar con    to get along with

singularizar    to distinguish, single out

sintetizar    to summarize

sintonizar    to tune in to

solazar    to amuse, entertain

sonorizar    to voice

suavizar    to smooth

tamizar    to sift

teorizar    to theorize

totalizar    to add up

tranquilizar    to tranquilize

tranzar    to break off

trazar    to trace

trivializar    to trivialize

utilizar    to utilize

valorizar    to value

vigorizar    to fortify

visualizar    to visualize

vocalizar    to vocalize

vulgarizar    to popularize

## -zar Verbs with *e* to *ie* Stem Changes

comenzar    to begin

empezar    to begin

tropezar    to hit, stumble

## -zar Verbs with *o* to *ue* Stem Changes

almorzar    to eat lunch

esforzar    to strengthen

forzar    to force

reforzar    to reinforce

## -zar Verbs with *o* to *üe* Stem Changes

avergonzar    to shame

## -ar Verbs with *e* to *ie* Stem Changes

acertar    to ascertain

acrecentar    to increase

alentar    to breathe, encourage

apretar    to frighten

arrendar   to lease

asentar   to seat

atraversar   to go through

calentar   to heat

cerrar   to close

concertar   to arrange, agree

desconcertar   to upset

despertar   to wake up

enmendar   to correct

encerrar   to lock up, enclose

encomendar   to trust

enterrar   to bury

helar   to freeze

merendar   to have a snack

nevar   to snow

quebrar   to break, smash

recalentar   to reheat

recomendar   to recommend

remendar   to mend

reventar   to burst

sentar   to seat

temblar   to tremble

tentar   to touch, try

## -ar Verbs with o to ue Spelling Changes

acordar   to agree

acostar   to put to bed

aprobar   to approve

colar   to filter, strain

comprobar   to verify

concordar   to reconcile

consolar   to console

contar   to tell

costar   to cost

demostrar   to demonstrate

derogar   to abolish

desacordar   to disagree

descollar   to protrude

descontar   to discount, disregard

encontrar   to meet

mostrar   to show

poblar   to settle

probar   to try (on)

recordar   to remember

reprobar   to censure, condemn

resonar   to resound

rodar   to roll

renovar   to renovate

sobrevolar   to fly over

soltar   to loosen, let go

sonar   to ring, sound

soñar   to dream

tostar   to toast

tronar   to thunder

volar   to fly, blow up

# -er Verbs

absorber   to absorb

acceder   to agree

acometer   to attack

aprehender   to apprehend

aprender   to learn

barrer   to sweep

beber   to drink

ceder   to yield

comer   to eat

cometer   to commit

competer   to be up to

comprender   to understand

conceder   to concede, grant

condescender   to consent to

correr   to run

corresponder   to correspond

corromper   to corrupt

deber   to owe, must have to

depender   to depend

desprender   to remove

embeber   to soak in

emprender   to start

entremeter   to insert

esconder   to hide

exceder   to exceed

interceder   to intercede

lamer   to lick

meter   to put in

ofender   to insult

preceder   to precede

pretender   to try to do something

proceder   to proceed

prometer   to promise

remeter   to put back

repeler   to repel, disgust

reprender   to tell off

responder   to answer

retroceder   to go back

revender   to resell

romper   to break; **Irregular past participle only: roto**

socorrer   to help

someter   to subdue

sorber   to sip

sorprender   to surprise

suceder   to happen

suspender   to suspend

tejer   to weave

temer   to fear

vender   to sell

## -eer Verbs

creer   to believe

leer   to read

proveer   to provide

## Vowel + -cer Verbs

ablandecer   to soften

aborrecer   to abhor

acontecer   to happen

adolecer   to suffer from

agradecer   to thank

aparecer   to appear

apetecer   to crave

carecer de   to lack

coercer   to restrict

compadecer   to pity

complacer   to please

conocer   to know, be acquainted with

crecer   to grow

decrecer   to decrease

desobedecer   to disobey

desaparecer   to disappear

encarecer   to make more expensive

endurecer   to harden

enfurecer   to infuriate

engrandecer   to exalt, increase

enmudecer   to silence

ennoblecer   to ennoble

enriquecer   to make rich

enrojecer   to make red

ensombrecer   to cast a shadow on

enternecer   to move, touch

entorpecer   to hinder

entristecer   to make sad

entumecer   to numb

envejecer   to grow old

escarnecer   to ridicule

establecer   to establish

estremecer   to shake

favorecer   to favor

florecer   to flourish

fortalecer   to strengthen

guarecer   to protect

humedecer   to moisten

languidecer   to languish

palidecer   to get pale

parecer   to seem

perecer   to perish

prevalecer   to prevail

merecer   to merit, deserve

nacer   to be born

obedecer   to obey

obscurecer   to darken

ofrecer   to offer

padecer   to suffer

parecer   to seem, appear

permanecer   to remain

pertenecer   to pertain

placer   to please

reconocer   to recognize

rejuvenecer   to rejuvenate

resplandecer   to shine

restablecer   to reestablish

reverdecer   to revive

robustecer   to strengthen

## Consonant + -cer Verbs

convencer   to convince

ejercer   to exercise

vencer   to conquer

## -cer Verbs with c to z Spelling Changes and o to ue Stem Changes

cocer   to cook

torcer   to twist

## -*ger* Verbs

acoger   to welcome

coger   to seize

converger   to converge

emerger   to emerge

encoger   to shrink

escoger   to choose

proteger   to protect

recoger   to gather, pick up

sobrecoger   to startle

## -*er* Verbs with *e* to *ie* Stem Changes

atender   to attend to

ascender   to climb

defender   to defend

descender   to descend

encender   to incite, light

entender   to understand

extender   to extend

perder   to lose

querer   to wish, want

tender   to extend, spread

transcender   to transcend

verter   to pour, spill

## -*er* Verbs with *o* to *ue* Stem Changes

absolver   to absolve; **Irregular past participle: absuelto**

disolver   to dissolve; **Irregular past participle: disuelto**

envolver   to wrap up; **Irregular past participle: envuelto**

resolver   to resolve; **Irregular past participle: resuelto**

revolver   to revolve; **Irregular past participle: revuelto**

volver   to return; **Irregular past participle: vuelto**

conmover   to move, touch

demoler   to demolish

doler   to hurt

llover   to rain

moler   to grind

morder   to bite

mover   to move, persuade

promover   to set up

poder   to be able to

remover   to stir

soler   to usually do something

# -ir Verbs

abatir   to knock down

abolir   to abolish

abrir   to open; **Irregular past participle only: abierto**

aburrir   to annoy, bore

acudir   to attend, respond

admitir   to admit

añadir   to add

apercibir   to warn

aplaudir   to applaud

asistir   to attend

asumir   to take on

aturdir   to stun

batir   to beat

coexistir   to coexist

coincidir   to coincide

combatir   to fight

compartir   to share, divide

concurrir   to attend

confundir   to confound

consistir   to consist

consumir   to consume

convivir   to live together

cubrir   to cover

cumplir   to fulfill

debatir   to struggle

decidir   to decide

definir   to define

difundir   to spread

deglutir   to swallow

departir   to converse

deprimir   to depress

describir   to describe; **Irregular past participle only: descrito**

descubrir   to discover; **Irregular past participle only: descubierto**

desistir   to give up

discutir   to discuss

disuadir   to dissuade

dividir   to divide

eludir   to avoid

emitir   to emit

encubrir   to conceal

escribir   to write; **Irregular past participle only: escrito**

escupir   to spit

evadir   to avoid

exhibir   to exhibit

eximir   to exempt

existir   to exist

expandir   to spread

exprimir   to squeeze

impartir   to give

imprimir   to print

inhibir   to inhibit

inscribir   to inscribe; **Irregular past participle only: inscrito**

insistir   to insist

interrumpir   to interrupt

invadir   to invade

nutrir   to nourish

occurir   to occur

omitir   to omit

oprimir   to oppress

partir   to leave

percibir   to perceive

permitir   to permit

persistir   to persist

persuadir   to persuade

preconcebir   to preconceive

prescribir   to prescribe; **Irregular past participle only: prescrito**

presumir   to presume

prohibir   to prohibit

pudrir   to rot

pulir   to polish

recibir   to receive

remitir   to remit

repartir   to divide

reprimir   to suppress, repress

rescindir   to rescind

residir   to reside

resistir   to resist

resumir   to summarize

sacudir   to shake

sobrevivir   to survive

subir   to go up

su(b)scribir (subscribir)   to subscribe; **Irregular past participle only: suscrito (subscrito)**

subsistir   to subsist

sucumbir   to succumb

sufrir   to suffer

sumir   to plunge

suplir   to replace with

suprimir   to suppress

surtir   to stock, supply

transcribir   to transcribe; **Irregular past participle only transcrito**

transcurrir   to pass, go by

transgredir   to transgress

transmitir   to transmit

vivir   to live

## Vowel + -cir Verbs

conducir   to drive, conduct

deducir   to deduce

inducir   to induce

introducir   to introduce

lucir   to illuminate

producir   to produce

reproducir   to reproduce

reducir   to reduce

relucir   to shine

seducir   to seduce

traducir   to translate

## Consonant + -cir Verbs

esparcir   to spread out

fruncir   to frown, purse (lips)

resarcir   to compensate

zurcir   to mend; **c to z**

## -gir Verbs

afligir   to afflict

divergir   to diverge

dirigir   to direct

erigir   to erect

exigir   to demand

fingir   to pretend

infligir   to inflict

infringir   to infringe

infundir   to inspire

resurgir   to resurge

rugir   to roar

sumergir   to submerge

surgir   to appear, spring forth

surtir   to supply with

transigir con   to agree to

urgir   to urge

## *-gir* Verbs with *e* to *i* Stem Changes

colegir   to collect

corregir   to correct

elegir   to elect

regir   to rule

## *-uir* Verbs

afluir   to flow

atribuir   to attribute

concluir   to conclude

confluir   to converge

constituir   to constitute

construir   to construct

contribuir   to contribute

destituir   to deprive

destruir   to destroy

disminuir   to diminish

distribuir   to distribute

excluir   to exclude

fluir   to flow

huir   to flee

imbuir   to imbue

incluir   to include

influir   to influence

instituir   to institute

instruir   to instruct

intuir   to intuit

obstruir   to obstruct

recluir   to shut away

rehuir   to avoid

restituir   to refund

retribuir   to repay

sustituir   to substitute

# *-uir* Verb with *ü* to *u* Spelling Changes

argüir   to argue

# *-guir* Verbs

distinguir   to distinguish

extinguir   to extinguish

# *-guir* Verbs with *e* to *i* Stem Changes

conseguir   to get

perseguir   to pursue

proseguir   to continue

seguir   to follow

# *-ir* Verbs with *e* to *ie* Spelling Changes

adherir   to adhere

advertir   to advise, warn

arrepentir   to repent

asentir   to assent

concernir   to concern

conferir   to confer

consentir   to allow

convertir   to convert

deferir   to defer

desmentir   to deny

digerir   to digest

discernir   to discern

disentir   to dissent, disagree

divertir   to amuse

herir   to wound

hervir   to boil

inferir   to infer

ingerir   to ingest, consume

interferir   to interfere

invertir   to invert

mentir   to lie

preferir   to prefer

presentir   to foresee

proferir   to say

referir   to refer

requerir   to require

revertir   to revert

sentir   to feel, regret

sugerir   to suggest

transferir   to transfer

# *-ir* Verbs with *i* to *ie* Spelling Changes

adquirir     to acquire

inquirir     to inquire

# *-ir* Verbs with *e* to *i* Spelling Changes

competir     to compete

concebir     to conceive

derretir     to melt, dissolve

despedir     to say good-bye to

expedir     to send

gemir     to moan

impedir     to impede

investir     to invest

medir     to measure

pedir     to request

repetir     to repeat

revestir     to cover

servir     to serve

vestir     to clothe

# *-ir* Verbs with *o* to *ue* Spelling Changes

dormir     to sleep

morir     to die; **Irregular Past Participle: muerto**

# Appendix G

# Common Reflexive Verbs

| Spanish Verb | English Meaning |
|---|---|
| abrocharse | to fasten |
| aburrirse | to become bored |
| acordarse (de) | to remember |
| acostarse | to go to bed |
| afeitarse | to shave |
| ahogarse | to drown, suffocate |
| alegrarse | to be glad |
| apoderarse (de) | to take possession (of) |
| apresurarse (a) | to hurry |
| aprovecharse (de) | to avail oneself (of), to profit (by) |
| apurarse | to get upset, worry |
| arrepentirse (de) | to repent |
| asegurarse (de) | to make sure |
| asustarse | to become frightened |
| atreverse (a) | to dare |
| bañarse | to bathe oneself |
| burlarse (de) | to make fun of |

*continues*

*continued*

| Spanish Verb | English Meaning |
| --- | --- |
| callarse | to be silent, keep still |
| cambiarse | to change (clothing), to move (home) |
| cansarse | to become tired |
| casarse | to get married |
| cepillarse | to brush (hair, teeth) |
| colo**car**se | to place oneself |
| conven**cer**se (de) | to convince oneself (of) |
| cuidarse (de) | to take care of (to worry about) |
| **dar**se | to give in |
| desanimarse | to get discouraged |
| desayunarse | to have breakfast |
| desmayarse | to faint |
| des**pedir**se | to say goodbye, take leave of |
| des**per**tarse | to wake up |
| des**ves**tirse | to undress |
| di**ver**tirse | to have fun |
| d**or**mirse | to fall asleep |
| ducharse | to take a shower |
| ejercitarse (en) | to train (in) |
| empeñarse (en) | to insist (on) |
| enfadarse (con) | to get angry (with) |
| engañarse | to be mistaken |
| enojarse | to become angry |
| enterarse (de) | to find out about |
| equivo**car**se | to be mistaken |
| escaparse | to escape |
| esconderse (de) | to hide (from) |
| fiarse (de) | to trust |
| figurarse | to imagine |
| fijarse (en) | to notice |
| **hacer**se (a) (con) | to become; get (used to) (hold of) |
| **ir**se | to go away |
| lavarse | to wash oneself |

| Spanish Verb | English Meaning |
|---|---|
| levantarse | to get up |
| llamarse | to be named, called |
| maquillarse | to put on makeup |
| marcharse | to go away |
| mojarse | to get wet |
| moverse | to move |
| negarse (a) | to refuse (to) |
| olvidarse (de) | to forget |
| pararse | to stop |
| parecerse (a) | to resemble |
| pasearse | to go for a walk |
| peinarse | to comb one's hair |
| **poner**se | to put on, become, place oneself |
| preocuparse | to worry |
| protegerse | to protect oneself |
| quedarse | to remain |
| quejarse (de) | to complain (about) |
| quitarse | to take off (one's clothes) |
| reírse (de) | to laugh at |
| relajarse | to relax |
| resfriarse | to catch a cold |
| romperse | to break |
| secarse | to dry oneself |
| sentarse | to sit down |
| sentirse | to feel |
| tratarse (de) | to concern |
| vestirse | to get dressed |

# Conjugating Reflexive Verbs

LLAMARSE (to be called) **Gerund:** llamando; **Past participle:** llamado

**Commands:**   llama (tú), no llames (tú)

llamad (vosotros), no llaméis (vosotros)

llame (Ud.) llamen (Uds.), llamemos (nosotros)

## Simple Tenses

### Present

| | |
|---|---|
| me llam**o** | nos llam**amos** |
| te llam**as** | os llam**áis** |
| se llam**a** | se llam**an** |

### Preterit

| | |
|---|---|
| me llam**é** | nos llam**amos** |
| te llam**aste** | os llam**asteis** |
| se llam**ó** | se llam**aron** |

### Imperfect

| | |
|---|---|
| me llam**aba** | nos llam**ábamos** |
| te llam**abas** | os llam**abais** |
| se llam**aba** | se llam**aban** |

### Future

| | |
|---|---|
| me llam**aré** | nos llam**aremos** |
| te llam**arás** | os llam**aréis** |
| se llam**ará** | se llam**arán** |

## Conditional

| | |
|---|---|
| me llama**ría** | nos llama**ríamos** |
| te llama**rías** | os llama**ríais** |
| se llama**ría** | se llama**rían** |

## Subjunctive

| | |
|---|---|
| me llam**e** | nos llam**emos** |
| te llam**es** | os llam**éis** |
| se llam**e** | se llam**en** |

## Imperfect Subjunctive

| | |
|---|---|
| me llam**ara** | nos llam**áramos** |
| te llam**aras** | os llam**arais** |
| se llam**ara** | se llam**aran** |

# Compound Tenses

## Present Perfect

| | |
|---|---|
| me he llamado | nos hemos llamado |
| te has llamado | os habéis llamado |
| se ha llamado | se han llamado |

## Preterit Perfect

| | |
|---|---|
| me hube llamado | nos hubimos llamado |
| te hubiste llamado | os hubisteis llamado |
| se hubo llamado | se hubieron llamado |

## Pluperfect

| | |
|---|---|
| me había llamado | nos habíamos llamado |
| te habías llamado | os habíais llamado |
| se había llamado | se habían llamado |

## Future Perfect

| | |
|---|---|
| me habré llamado | nos habremos llamado |
| te habrás llamado | os habréis llamado |
| se habrá llamado | se habrán llamado |

## Conditional Perfect

| | |
|---|---|
| me habría llamado | nos habríamos llamado |
| te habrías llamado | os habríais llamado |
| se habría llamado | se habrían llamado |

## Perfect Subjunctive

| | |
|---|---|
| me haya llamado | nos hayamos llamado |
| te hayas llamado | os hayáis llamado |
| se haya llamado | se hayan llamado |

## Pluperfect Subjunctive

| | |
|---|---|
| me hubiera llamado | nos hubiéramos llamado |
| te hubieras llamado | os hubierais llamado |
| se hubiera llamado | se hubieran llamado |

# Irregular Past Participles

The following verbs and their compounds (listed in Appendix G), some regular and some irregular, have irregular past participles.

| Verb | Meaning | Past Participle |
|------|---------|-----------------|
| abrir | to open | abierto |
| absolver | to absolve | absuelto |
| cubrir | to cover | cubierto |
| decir | to say, tell | dicho |
| disolver | to dissolve | disuelto |
| escribir | to write | escrito |
| freír | to fry | frito |
| hacer | to make, do | hecho |
| imprimir | to print | impreso |
| morir | to die | muerto |
| poner | to put | puesto |
| proveer | to provide | provisto |
| pudrir | to rot | podrido |
| resolver | to resolve | resuelto |
| romper | to break | roto |
| satisfacer | to satisfy | satisfecho |
| ver | to see | visto |
| volver | to return | vuelto |

# Index